The Young Lawyer's Jungle Book

Sara—
Congratulations!.
I'm very proud of
you! I thought this
might help in your
transition from
student to lawyer!

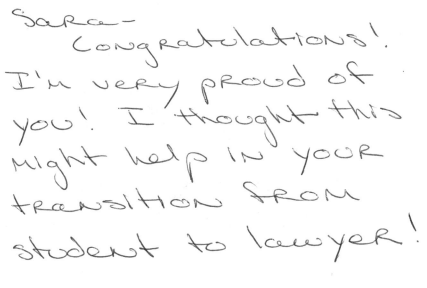

The
Young Lawyer's
Jungle Book

A Survival Guide

SECOND EDITION

❋ REVISED AND EXPANDED ❋

THANE JOSEF MESSINGER

THE FINE PRINT PRESS
HONOLULU

This is a work of experience, observation, and opinion. Any resemblance to
events, places, or persons (living, dead, or practicing) is entirely possible.

Copyright © 1996, 2000 by Thane Josef Messinger.
Front cover artwork by Ngoma Muanda Kizito and Delfi Messinger.
Front cover artwork commissioned in The Congo (formerly Zaire).

Library of Congress CCN 99-71107
ISBN 1-888960-19-1

The Fine Print Press, Ltd.
350 Ward Avenue, Suite 106
Honolulu, Hawaii 96814-4091
Email: fpp@hits.net

Publisher's Cataloging-in-Publication Data:

Messinger, Thane Josef
    The Young Lawyer's Jungle Book: A Survival Guide—2d ed.
    Index.
    1. Practice of Law   2. Legal Profession
3. Lawyers—Practical Guides
KF300 M48   2000   99-71107
347.0504   1-888960-19-1

PRINTED IN THE UNITED STATES OF AMERICA

05 04 03 02 01   9 8 7 6 5 4 3 2

Both paper and author are acid-free.

Dedication

No book is the product of only one mind. Recognition is owed (in reverse alphabetical order) to Tim, Mara, and Laura Tack; Pam, Dylan, and Bill Sublette; Tim Stumpff; Tim, Jan, Carey, and Blake Ryan; Mark Rumple; David Ronin; David Rair; Martha Cecilia Prada T.; Zuleika Pinzón Mendoza; Jim Obrien & Vera Michalchik (and Isabel, too); the late Marcus Nedlic; Phyllis and Peter Nimkoff; Judy, Jennie (aka "Jennie Unit"), Bob, and Amanda Mieger; Milton, Ivri, Delfi, and Dawn Messinger; Muffy McCafferty; Jeannie Latenser; Brian Kressin; Scott Harmon ($Scott_{sw}$); John Bourgeois; Scott Benbow ($Scott_{AG}$); and Scott ($Scott_y$), Sally, Josh, Doug, and Adam Beitz.

Thank you for your copious comments, philanthropic friendship, and plentiful patience, without which this would be incomparably worse. *Oana ke fwakyuk Kosrae, kulo na ma lulap!*

Special recognition is owed to Mark, without whose influence this sentence wouldn't have been written.

To Kizito and Delfi, *merci*.

To Milton, Dawn, Delfi, Ivri, Daaven, Brus, Autumn, and to their affiliated Spousal, Offspring, and Other-Related Units, ILANU.

And to Baolan, 親愛的寶蘭，謝謝你的耐心，信心，幫忙，再次謝謝。我愛你。

Table of Contents

– Preface to the Second Edition –

Some who read the first edition have assumed that this book is only for those law graduates who will work in the largest firms. Untrue. With few exceptions, *all* law offices—including public-service ones—follow a big-firm model. More importantly, the *issues* that new attorneys face in adjusting to practice are universal.

This book applies broadly for another reason: it is the product not only of my experiences, but also of my observations of others' experiences, and of the varied experiences of contributors.

Some have criticized my characterization of law practice—especially for the beginner—as a game. Or, more charitably, they dislike my unintended encouragement of new generations to play this game.

Well, sir or madam, it *is* a game. (...And so are you, in another sense of that word.) It cannot help but be. But it's not just *any* game: the stakes (your career) are all too real. Rules, expectations, rewards, and punishments. Tied to talent, deportment, connections, and luck. No instruction manual. No warnings. No third chances. (Sometimes no second or even first chances.) No respite.

I wish it were not so harsh. I wish the Rules of this Game were applied more consistently, and gently. But who cares what I think? My task is to give notice: to disclose the reality. My hope is that, in so disclosing, perhaps the crueler realities that face today's generation will someday fade.

I had not realized, when I started this book in the mid-1990s, how close I would come to a central danger: law students do not learn in law school how to *practice* law, and law firms are increasingly hard-pressed to take up the slack. (I am not alone in this assessment. Many senior practitioners, and more than a few academics, share the alarm.) Moreover, there's a perilous assumption that three years of law school ends with a mastery of the law.

No. Law school will not—cannot—teach all that you must learn to become an attorney able to represent the interests of a client, in all its many modes and nuances. Clichéd as the saying is, law school is only the beginning for a lifetime's continued learning. *If* you decide to practice law, do it right. It's not a part-time or transient "job"; the reputation you develop will follow you your entire professional life.

Why the hard edge in parts of this book?

First, I'm a Texan. (Well, I'm no longer *in* Texas, but...once a Texan, always one. And I can't be sure that Austin is *really* part of Texas, but that's another story.) No matter on which island I happen to find myself, I cannot help but admire the no-nonsense upbringing of my youth. I'm a little amused, and more than a little dismayed, in the odd viewing of a pulp Western showing townsfolk in the Old West cowering before the big, bad guys. *Yeahh*...right. These townsfolk had risked their *lives*—in their longing to carve better lives for their children and escape the miseries of the East—just to *get to* where they settled...after their parents had fought off starvation, seasickness, vultures (of both species), chronic deprivations, indentured servitude, and all manner of horrors we would have difficulty facing for a day. You needn't have quite as much backbone as they, but you *do* need a healthy appreciation for what will follow. Some of it will not be pleasant. And, unlike Ally, if you come apart every other episode, you won't be long for the line-up.

I've tried to take some of the edge off in this edition. I fear that I haven't been entirely successful. For reasons that I hope are obvious, this is not a standard text. Nor is it a standard guidebook. I intend, instead, to attempt a gentle, friendly, yet *no-nonsense* one-on-one conversation with you, the reader. Thus, please take the contents of this book in the spirit intended: imagine a pitcher of your favorite frozen beverage, and a two-thirds eaten pizza in front of us, as we ponder your fate. Whether you believe me, or even like me, is your choice. But it shall not alter the truths I feel it my duty to disclose. And I do wish you good luck, whatever your path.

I also admit to some incredulity at the transformation of the legal services industry. (Yes, it is an industry, which is part of the point: the genteel ways of the past are increasingly archaic, yet succumbing wholly to the vagaries of commerce presents its own problems. The lessons of leading and managing people—*the* most difficult and important part of *any* business—might be brought to bear to the benefit of clients and new attorneys, alike. But that's the subject for another book.) Ours is a profession between two worlds. The reality isn't as troublesome as the reactions among some. Still, it's easy to get caught up in the hectic atmosphere, to become cynical. Do your best to avoid this trap. (To paraphrase a historical figure, in court on trumped-up charges and accused of showing his contempt, "On the contrary, your Honor, I'm trying my best to conceal it.")

Yet another reason for the hard edge is its need. Believe it or not (at your peril), law firms and senior practitioners are too *gentle*—and too busy—to manage their own people as their clients must manage theirs. Rather than correcting a problem—you—they'll quite likely let it slide, instead. As crazy as it sounds, heed the warning: Law office life is too frenzied for serious, continuous feedback. They will *already have made their decision* that you're not "cut out" for partnership, and if you don't take the hint, they'll (eventually) help you with the punchline. You might not even *know* you're off track, until it is too late. (Know, also, that if it doesn't work out, you'll have only days, or even hours, to clear your office.) It's not a pleasant kill.

I once spoke with a law firm consultant, who stated in not-so-gentle words a response to my comment that law firms have much to gain by paying just a *little* more attention to junior associates: *"Yeah, that* may be true, but they really don't care." I'm not convinced it goes that far, but, sadly, for many firms it *is* a numbers game. Partners *can* identify, quickly, those associates with the "Right Stuff". Actually, it's pretty accurate, if falsely narrow. Though the economics are odd (and short-sighted), that doesn't change reality: don't *you* get trapped with the *wrong* stuff. Your survival is not-at-all assured, and you must fight to stay on track. (And you must know where the track is.) Anything that sets you up for a potential fall is deadly.

I do not mean, by the way, to be disparaging of law firm managers, and neither should you. They have an exceedingly difficult job, in which you, initially, play only the most minor supporting role. The history of firms provides the backdrop: law firms were partnerships among trusted, known, almost always upper-class attorneys...who managed themselves. New blood came from old blood: young lawyers were the sons (...*yup,* sons) of *very* established partners (or clients). Fast-forward a few decades, and firms are still catching up to the astonishing changes in our business world...while inexorably stuck partly in the old. Though you might not yet appreciate it, you should appreciate *them,* sincerely, for the pressures they face in that cold, cruel world. As a tycoon once said, "Someday, this'll all be yours."

Get mad at me, if you wish. I won't retaliate. Even I—ever the cynic—would not have believed, way back when, what I now write. I might well have responded poorly, in disbelief and disdain. The important point: Don't act out self-destructive frustrations at the office. That's a guarantee of disaster. At the office—no matter how stressful it gets, or how frazzled you get—keep it professional. Whatever your eventual career path, don't erase the present one, lightly.

In several parts of this book, I encourage you to focus, immediately, on an area of practice. Specialization. A dirty word, in some corners (...with some justification). Yet an absolute career requirement. You cannot, cannot, *cannot* become an excellent lawyer in more than a few (related) areas, especially at first. Some cannot, ever. You must develop expertise (immediately) and professional presence (soon).

You must also develop a *purpose.*

Many, if not most, new lawyers have little idea of their own preferences. This is understandable, but dangerous. I repeat this point not for the immediate benefit of gaining expertise in a narrow area of law, or for the added benefit of self-confidence (or for the practical benefit of greater paychecks), but for a more basic point: in law practice, you're it. A few lucky new lawyers work for senior practitioners who care about both (1) the law and (2) transmitting that knowledge and care to the next generation. You. Few mentors have the time (and energy, and commitment, and skill) to diagnose your strengths, and forgive and correct your weaknesses. Few will guide you in a direction you probably can't yet see—especially if it is outside that mentor's specialty—but one into which you can grow with the right help.

The trap should be obvious: instead most new lawyers struggle, alone, merely to survive. As in the jungle, quite a large number don't make it. And of those who do, their "success" is too frequently marked by a multitude of scars...which only worsen the injuries inflicted in future scrapes. Perhaps they survive, but not as they might have liked, and rarely as they should. Others fall prey to various predators: malpractice, malfeasance, the market. It's a scary path, for many.

It needn't be, for you.

Thus another reason for the book: when you're in the trenches, it's all too easy to feel that you're the only one going through the immediate difficulties you'll face. Take heart: *You are not alone.*

Sadly, how you start in life is ever more important to how you end. This applies with full force in the law. With few exceptions, your first law job is *crucial:* it is not much of an exaggeration to write that your future opportunities will be granted (or denied) by where you start. This is true because—rightly or wrongly (and mostly wrongly)—the past is and will remain the sieve through which potential employers screen candidates.

If you come from a big firm—no matter how you got there—you'll have a wide range of options. If you work in a "lesser" office, you'll work harder for those same opportunities. (And many will be closed to you, period. More often than not, you'll not even be in the running without the "right" background, and backing. Period.)

I have witnessed, first-hand, the filling of many positions. In almost every instance, *the wrong person won.* (And where the right person wins, it is almost always for the wrong reason.) I have landed two law jobs almost solely because of my credentials, and I've lost other jobs for which I was—reasonably objectively, I think—a perfect match, to others with a closer credential fit. Even I fall into the trap when sifting through stacks of résumés. How else to winnow faceless papers to a manageable few? The tendency to rank—to assign a mathematical precision to that which is inherently imprecise—is overwhelming. Beware. Don't belittle this human tendency.

If the choice is yours, choose wisely.

Finally, please read this in the spirit intended: to give notice, to help prepare you for some of the challenges you'll face. Through it all, keep your *own* goals in sight. As with any profession, the law expects much. Yet she also gives. Money. Power. Connections. Knowledge. Justice. Civilization. Accomplishment.

Give the law a chance. After three years, much energy, and many thousands of dollars, you (and we) deserve it.

And, through it all: Good Luck.

Honolulu, Hawaii
August 1999

– PREFACE TO THE FIRST EDITION –

Your first year as a lawyer will be one of the most stressful you will ever face.

No, that's not quite right. Your first year as a lawyer will be *the* most stressful you will ever face. Even your first year in law school won't quite compare, because there, at least, you were your own taskmaster. You could in some small way control the day-to-day goings-on in your frantic rush to master those Byzantine rules of law swirling about. In real law, you'll have no such luxuries.

Well, that's not quite right, either. You *will* have fairly broad minute-by-minute control over your workday, but at a steep price: the pressure on you to rack up the hours and finish the rapid procession of projects will make each of those minutes seem like ungrateful brats zipping past. As young professionals in every discipline soon learn, your life is not your own.

Physicians are expected to attend to their patients based upon the exigencies of medicine and chronic understaffing, not a clock. Editors are captives to the circling of similar clocks, while accountants count to the rhythm of their snootier brethren, calendars, to meet periodic deadlines...which only serve to focus the energies of workaholic executives, who take their frustrations out on overworked, underappreciated, and unrealistically deadlined engineers. Few are spared.

And you. *You* will be expected to serve the needs of your clients. This is both better—and worse—than it sounds. Better because being King's counsel has its privileges. Worse because the King can be—and often is—both demanding and unforgiving. In this legal feast, surviving the peril of Damocles is tricky, at best.

I want to tell you what you'll face because, in part, no one ever told me. My first years as a junior associate were miserable not only because of the stress inherent to the experience, which I truly did not mind, but also because of the uncertainty that came with a nearly complete lack of guidance, which I did.

Thus, one justification for this book is that ever-familiar concept of notice. (Our profession is one of the worst violators of this doctrine, which we happily foist on others.) Despite—or perhaps because of—my many missteps, this book should prove helpful to you, the eager new attorney, who, with your compatriots, will populate offices of all varieties from sea to shining sea. Whether in big firms, small firms, courts, agencies, corporate suites, or the military, the principles in this book apply to all.

In all immodesty, these principles apply as well to the initiation process that is the hallmark (if not the watermark) of the rites of passage in each young professional's life, whatever the chosen discipline.

For convenience, and as a captive to the law of averages, you'll read about firms, firms, firms. The archetypal big law firm is the model here and in life. Many are less formal. As will be your responsibility in life, however, you must adapt to meet your environment as it meets you. (If you don't, you'll be astounded at the jungle's quenchless capacity to overtake any attempt to contain it.) Thus, a worst-case legal scenario for the most hearty pessimist.

So look to 𝕿𝖍𝖊 𝕵𝖎𝖗𝖒, if only because, as an only partially cloaked service business, it tends to intensify the stresses inherent in the transition from law school graduate to lawyer. Still, you ADAs and PDs and O-2s and GSP-11s out there are, or will be, in a world of enigmatic wonder as you struggle to get your law legs.

And, even if you *do* discover a legal paradise, where you're treated with smiles and kindness every day, take your motto from the Boy Scouts: Be prepared. (If you are off on a divergent—and often vastly more interesting—path, just picture a law firm façade describing your gallant efforts.)

You're not a lawyer when you graduate from law school. You're not even a lawyer after you pass the bar exam and're admitted to the bar. When you can face a client or an opponent—or a judge—without an overwhelming urge to throw up...*then* you're on your way.

The assumption among many partners (reinforced by their existence) is that, if you are *worthy*, you'll divine what is right (if, indeed, you don't already magically possess it). That is profoundly unjust. Few fresh JDs have what it takes from the word GO, and those few who do are more—not less—prone to trouble by their precociousness. A fairer demand by partners is a smooth and speedy transition from legal novice to dependable (and profitable) junior partner.

In this rarely smooth (and often sluggish) transition, most suffer in silence. Although no maturation process can be cleansed to painlessness, the one in law is especially caustic. Feedback, when (or *if*) it comes, is often too late, too demeaning, and too spiteful. Or, perhaps worse, too shyly given; we lawyers can be a dense lot.

Sometimes, it's negligently overlooked. Yet new associates who are told they took a wrong turn aren't even given a map to know where the turn was.

Here's a map.

Part of a winning strategy is being wise and lucky enough to find and cultivate a mentor—a legal patron saint—to assist you in this transition. Part of *your* job is to reduce the importance of luck in that strategy. Although luck might be a large part of every success, many bones are tossed in each career. It's up to you to recognize them as they arc past, snatch them from the air, and bury them in your own secret little part of the legal backyard. That's what'll separate the prized greyhounds from the unwanted mutts.

You can take the hard road, or an even harder one. This is the former; life is harder. Trust me. No, *don't* trust me. Instead, think back to your own hard-learned lessons in life. Though you might not have listened, chances are there was someone who could see from a better vantage warning you of the shoals. (One problem in law is that many new lawyers steam about without any such warnings—a sure sign of danger.) Don't let 'em sink you before you've even been out to sea. In the beginning, *all* are ignorant. Relax. There's a first time for everyone. Sure, you need to learn, and learn well. Just don't let your anxieties run you aground before you've mastered the currents.

This book may, at times, seem a little pedantic. Perhaps the best plea is *nolo contendere*. Okay, okay. Guilty. In making you into a proper young partner omelette (*sans fromage,* if you prefer), I might break (or at least crack) the occasional legal egg or two.

One more note. I use the masculine pronoun *he*—not *he or she, s / he,* or *he* and *she* alternating like nervous contrarians. I'll also take advantage of handy, if sexist, references to the law and her many features. I like to think I'm not a sexist pig. But literary egalitarianism is anathema to concise writing, historically not quite as objectionable as our modern ear hears, and tiresome. Before the fifty or so percent of you out there sharpen your knives, I'm a testosterone-modified feminist, so don't slice, dice, or lecture.

Oh. I also, sometimes, play a little fast and loose with grammar. Lighten up. Rules must be known, if only to have a reference with which to play. As you might read between the lines, such playfulness is both an allegory to the world of the law (you must learn the Rules before bending them)...and a heresy to be soundly suppressed during your first years as an attorney.

Kosrae, Micronesia
April 1996

— Recommended Reading —

In scribbled notations over the past few years on a battered copy of the first edition, I added references to specific practice guides. I then realized a better venue was at hand: The Net.

I thus started a list of books of interest to lawyers (and soon-to-be-lawyers) to which other attorneys have added their recommendations. If you run across a section that recommends a practice guide, you might check:

http://www.hits.net/~fpp/greatlawbooks.html

You may type in the root address only, http://www.hits.net/~fpp/ or www.fineprintpress.com to save time. A link is provided on the first page.

Postscript: A few *days* before the final draft of this second edition was supposed to go to press—or, according to the lords of publishing, a few months *after* the final draft of this second edition was *supposed* to go to press—I ran across a copy of a title that might well have displaced mine: *The Successful Practice of Law,* by John Evarts Tracy, a law professor with twenty-six years' practice experience. (Beats me by a good score.) There's no need to rush to Borders to buy it, however; it was published in 1947.

Despite the late hour, I added a few of the nuggets, where I could, from his book. (At times, his advice adds just that inter-generational sparkle that we lose every other cycle. For instance, at one point he discusses the wisdom of using women as witnesses: "Some attorneys see no difference between the sexes and would as soon use a woman witness as a man. Other attorneys will never use a woman under any circumstances." He avoids either extreme: "My own feeling is that it is dangerous to use a woman as a witness if you can prove the fact in any other way." He goes on to explain: "The reason for my hesitancy on this point is that we attorneys have learned, from experience, that a woman is a born partisan. It is impossible for her to take an unprejudiced view of the case.") Lest you assume him the obdurate misogynist, he goes on to relate in open admiration a case in which injustice was averted—against the testimony of *ten* opposing witnesses, including two physicians—only by the testimony of a reluctant and most honorable witness, a nun.

In the main, his advice is heartfelt and helpful. You might check your local law library, if you're curious. As to my shameless use now, I trust that he (and his spirit) don't mind, and I thank them both for their thoughtful contribution to generations then unknown.

— Official Disclaimer —

No words of law are complete without some attempt to disavow responsibility for the outcome—proximate, foreseeable, or otherwise—for advice-takers. I shall be no brave exception.

Responsibility for your life, loves, and career is *yours.*

The advisory tidbits offered herein are intended to give you an added perspective to which you probably won't have access otherwise (until you acquire it the hard way). Too often during the battles of life, we are each too buried in our own foxholes to see the horizon above the embankment. When we rise—or retreat—to better fortification and look back on what were, then, momentous engagements, our immediate reaction is usually snickering. Remember the math test you took in Mrs. Anderson's third-grade class? I thought not...though it seemed pretty important at the time. Well, it *was,* along with countless other little academic pit stops. Now you're in the big leagues, and the school-to-practice swap is often the most wrenching of all.

Too many variables affect the truth of these many generalizations, not the least of which is *you.* As circumstances alter cases, so too must your own situation—and your place in it—alter *your* actions. Often, the answer is to do nothing. This should imply not sloth, but acute feline-like steadiness before the vocational or personal pounce.

Learn who you are and what you want. From there, select from the varied and ever-changing palette of life's offerings. As an old, chirpy Air Force poster of my father's admonished: "Take what you want from life...but be prepared to pay for it."

The trials (real and figurative) that you're about to face will be less than pleasant. Here's to your eventual success, in whatever form.

Okay then, how about an introduction to the strange, sometimes savage new world you're about to explore?

An Introduction to the Law

Hello. I'm the Law.[1]

Nah...not really. I'm just a former junior associate, but I'll do, I suppose. I've been there. I've seen and done, and now it's time for me to show and tell (...or at least tell).

Why so much to tell, and such need?

The world of the junior associate is one marked by stress, long hours, uncertainty, more stress, sudden affluence, a new professional persona, still more stress, undefined expectations, a change to a new, unfamiliar measurement system, and, finally, some additional stress. Part of these multiple stresses is a result of the lack of information, even anecdotal, about the strange new world of law practice. Part is the sudden change from an extended studenthood to true professional responsibilities. Another part is the desire to live up to expectations as to which you're yet a stranger: In law practice, it's *assumed* that you'll complete your work at both high quality and high quantity. Just being good enough...isn't enough. (Though it's not all that easy.) You must also be professional, presentable, and profitable.

For a newcomer, law practice raises the same fears of ignorance and inadequacy that were particularly evident in law school. Worse, the stakes are higher. Your livelihood—in addition to your ego—is now on the line. Screw up and you do not pass go. Forget Park Place. Baltic'll start looking good. After you've been wallowing awhile, the realization hits: *real* people—with real concerns and real money at stake—are depending upon your lawyering skills...which are, as yet, undeveloped.

---

1   Hello again. I'm your first footnote. I'm also the last, because law in the real world is unlike the often excessively erudite (and even more often footnoted) academic world you're used to.

While I'm here, however, I may as well concur with the salutations offered by my elevated Big Brother, the Main Text, and tell you what I was thinking of. ("...of what I was thinking"? *Hmm*.) You see, a funny thing happened when the author typed "Hello." In true Freudian form, he typed, instead: "Hell." Come to think of it, that may be equally accurate in describing the introduction to law practice that some are unfortunate enough to face. Honestly, for most, it's usually not as bad as it's made out to be, but it *can* be worse. So much depends on variables outside your control. But not everything. Part of the reason for this book is to minimize the *Hell* part, and increase the likelihood of a reasonably happy *Hello,* instead. As in the jungle, survival is its own reward.

And each participant brings a few spare quandaries to the office. All converge to form one giant question mark: a nagging doubt as to your abilities and new station in life.

Well, like it or not, you're at the bottom rung of the social ladder... again. Before, however, you'd move to the bottom of each progression from elementary to junior to high school, and on to college and law school. At the beginning of each new experience, you were rightly unsure and nervous. But you were fairly comfortable in the familiar world of school, and pretty much knew that you'd rise to the top academically. The difference with practicing law is that the skills that served you so well in school might not be such an advantage—and might actually be a *hindrance*—in practice. Mere knowledge is useless; it must be wielded, and wielded well.

Your job now is to mold your known academic talents into a new, real-world strength.

MEMBERS OF THE TRIBE

Some are born to advantage. For those of you fortunate enough to have a family with the stray lawyer or two, or the test-taking profile rewarded on law exams (or, more likely, both), you will likely proceed down the well-carpeted path to high-powered law practice. You enter this world reasonably comfortable with its trappings. If so, you're miles ahead of your compatriots precisely because of that familiarity, which (...no one tells others) is nearly half of the game. If not, you won't. Fair? Not even close. Get over it.

The game? It's rigged. Is. Was. Always will be.

This book is written for someone else: the law virgin. For those of you—like, once upon a time, me—for whom law practice is an alien world, you must find your footing, quickly. Much of this process relates directly to the attitude and maturity of one person: *you*. Your handicaps are largely self-imposed, and your successes and final transformation will be a new you—the attorney—emerging from your student cocoon.

Some are "natural" lawyers, who seem born (if not inbred) with a sixth sense to the ways of the profession. In reality, this is most often a well- (if not over-) developed sense of self-confidence, often bordering (if not wildly exceeding) the bounds of arrogance. Others seem ill at ease even in their own offices. For most, the path lies somewhere in between. For now, realize that lots of very different people have succeeded in law. You should develop self-confidence, which is primarily a function of familiarity, while not succumbing to the Darker Side of the Force. Assuming you enter this strange new world alone, you should, first, relax, and, second, be particularly open to the advice of your superiors and me, for we both wish—for very different reasons—to see you make it.

DREAMERS AND OTHER SUBVERSIVES

Remember Confucius? Well, old Master K'ung Fu-zi (pronounced "Gong Foo´-dz", if you're curious) laid the foundation for Chinese philosophy for the two-plus millennia that succeeded him. More than that, he molded Chinese thought and developed the (now) traditional Chinese principles of ethics, morals, and social and filial obligations. These principles run very, *very* deep in modern China (and, indeed, in most of east Asia). He became, and still is, a revered figure for one-quarter of the world's population. And he is reasonably well-known and regarded among the remaining three-quarters.

So what's the point? *He died poor.*

He was a misfit. A troublemaker. And, eventually, a wandering outcast in a society of unyielding conformity. Sound familiar?

Most idealists starve. Many are unappreciated until long after they have passed from the scene (...which isn't much comfort while on stage). Confucius was one among a vast procession of unrewarded, frustrated thinkers that continues like a cruel joke. Though it might not help if Quixote's in *your* blood, take a look around. There're a whole lot of windmills out there—and *they* can tilt, too.

It's almost axiomatic that those who truly care...don't succeed. They're too busy caring, and too unsympathetic to the realities of human maneuverings. Those who succeed...care mostly about succeeding.

If *you* have severe idealistic leanings, which is not uncommon among law school crowds, take their lessons to heart, and maneuver yourself into a teaching position (if possible in today's exceedingly constrained market) or something similar that will stave off your creditors whilst you dance among the clouds.

The lesson for the rest is just as important, for Confucius *did* have ambitions. Ordinarily, one with his talents could, eventually, have become a powerful, entrenched leader. Yet for him it was not to be. He was too pig-headed to bow to the narcissistic demands of court life in ancient China, where the powerful expected endless flattery and sycophancy from upstart young hangers-on. Though this was beyond the abilities of poor Confucius, who was too enamored of the Truth, the lesson holds as well two thousand years later.

For you, the lesson is this: *Your success in law will be determined by others.* Specifically, by *Senior* others.[2]

---

2   OK, I lied. While we're at it, though, you may as well get used to legalese. So from now on, "senior attorney"—which includes both senior and junior partners and very senior associates—will be shortened to "Senior". Junior associates, comprising that bright-eyed group of legal virgins in their first few years, will be referred to as "Juniors". Mid-level associates ("senior Juniors") are breaking out of their own neophyte shells into legal adolescence, so it's usually best to smile at, listen to, and learn from them. Yes, you'll do the

Your talents are a necessary but not a sufficient condition for your success: You must have what it takes, but that alone isn't enough. You must also have the right attitude and the solid support of at least one Senior. (This should not imply abdication. Your success in *life* is determined by you, with a healthy dose of luck thrown in for good measure, but in the *law*—as in other professions—you're dependent upon the graces of those for whom you toil.) This reality you must accept...*now*.

It is a hateful process because you are at once unsure of your footing in this alien world...and dependent upon the mercy of someone else—a Senior someone else—who has his own doubts about the process. It is he who will be understanding—or not—of your inevitable missteps. While most are forgiving, their lessons are no less unpleasant.

Before you rail against the unfairness of it all, ask yourself how else it could be. Ours is a species of social constraints and hierarchy. We've seen what happens when alternatives are tried. (While we're on China, remember the Red Guards? Or, if Europe's more your style, how about the *Hitler Jugend* or Soviet *Komsomol?*) It is unfair, generationally, but, in those trite words of wisdom, who ever said life was supposed to be fair?

When the model works well, Seniors, who have the best interests of their Juniors at heart, guide them along the path to professional maturity. The important point for you is to find Seniors who do care, and help them to have *your* best interests at heart, for the one who is hurt most painfully when the model doesn't work is *you*.

MEMBERS OF THE TRIBE—PART TWO

And now for a less pleasant reality of law practice: Few are welcomed into the exclusive clubs of high-powered firms. Beginning with the first day of law school, the process is calculated to separate the superstar from the mediocre. The problem isn't that there *is* a disparity, but that, by disdain from above and acceptance from below, this disparity is embraced with an *assumption* of natural selection.

A friend, commenting on the "intimidation process" in law school and beyond, once wrote:

> [The top law firms] start the intimidation process in law school: They hire only the top of the class, and if you weren't in the top of the class, you feel inadequate when you come up against those who were —in part because you know damn well they got better training when they got *out* of law school and can draw upon the best mentors in the business when needed.

same with the Seniors, but you will rarely get the opportunity to develop as close a personal relationship as you will likely have with senior Juniors.

[O]bviously, the firms like the system as it is: Most law school graduates don't know squat, and take a long time to learn it. (If, indeed, they ever do. Based on my observations, a lot of lawyers are malpractice incarnate.) [The big firms] hire the cream of the crop, and then make damn sure the new associates learn the law. Hence, they do indeed have a big advantage once they start dealing directly with the outside world.

It isn't because they're smarter, usually. It's because they know what they're doing—and that can make all the difference in the world. So, from the big firms' point of view, the incompetence and indifference of law schools re. legal education suits them just fine. As a result, [they] have yet another big advantage when they go against "lesser" attorneys.

Sadly, there's more than a small grain of truth to his indictments. The point for you? Whatever *your* circumstances, take advantage of the knowledge offered by more experienced attorneys to maximize your toehold at the top, or minimize the disadvantage at the bottom.

AUTUMN ATTORNEYS

A few months after the first edition of this book was published, I received an email from moderately irate reader. She, along with others who have already lived a fair portion of their lives, faced a wall of exclusion: Exclusion of older law graduates from the ranks of the powerhouse firms. She wished that I change the title of the book to *The New Lawyer's Jungle Book,* or some such. (To be honest, I had considered that title, but I didn't think it had the same punch.) And, after much deliberation, I thought *Young* better, for two reasons. But first, an explanation in contrition.

A reality: it is unlikely that the older law student will be offered a position at the largest (and most prestigious, and best-paying) firms. Why? On behalf of the profession, I apologize. I think the justifications are thin, and outweighed by what older Juniors *do* have to offer. Nonetheless, the largest firms operate on a different model; they require the slavish dedication for which few older folks—literally—have the energy. (Even graduates entering the downside of their *twenties* quickly find the pace intolerably draining.)

She thus faced, in immediate and hurtful relief, a burden not faced by her younger "peers". I sensed her irritation...though I think it somewhat misplaced. *Young* is better in large part as a *compliment* to older Juniors: they've already lived life, and have learned the lessons of professional deportment. *This is half the battle.*

Also, older Juniors have a somewhat different problem: while they face a higher hurdle at large firms, they generally face a more hospitable reception at smaller firms—and in government offices—which to be fair are more suited to the more mature new attorney. To be blunt, large-firm hiring folks face a difficult reality: older Juniors will pose a *different* interpersonal dynamic; they will disturb the power/age equilibrium; and a good percentage simply won't have the *energy* to devote eighty-to-one-hundred-hour weeks for eight-to-ten *years* before professional acceptance among their generational peers—and even longer before *true* partnership.) Sadly, in practice, *different* equals *wierd,* and *wierd* definitely equals *bad.*

If this section applies to you, please do not take offense, or rail against the intergenerational unfairness. Instead, look ahead to the greater contributions you can make. You *are* better than your younger peers—not in terms of any of the variables that are distributed in varying degrees to each—but in qualities more important: experience, emotional balance, judgment, and insight.

Further, many older *Young Lawyers* are able to take advantage of their earlier careers to...great advantage. Three fellow first-year students were physicians. Two became medical malpractice attorneys (one each for either side), and the third, an anesthesiologist, started with an intellectual property firm. Indeed, all three started while still in law school, and have done quite well. (At least one made partner early. Astonishingly early.)

METRO GREEN, METRO BLUES

Money is a large part of the attraction to law practice. Much is made —by firms and associates alike—of stratospheric starting salaries. Generally, such salaries are available only with the largest firms, in the largest cities. Even so, cities offer higher salaries than elsewhere, leading to an annual urban migration of that most odd creature: *Officus recentgraduatium*. (Easily recognized by the new suit, bright tie, and severe haircut. Notice also its nervous mannerisms, especially when nearing others of its kind.)

Consider, as well, the cost of living. Yes, you might earn that nosebleed-inducing salary—if the planets are correctly aligned—yet such a salary in Manhattan (the one in New York, not Kansas) earns a lower standard of living than a more modest salary in, say, Denver. It's not unusual for the cost of living in smaller cities to be *half* that of their larger cousins, especially for new residents. (Resort areas are also notoriously pricey, which rarely hits home until you live there.) In smaller towns, it's half again less expensive. If you want to buy a nice house, in a nice neighborhood, the difference is even greater.

In terms of *quality* of life, it's not even close. (You'll have surprisingly little time for those many museums.) Something to think about when striving for that 200th billable hour at the end of each month.

Sure, if you're a big-city aficionado, by all means. But it *will* require a healthy chunk of those means.

CHOOSING YOUR POISON

If you're still in school, take heed. Too often, law students look to the world of firms with understandably uncritical eyes. This problem is compounded by most students' unfamiliarity with law practice, by necessarily imbalanced recruitment goals, and by firms' dominance of the process and duplicative self-promotion. To many a student, the procession of interviewing firms melds into one endlessly named monolith. Each firm seems to tout the same things, and interview questions flow into each other for their repetition and vapidity.

Don't succumb to this trap. As much as you can afford to, reverse (or at least balance) the scenario. It really is (or should be) a two-way street; you should be appraising the firms while they're maneuvering about you.

Take a long, hard look at yourself. What do you *really* want? What is your personality best suited to? If you're truly of the pinstriped set, and have the grades, then shoot for that; there's plenty to choose from. But you still need to be critical, not complacent. You should look to more than nice offices, panoramic views, or fancy lunches. Look to *personality*. Seriously. For it is there that you will feel, months and years hence, either at home or in a hell of Dantean dimensions. Look beyond the L.A. Law/Ally McBeal hype. That's pretend lawyering. Look instead to where the firm is *really* coming from.

If you feel lost and unsure of your legal desires, then find a firm whose partners take mentoring seriously. Ironically, bigger firms are usually better at this—because they *have* to be. If you like smaller firms (...and smaller firms are, generally, nicer places to practice) then you should understand that, more likely than not, a far greater part of your learning—and self-teaching—responsibility will fall upon *your* shoulders. If you're not self-directed, then go with a bigger firm, at least until your training wheels fall off.

If you're a total cynic, save yourself and law firms the trouble of dealing with you...find something else. The parallel construction of the preceding sentence was intentional, by the way: You won't be much fun to others—*or to yourself*—if you're miserable. Expand your search; there's a whole lot out there for those willing to explore.

The point is to disabuse yourself of the notion that you should bluster through as many interviews as your grades allow, go to office interviews at those firms on whose original interviewers you didn't throw up, and accept with gratefulness the "best" (i.e., best-paying) offer that comes your way. Sure, the wildly cyclical job market has a lot to do with your level of gratitude—and desperation—but do try to take *your* part of the process seriously.

For a good long-term fit, it *is* important for you to judge them as much as they judge you. If this means a lot more work in your cozy placement office (which it does), then have the pizza-delivery number ready. Spending a few dozen hours of your student time might save you from thousands of hours of costly, and resented, billable time.

Read legal periodicals—your state's bar journal, the ABA, American, and National law journals, *The Young Lawyer, The National Jurist, The Associate*, and the like—while you're still in law school. This will give you a better feel for what's going on among practitioners...even if you don't intend to enter private practice. It might also give you a leg up in the interviewing process, where *interviewers* are numbed to exhaustion by an endless procession of student names connected to bodies whose masters haven't a clue.

It's a paradox of life that we rarely know what we want until it's too late. This is only worsened by modern careers, which must be chosen and developed earlier and earlier. Do what you can to be one who chooses wisely the first time around.

CLASSES

If you're still in school, and're undecided about what classes to take, here's a contrary view: Do *not* take classes because you think they'll be helpful for the bar exam. You'll spend time enough with bar-review study, and having taken a course in, say, commercial paper will be only marginally helpful—if at all—in the exam.

Sure, if you feel the litigator deep in your bones, you may as well load up on evidence and trial courses. (Clinics are good for non-litigators, too; they'll give you a taste of what you'll be missing.) And if you're destined for that glorious tax practice, you should excise all thoughts of Pre-Renaissance Entertainment Law of Southern Europe and encumber yourself, instead, with other exciting, if somewhat more exacting, courses. (Even better, if you know what and where you'll likely practice, *read the state's statutes for that topic*. You'll be parsecs ahead of everyone else.)

You should take (and ace) Family Law and Wills & Estates: two areas in which all lawyers are expected to have ready dinner-party answers. Remedies, Alternative Dispute Resolution, Conflict of Laws, Jurisprudence, and the like are nice components of a legal education. Consumer Protection, Employment, Environmental, Immigration, International, and Tax courses are other prospects, depending upon your desires. (Unfortunately, each is usually too concerned with depth, at the expense of breadth or sense, to be of true benefit to most students.) Survey courses, if available at your school, are a nice way to learn an area of law, without wasting time on details that will change, if not fade immediately from memory.

You should also take courses offered in other disciplines. Business courses, though time-consuming, are a natural complement to future commercial lawyers...and they're *fun*. (Well, most of them—although all are a nice break from the redistributive world of law.)

Don't like money-grubbing? Take courses in the social sciences, the hard sciences, the arts...whatever. If you have a sincere interest in something, you'll likely be able to talk your dean into approving law school credit for...just about anything. It'll transform your law school years into the intellectual delight that they should be. As long as your grades impress, it'll rarely make any negative difference to interviewers (if it *does,* would you *really* want to work there, anyway?), though it might make a positive difference to some. More importantly, it'll make you a better person...and a better lawyer.

Don't feel bound by your law school catalog.

And don't listen to those who insist that you must take the most boring classes ever offered to succeed in practice. It ain't so. When necessary, you can prepare yourself adequately in the real world by reading an outline over a weekend. (And don't worry...you *will.*) They won't be the most enjoyable weekends, true, but once you've learned about law, generally, condensed references are the best way to learn about law, specifically.

A legal education—indeed, all education—is not *supposed* to teach you...stuff. That's called training. Rather, education should teach you *how to learn*...and how to figure out how to apply learned knowledge. Clichéd as the saying is, this won't sink in until after you've practiced awhile: the law you learn in school will not be the law you practice. Besides, there's a word for relying on your law school lectures for law practice details: *mal*practice.

So how do you practice if not from memory? That's coming up.

For now, don't make yourself miserable for what's left of your law school career in the misdirected hope that it'll make more than a modest difference. It won't.[3]

LAW REVIEW

For those who "made" the penultimate law school hurdle to Law Review, the psychological—and fiscal—boost is considerable, particularly at the starting gate. This advantage doesn't hold perfectly...especially after the tenuous correlation between law review dweebdom and law practice performance becomes apparent.

For a significant number of the other ninety percent who did not, a mention of law review often touches a raw, exposed nerve.

I'll go on record: were I Emperor, law review would be *mandatory* for *all* law students. For, you see, law review presents an interesting

---

3 As a contrary view to my contrary view, there probably *is* a correlation, but not between classes and success. Rather, it's probably between boring-class temperament and practice success. An editor asked if I meant that "those willing to get down in the trenches are more likely to succeed than those with their heads in the clouds." Exactly.

chicken-and-egg question. Whether it is: (1) mere recognition of latent genius, or (2) an incubator of legal skill is unexamined and, more practically, is a rare concern among hiring Seniors; they simply favor the halos. It's not really their place to care.

(The answer, by the way, is: *both*—and probably more of the latter. Through a process of dreadfully boring work, law review *does* give its members an added educational benefit to which other law students are now denied. The meat of the common law is the synthesis of endless statutory and case law and secondary sources, which is the forte[4] of law reviews. This skill, which is probably the more important of the two functions of law reviews—student training and academic dissemination—is glossed over, if not completely ignored, during law school for non-review students.)

I am grateful that my own law review experience gives me credibility to castigate from within. It is most emphatically not true that "others" are unworthy of law review. Ninety-plus percent of all law students are perfectly capable and motivated to do as good a job as is legitimately required...and the ten-minus percent who cannot, arguably, shouldn't be lawyers. For law review admission, however, the proportions are instead reversed, leading to no small misery and adversity among the talented but misfortunate majority. These soapbox paragraphs notwithstanding, law review has odd consequences in law practice.

If you were on law review, chill out. You're not quite as valuable as others make you believe. A little modesty, *s'il vous plaît*. More importantly, put your law review skills into perspective. They'll make legal research a little less scary, but, at the same time, will encourage you to go overboard. Be careful. Few Seniors want law review-type memos to cross their desks. They want, instead, to see short, sweet, and *quick* results. Particularly for you true dweebs out there, this is a conundrum. (I take liberty to condescend because I am one.[5]) Fortunately, most of you were sufficiently distracted, bored, or lazy enough during your second and third years to not take things too seriously.[6] You *do* need to be serious, but judicious, in practice.

If you were *not* on law review, chill out. You're not quite as worthless as others—and you—made you believe. A little perspective,

---

4   Which, for you upper-crusters-to-be, is pronounced "fort", not "for tay". The pronunciation "for tay" refers to an instruction in music to play in a loud or forceful manner. The pronunciation "fort" referred originally to the middle, and thus strongest, part of a sword or foil blade near its hilt (handle). "For tay" is mispronounced so commonly on this side of the Atlantic, however, it has achieved legitimate, albeit secondary, status. Perhaps, depending upon your view, this is just another of our many American foibles.

5   ...a dweeb, not a conundrum.

6   When not splitting hairs, I take my frustrations out on infinitives.

s'il vous plaît. Practice and academics have very different purposes. Law review is even farther off the theoretical end of the scale. If you want to be a successful practitioner, yet are embarrassed by your law school "failure"—remember that you're in populous country: a healthy percentage of successful practitioners were *not* at the very top academically. This is more than statistics at work; practice rewards street smarts as much as the other variety.

If you're coming up from behind the power curve, credential-wise, you'll need to work that much harder to prove yourself, if that's important to you. (Remember too that discussions of law review come up rarely in practice, except among the insecure.)

If you're in litigation, law review is the least helpful, and might even be *inversely* correlated with a smooth transition; the best litigators are comfortable in the courtroom, not the library. Smart Senior litigators look for the lean and hungry look, which is rarely found in hallowed halls. When assigned a case, grab hold and do an aggressive, comprehensive job. This should not imply that you need to be rude, or dishonest, or needlessly crafty. Nine-tenths of litigation success is in outpreparing your opponent. (Which might just understate things by about ten percent.[7])

If you're competing with snotty reviewers, pick up your unused Bluebook and double-check citations as you go along. This is, after all, how law reviewers learn.[8] But don't go overboard: few Seniors still know, or follow, the technical conventions of law reviewdom. Guard against the dangers of overcompensating; converts are usually the most devout...and annoying.

And snotty people are best ignored. Don't give them the satisfaction of acceding to their caste regime.

HUBRIS

I wrote a review for a book that was recently published for law students. In reading the book I was struck by a phenomenon that strikes nearly all who make law review: the nearly overwhelming impulse to become insufferably snotty.

Those who do well in law school just naturally assume that they succeeded by their brilliance, and their brilliance unaided. Wrong. There are *lots* of brilliant people in law school...and a significant percentage will fail. Perhaps not literally, but "failure" is relative, especially among the talented folk who populate law schools.

Those who have "made it" cannot know—they cannot *truly* understand—*why*. But that's not the worst of it: They move on—with real

---

7   Though a good set of facts and favorable law help, too.

8   You *do* need to learn how to cite properly. More on that, later.

and imagined imperatives in maintaining the fiction that they were predestined for greatness, while the rest are too embarrassed, confused, and defeated to figure out what went wrong.

Yes, there *is* a correlation. Law reviewers *are,* on average, smarter than non-law-reviewers. But that datum is neutered in comparison to three more important realities. First, it's an *average*.

I've grown weary at our species' profound inability to comprehend the meaning of that word and concept, and to apply them properly to individuals: you *can't*.

Even if the statement is categorically true—that law reviewers are, on average, smarter than non-law-reviewers—that *necessarily* implies that *some* non-law-reviewers are smarter than *some* law reviewers. Given the distribution of talent in law school, and given my own experience, *many* non-law-reviewers are smarter than many law reviewers.

Second, law school exams test only a part of lawyering skills, and actively distort appreciation of deeper intelligence. Thus, the correlation between law school grades and intelligence is low. I'd guess a (positive) zero-point-two to, perhaps, a zero-point-four.

Finally, law review—indeed, intelligence generally—isn't the most important factor in success. It comes in a distant second.

In the science fiction novel *Dune,* the protagonist is the cosmic combination of both mathematical and emotional omniscience. His royal training encompassed both, and his task was equally daunting. Through it all, he remained a decent human being.

In real life, chances are better than even that anyone getting such attention would turn into a sphincter of equally regal proportions. One of our oddities is our tendency to turn advantage into unworthiness, as those who are given too much appreciate it too little.

The point? If *you* were lucky, you might avoid the gods' wrath by appreciating their generosity: go easy on the hubris. For practical reasons, it will harm you. For emotional reasons, it will destroy you.

SUMMER CAMP

If you were lucky enough to secure a comfy summer clerkship, you'll already have a few toes in the water. As modified—and grossly overpaid—apprenticeships, summer clerkships provide a profitable role for the young lawyer. Less is expected of most summer clerks, yet much is learned during these mercury-enhanced months. Names. Office routines. Fancy lunches. Memos. Picnics. Softball. Golfing. Preliminary power pow-wows. Important and heady stuff for a young legal eagle.

In fairness to firms, and unfortunately for new generations of law students, summer clerkships are becoming less and less the playful extravaganzas that played so prominently in the '80s, which were not only alarmingly expensive, but didn't truly test the students' mettle. And they were a *definite* violation of truth-in-advertising. So don't expect quite the picnic your older sibling got.

In larger firms, you'll likely be rotated through several practice areas. Don't resist, or insist that you've already "chosen" an area for yourself. Instead, take advantage, and keep an open mind. In smaller firms, you'll likely be passed among many or all of the Seniors, to help as needed, ad hoc. Don't resist. Instead, take advantage.

If you're still in school and can't secure a summer clerkship, try like hell to get something. Anything. Even volunteering is better than nothing, particularly if you can get law school credit for it (which you likely can). Talk with your deans. Talk with your favorite profs. Talk with your placement counselors. Talk with your Senators.[9] Talk to *everyone.* This is far more important than it should be in getting your professional life started.

INTERVIEWS

I once had a particularly important interview, and happened a few days before to meet up with my brother, who was traveling through Texas. On a trip to San Antonio, he insisted that I role-play the part of the hapless interviewee, and he the intrepid interviewer. He was well-suited to the role, having just spent several hundred dollars on a private consultation with an airline expert. (His dedication apparently paid; he landed a job with American Airlines, in a difficult market.) As silly as it felt, I knew it was valuable help. As I started every answer with some quasi-thoughtful response, I was gruffly interrupted.

"*No!* Don't say that! Say it this way...."

Upon which he proceeded to spin a saccharinely emphatic string of phrases that would give bullshit a bad name. I remember joking that if someone had thrown such blatantly brown-nosing tripe to *me,* I'd've suffered an instant urge to, well...I'd better not recount the exact conversation. Yet he was dead serious. And right. I was annoyed. Not at being interrupted, or corrected. But at the emptiness of it all.

---

9   Another joke? Actually, no. It's a hateful process for you, and an annoying one for them, but the various offices that exist to make, execute, and interpret the law are filled with folks who might just be willing to help. The opportunities are there, in every market; all you need is *one.* But it's up to you to find (...or create) it.

The author of *Planet Law School* (published by the same press) has written perhaps the best discussion of this dilemma for those law students without an automatic "in". Further, he approaches it from the right perspective: lay the groundwork *before* you *need* the job. (I've been accused of writing *Planet Law School,* which is both odd and untrue. I did review a manuscript and write a review for the publisher.) Although I disagree with some of the author's conclusions, I do believe it's the best book available on law school.

Thus a Great Truth: *interviews are artificial*.

If we wanted to be honest—there I go again—they are an almost unqualified waste of time.[10] Interviewing is not about the positives. It's about *not* being negative. Interviewers don't *really* want to know the whole story, even if they say they do. They don't want to know your *life's* story. They only want to know that you'll do the job...and won't make them look bad in the process. Credentials. Image. Politics. Self-interest. (Note your lack of control over many. Note too that you don't know what they're *really* looking for.) Say *nothing* negative, and focus only on the positive. Yes, tell the truth, but only half: the *positive* half. This isn't about full disclosure. It's about landing a job.

Play defensively.

I've blown more interviews in life than I've passed, in part because I find it so difficult to suppress those prickly subordinate clauses. Interviews are no place for introspection. Nor are they for nuance. I look back on that drive with my brother, and remain stunned at my own naïveté, then and after. What struck me as grossly, offensively sycophantic is *expected* among interviewers. And, even if they try otherwise, they *will* be turned off by the negative. In many interviews, it's *already your job*...to lose.

JUDICIAL CLERKSHIPS

"Clerkship" always struck me as both archaic and vaguely insulting. Though it's a little of the former, it's the latter only for non-lawyers. No, it doesn't refer to the office equivalent of burger-flipping (depending upon the boss). Rather, it refers to an honored position as research assistant and confidant to a judge.

If you're still in school, and have anything close to the necessary credentials, you *must* seek a judicial clerkship. If not appellate, trial. If not federal, state. If not state, local. If not judicial, administrative. If not easily obtained, hard.

It might seem, in your youthful haste, like a waste of a year or two. It is not. It is, instead, a finishing school for the young attorney. You will learn things about which your non-clerkship brethren will be clueless. It provides invaluable exposure to the legal system—especially for future litigators—from a vantage inaccessible even for senior practitioners (...except that many Seniors were themselves judicial clerks). More cynically, it sometimes means the difference between a high-powered job and an ordinary one, or, in a few markets today, a law job or none at all.

---

10 I'm not kidding. It would be almost as efficient (and in some cases moreso) —and *considerably* less costly—to allocate entry-level positions by lottery. *Ah*...then the illusion would be exposed. (Managers would be forced as well to evaluate, train, and *lead* their charges more effectively.)

If you want to teach law, a clerkship is almost mandatory. (Indeed, just *any* clerkship won't do; it must be a *prestigious* one.[11])

If you think you'd like to be a judge, a clerkship is a wise move. If your tendency is intellectual, it is downright *fun*. It's like law school... on steroids.[12]

You'll almost certainly get credit for the time, and, not least, it is yet another effective delaying tactic from the cold, cruel real world.

BAR ADMISSION

Sometime before you sit for the bar exam, you'll fill out a pile of forms that would've done the ol' KGB proud. To paraphrase Arlo Guthrie, you'll be inspected, dissected, neglected, reinspected, corrected, perhaps disinfected...and, with a little luck, not rejected but accepted.

Take this process *seriously*.

Now is not the time to draw pictures in unused questionnaire spaces (well-drawn though they might be), or write "As often as possible" in the "SEX: " space.

It is also not the time to decide that check-kiting is really more misunderstood than malevolent, or to realize your most radical dreams of restructuring society.

Wait until *after* you've passed the examiners' gaze, and've received their seal of approval.

THE EXAM

Few of life's experiences will match the drama (and, possibly, tragedy) of the bar exam. Like all law school exams rolled into one, it will keep you on edge for a good half-year or so. Worse, it's pass/fail, which means that you'll have no choice but to overprepare for everything. Even more wondrous, preparing for the exam will *finally* expose you to *real* law! Much that was unclear in class is synthesized in bar review courses, and becomes obvious the second time around.

The bar exam is your final rite of passage for official entry into the profession. (Final, that is, except for your Junior years to follow.) Like your Junior years, give it all you've got...and get it behind you.

If you're joining a firm, they'll probably pick up the tab for a bar review course. If it's a larger firm, they're probably quite generous in

---

11 A few years as an associate in a prestigious, national law firm is okay. (Which, of course, requires either Top 10% of the Top 10 status, or a federal clerkship...which in turn requires the former. A few exceptions—perhaps Top 20% of the Top 20 and some other hook—only prove the rule.) Know, also, that after only those few years in the real world, you become "tainted" in the academic one; make the shift ASAP.

12 ...but more legal.

giving you paid leave to study. Use it. Even if your firm doesn't have a policy—or deducts vacation time instead—*take the time off.*

Sitting through four hours of bar review lectures six days a week after eight-to-twelve hour workdays is not a realistic long-term study plan.[13] (And you do not want to face the consequences for your continued employment if you fail.)

If you're still on your own, you'll be stuck with yet another thousand-plus-dollar tab in addition to your mounting student debt. (It's still cheaper than taking it twice.) Unfortunately, signing up for commercial courses is not a luxury easily avoided.

(Were it up to me, vigorous bar review courses and even *harder,* phased exams would replace the final semester of law school. Not a chance: ABA dictates and self-interest will keep such radical thoughts at bay.)

Few (former) law students have the self-direction to make a decent go of self-study. Unfair or not, just figure this expense as yet another mounting cost to the legal feather in your cap.

Hang in there. It'll all work out okay.

Whether you pay for it or not, take advantage of each bar review class. Usually, you can sit back and absorb most of the lectures.[14] Like law school (and practice), however, you must learn to think methodically...and write it down, quickly. But this is the *final* final.

Compile your own outlines, boil one for each subject down into one-to-three page nuclei, burn them all in a ritualistic cleansing,[15] and take the exam.

Good luck.

---

13   For the record, I violated then my own advice now. Although the result was positive, the effect on me was not.

14   While you're at it—and regardless of what area of law you think you're interested in—pay special attention to the basics: criminal law, family law, wills and estates, and such. Fifty dollars to the first lawyer who goes a season without being asked a dinner-party question in one of these areas. I revoke the preceding sentence, by the way, for those who saw an offer therein.

15   Don't forget to douse the embers with the sludge that's left at the bottom of your coffee urn.

IN AWE OF LAW

A large part of the problem with your first years as a lawyer is that you're walking a tightrope...and you'll have only the vaguest notion where that darned rope is.

The first day on the job you (along with new employees of all stripes) walk into your office, scared. Just as you felt before your first day of junior high, and at each of life's milestones, realize that "they" are not out to get you, and will honestly try to make you feel less nervous.

Relax. Usually, you'll do mindless housekeeping for the first morning or so, then it's off to an expensive lunch—on the firm—with your new compatriots. Relax and smell the cappuccino. There is a flow to this learning process, as there is a flow to every learning experience. *Go with the flow*.

Accept that there's much out there you don't know. (There's much out there *Seniors* don't know.) Sometimes, sadly, this unavoidable ignorance affects real people, in real bad ways. This is a reality of any practice. *Your* goal should be to prepare yourself well enough to avoid—or at least recognize—the traps set for the unwary.

THE PREGNANT YEAR

Twelve months is an awful long time to carry around heavy (much less unrealistic) expectations.

You're no longer in the academic game; you are in law *practice*. Perhaps the greatest source of frustration for Juniors is the difference between the two. Those who adjust most easily are often those who were most cynical (or cared least) about their academic games.

Much of the game—*any* game—is a question of expectation. Is a B good? A rather telling question, depending upon your response. To someone who usually gets a D, a B is spectacular. To you and most of your lawyer brethren, however, A's were the norm throughout your young lives. For this uppity group, responses to a B range from disappointment to devastation.

And now for a Truth that might go against the grain: Perfection is not always the best, or most realistic, goal...especially for the beginner. For most practitioners, *a B is the better target*—at least during your Junior years. It's not that an A is wrong, but you must be careful if you're a perfectionist, because that last ten percent of perfection will require a severely disproportionate, greater effort that you can neither spare nor handle. Excellence necessarily involves a higher risk of disappointment. Moreover, a perfectionist attitude will trip you up in a world of muddlers-through, for whom the rules of the game are designed. As Asian societies are fond of reminding their youngsters, the nail that sticks up is the first one hammered down.

The focus in practice is the *reverse* of academics. The educational system purports to teach process, but rewards results. Lawyers are hired to get results, but are primarily rewarded for the *process* of serving their clients. In the short-run, good results are a bonus.

Few clients know the difference between a superb A and a sub-par D memo, brief, or contract. Clients aren't professors. They don't want to pay for perfection, and they shouldn't have to. Unlike school, the emphasis is not product; it is, instead, perception. Bad results can be explained, but bad service is more distressing. Although your clients are ultimately retained by good results, for you the *process* is more important. This is one of those odd paradoxes created by the agency relationship between lawyers and their clients.

You do not have the time to reinvent the practicing wheel—being practical, *it's already there*—and your Seniors won't have the patience to withstand your eager dalliances. The client will wonder why *your* contract cost ten times as much as the last one the firm prepared. It's embarrassing for your Seniors, to whom complaints are addressed. They'll have little choice but to write your masterpiece off as a loss. And don't expect praise. Expect instead a lecture (or a less-kindly rebuke) for your sincere efforts. It's not worth it.

Here's an example: I prefer contractual language that is not only precise, but also elegant. Wrong. Real law—the kind you'll practice— isn't elegant; it's darned messy. I wasted time during my first years eliminating redundancies and reorganizing badly organized forms, when I should instead have been more concerned with making sure the document did what the client wanted, guarding against hidden bombs...and getting the thing *done*.

Later, *after* you've grown comfortable with your little niche in the law, can you burst forth with your brilliance and reap your rewards. For now, the hurdles are set a little lower. Take advantage of this. (Not, mind you, that you can rush out to celebrate lax standards. Your first year is just a warm-up to expectations that only increase.) Focus your energies on being above-average, and on-point.

ATTITUDE

As long as you're going to the trouble of being in the Game, you may as well do it right. Seniors are looking for someone to whom they can delegate work, freeing themselves for higher-order legal problems, golf, and rainmaking...without worrying about whether any risk of antagonizing clients will attach to your handling of their cases.

You will be frustrated, not so much by the quantity of work (which will be enormous), but more by the nagging feeling that someone's going to find out that you haven't the foggiest idea what's going on. In aviation parlance, this is "flying from the tail skid" and abates after you grow into your duties. (If it doesn't, confirm why.) Once you've truly become a professional, you'll still see questions to which you have no ready answer, but you'll be comfortable enough with yourself to handle them with aplomb (or at least without losing your lunch).

Attitude, attitude, attitude. You must *want* to be a lawyer.

Further, you must want to be a lawyer *with that firm*. And, still further, to succeed in the long-run, you must want to be a partner with the Seniors of that firm.

No, more than that. If you're there just because you have no idea who you are and what you want—but you know, deep down, that it ain't law practice—then you are taking someone else's slot, and you'll likely have a rough go of it yourself. You need to develop a sense of purpose...or move on. Either way, passivity is not the answer.

CARTOGRAPHY

Much of your initial confusion will be due to an ignorance of the terrain. Not only the global stuff, but also the local contours.

How many days do you have to do *x?* Where do you file *y?* How do you find out *z?*

Much of this information is under your nose. Worse, this is the type of knowledge that you must acquire on your own. Nonetheless, most Juniors are sent on their way with neither map nor compass... though they're expected to arrive, on-time, at the (secret) destination. When you start into a new legal area, ask your Senior to recommend a practice guide (there's a good HOW TO reference available for nearly every legal specialty, often from the local bar association or CLE vendors), and then—Surprise! Surprise!—*read* it.

So few new (or even old) lawyers actually do this, it's scary. They wait, instead, until something blows up...and then they dash about madly to figure out what's going on. In navigation, this is "backing in a fix"—or calculating a position *after* the fact—which usually means someone's screwing up. Often, that's just the way the world works. But, in your (relatively) protected years as Junior, take advantage of the opportunity to learn the basics. You'll be that much farther ahead of everyone else when the true challenges arrive.

I was once, very briefly, in the Air Force (but, instead of lusting after my coveted pilot's slot, I went to law school. Go figure.) In Officer Training School at festive Lackland Air Force Base in sunny San Antonio, eager young cadets are given a huge set of manuals covering every conceivable detail, and more, of Air Force training life. Nevertheless, many cadets—myself included—flail about without a clue. Wiser, former-enlisted cadets just smile, and read the manuals.

Take advantage of these maps—drafted by learned and caring minds—to learn the terrain the easy way. Sure, you won't have quite the same feel for the road as when you start on your own journey, but at least you'll recognize the route.

A CONTINUED LEGAL EDUCATION

CLE is a good way to learn the basics. Most firms pay for these (quite costly) courses, and some even give credit for your time. Either way, take advantage. (Careful, though; your billables tally is expected to be just as high.) CLE is a valuable tool, both for the practical details conveyed and for a quasi-formal acquaintance with the folks in your future legal circle. (Be on good behavior; you represent the firm, and you represent yourself.)

Although the CLE beast has become both bothersome and silly, in many jurisdictions it's mandatory. Thus, your task is to decide which courses most interest you. For most, the decision is easy: attend courses in your area of practice. Ask what the policies of the firm are. Usually, you'll clear your choice with a Senior or two, who won't be pleased if you fly off on too far a tangent...on *their* nickel.

Understand also the *purpose* behind such *expensive* training: it's not for the betterment of lawkind, nor for an excuse for you to get out of the office. It's for *money*. For the firm. You must become proficient, quickly. And CLE provides one way, alongside practice, to prepare yourself for the trials to follow.

You should focus your CLE requests in two areas: (1) legal fields of special strength in the firm and for which you have an *earnest* interest; and (2) "procedural" seminars—legal writing, speaking skills, social skills [no kidding], client skills, local bar hobnobbing, and the like. Look also to the CLE materials in your firm's library. Take them home (especially during a summer clerkship) and *read them.* (Don't forget to return them. It's mighty embarrassing to get caught for such low stakes.) Get the basics down, early.

Just to reinforce the expense part: larger firms spend tens or even hundreds of thousands of dollars on direct CLE costs...and many thousands more in your *time* away from the office. Appreciate.

THE WONDER YEAR

Your first years will involve much research, small projects, routine form-production, and even more routine scut-work.

In a high-powered office, you'll continue your summer clerkship rounds and get some meaty stuff, perhaps sooner than you'd like. Some big firms inundate new associates with mounds of make-work.

(This is less and less true, nowadays.) If you're in a smaller office, you might get a wider range of projects than others...with a scary dose of autonomous responsibility.

Most of you will face an innumerable variety of challenges; there are just too many possibilities. One thing is pretty constant, though: Juniors usually do Junior work.

Accept whatever work is given, with a smile, and do your best to tackle it. More on that later. For now, don't despair. Or criticize. Don't rebel against the "It's not your place" syndrome so stifling to impatient intellects. First, it really *isn't* your place. More importantly, you should cherish the relative security you'll enjoy as co-pilot. Take advantage of your legal teething period. Use this Junior opportunity to learn the ropes, learn the basic rules, learn some real law...and prepare yourself for the real adventures to follow.

Patience. There *is* a rough logic to it all.

Develop friendships with your office mates, secretaries, staff, night crew, janitors, and local legal importants—bureau clerks, vendors, and whomever. (You might even make a special effort to introduce yourself to folks in offices before which you appear; so few do this, you will be especially known and appreciated.) These friendships will reward you, both personally and professionally, in the years to come. And be *friendly*. Assholes are such a drag.

Once housekeeping settles, you'll get a mountain of small stuff. This will grow, not subside, with time. In short, it will seem as if your Seniors expect too much, too soon. And because each has survived the same process, with a dulled memory (if not a damaged psyche), they might seem unreasonably unforgiving—or worse, unmindful—of your insecurities. Get over it. You'll benefit from money and status and a far better array of problems than nearly all other office serfs face.

This is the price tag.

Legal work can be quite satisfying, and even fun, once you've acclimated yourself to its workings. Seriously. If you're in the middle of a legal maelstrom, and you're glancing wistfully at other folks scurrying about, take a closer look. Few professions are devoid of the same dimension of stress and proclivity to burnout (try teaching in an inner-city public school), and most carry far fewer financial and social rewards (try teaching in an inner-city public school). Plus, you'll soon be operating fairly freely in an advisory, somewhat aloof capacity... with other people's money or liberty (or lives) on the line. That should scare you a little, but it should also be a source of awe. Once you get past the vertigo, it's an exhilarating ride.

More on this later. For now, the important point (to restate) is that your Seniors want to be able to give you projects...without worrying about keeping the firm's liability carrier on the line.

PERKS: THE UPSIDE

Juniors enjoy bountiful material perks. For many (particularly those from working-class backgrounds), these perks are viewed almost suspiciously. Like the once-starving child who continues to stuff food into the pockets of his moth-eaten coat even after it becomes obvious that sustenance is no longer in doubt, these Juniors take advantage, in the negative sense, of these benefits.

Don't do that. First, it will be noticed. Second, it is unprofessional. Finally, it is unnecessary.

This often involves dining and wining on the firm's credit card. Mom & Dad Senior get the bill...but you'll hear about it if you cross the—sometimes undrawn—line. Learn what the policies of the firm are (...assuming there are any), and stay *well* within bounds. Sure, you might be able to get away with more, and you might even be well thought of by some Seniors for your bravado, but don't count on it. If you think you're being cheated, think again. Law is a fairly generous, if demanding, mistress. Treat her with respect.

PERKS: THE DOWNSIDE

While you enjoy these perks, you will probably notice little or no interest in your personal life. Whether your spouse is upset with you, or your kid is sick or...whatever, most Seniors would rather not know. Actually, it's a little deeper—and shallower—than that. It's not that Seniors are uncaring. It's just that they bump into problem after problem throughout each day, only to be followed, night after exhausted night, by their *own* lives. They really don't want to know that their subalterns also have lives. It's just too...*messy*.

Worse, life interferes with work. Even a well-planned vacation invariably causes some inconvenience or complication for someone. More often, it's quite a few someones. Seniors' lives are difficult—and stressful—enough as it is. They, along with all of us, shy away from additional complications.

These perks aren't free. Like the military, the firm exacts its pound of flesh for the goodies it doles out. You're expected to be a good soldier, forging ahead for its greater glory.

INDUSTRIAL PSYCHOLOGY (FOR THE INDUSTRIOUS AMONG US)

Many Seniors fail to appreciate that, managerially speaking, money is an incomplete motivator.

It's nice as an initial attractant (and, too frequently, it's the *only* attractant). It's useful as a peer scorecard. But it's also sometimes irrelevant when its novelty wears thin. Then other, usually personal, matters change from minor distractions to looming irritants.

Moreover, different people are motivated by different things. And to add complication to the brew, we're motivated by different things at different times.

For you, this will become particularly evident after the flush of law firm life wears off (while wearing you down). Along with most others, you'll start thinking about minivans, recliners, and naps. That last luxury, unfortunately, is a diversion from the consumptive demands of high-powered law practice.

Industrial psychologists know this phenomenon as the distinction between positive and negative motivators (or if you prefer, motivators and "hygiene factors"). Were a firm to entice you with, for example, its ultra-generous dental plan, you'd likely be unimpressed. Why? Because you expect *all* professional employment to provide roughly the same, *assumed* level of dental care. It doesn't positively motivate you, but its absence would negatively "motivate". Thus, firms tend to tout —and Juniors tend to drool over—generous compensation and accelerated partnership rewards. Yet what attracts you as a law student might not be what you lust after as an associate.

One example of coming to grips with this was the creation of the "Senior Attorney" position in large firms, which was a response to the umbrage taken against the rigid—and costly—"up-or-out" mentality of the partnership track. Seasoned lawyers were routinely kicked out upon failing the partnership test. Some had no desire for the high stress and managerial responsibilities of partnership, some were not overly motivated by the money that flowed from such exalted status, some might have felt that conflicting personal priorities raised the workload ante too much, some were damned by fate and excess competition, while others might have been decent associates, but either were not ready for, or were unlikely to grow into, rainmaking partnership. The institutional response was unthinking, and unwise. Thus lost were valuable, if static, players in the law game. This is now the response in fewer firms (and businesses generally). All are not meant for leadership or fame. When *you're* in charge, appreciate each for unique contributions and limitations.

There *is* an interesting, contrarian aside to this: A "revolving door" of sorts has emerged. The pace of practice is so frenetic few can keep up after a youthful start. Yet such a high billable demand is required to justify high salaries, which in turn are required to snare the "best" new associates. Economically, something's gotta' give. In practice, that something is the increasingly remote likelihood of the "average" superstar making partner. The new model: Run young associates ragged, with the assumption that most will opt out. Not a problem: those who do opt out form an informal rainmaking network for those few who stay. Thus, cynically, the firms have little to lose, either way. Importantly, this model leaves little room for vocational reconsideration. Thus, you really have only one shot. Make it a good one.

For now, realize that the Seniors' attention is diverted from your plebeian needs. If certain things are bugging you, pick the *important* points, pick the right time and right Senior, and present your case. Most times, it'll be no big deal. Just don't expect the coddling you've gotten since grade school.

And don't lose sight of your role. Barging in to ask for more money will almost certainly be met with indifference (at best). Unless you've just saved the partnership from dissolution by your timely rain dance bringing in a new Fortune 500 client (in which case you should demand partnership, not a raise), compensation is a topic not open for discussion, for Juniors.

YOUR PRIVATE LIFE

As much as possible, keep your private life...private.

Sometimes that's easier said than done. And, in all honesty, sometimes letting others know what's bothering you helps, where being the stoic does not.

Use your judgment, and don't be disloyal to your personality (...as if you could). But be careful when discussing your private feelings. As with military counseling, there is no such thing as a time-out rap session; what you say can and will be used against you. Well, it's not quite that impersonal, but the Seniors *do* have a responsibility to their firm and partners. Just realize that you're not among priests. (Know, too, that Seniors *will* talk about you, for good and ill, among themselves.)

If you're confronted with a serious personal problem, it's usually better to take yourself off-line for awhile, rather than to play it half-in/half-out, pleasing no one. This too depends upon your personality; some crave the diversion that work provides.

If, however, your personal life begins to interfere with your professional one, don't play the silent hero.

Talk with your friendly Seniors. Chances are they'd rather see you attend to your personal problem and return when things are settled. They've been there. And, after all, the firm doesn't (yet) revolve around you. Allow them the chance to be generous, while you still deserve it.

Temporary personal distress is rarely a career problem. If the trouble is recurring or involves a lifestyle or attitude choice, however, then *you* have a problem, not The Firm. Consider exiting gracefully— or changing your lifestyle and attitude—before you're unceremoniously and ignominiously yanked off the stage.

RENDERING UNTO CAESAR

As a corollary to keeping your private life private, try to keep your professional life, well...professional.

If Senior No. 18 walks into your office on Friday afternoon with a new project, keep your muttering to yourself. (This scenario is not at all uncommon. Think about it: *Clients'* businesses percolate during the week. Clients often wait to contact their lawyer—your Senior—for an answer...Monday morning.) When this happens, call home and explain that you'll be incommunicado again. If you can, head home for a quick bite and kisses for the little ones—then head back for more billable excitement.

Also, clear the decks when you start your new job. You'll barely have time enough as it is; you cannot worry about personal stuff, too. Keep your lunch hour open for the first week or so. You'll probably have lunch commitments with Seniors and office mates, so let your spouse know, ahead of time.

Try not to use office time for personal matters—including personal medical appointments. Seniors have sacrificed, too, and they won't appreciate your presumptuousness...on *their* dime.

Your job comes first.

Once, in my haste to play the gracious host to family visitors, I rushed out of the office early, and, in so doing, neglected some details in a deal that was simmering. I was—rightly—dressed down for my dereliction. Though no lasting harm was done, my first duty was to the client; I should have made other personal arrangements.

Don't let *your* personal life interfere with your professional one. Especially in your first year, your job comes first.

You must: (1) believe it, and (2) act like it.

LIVING WITH THE LAW

Lawyers, generally, aren't very nice people to live with.

Why?

Several factors merge to form one big pain in the butt...you. Stress. Combative pressures of practice. Office politics. More stress. Emotional connection with clients and their cases. The dreams of youth fading into the recesses of one's soul. An analytical mindset. The idiocies, minor and grand, that abound outside law. (Inside, too.) And still more stress.

The law hones one's personality traits into frighteningly sharp focus. Careful. What can be good in a lawyer can also be the kiss of death in a person. The structural friction that is so fruitful in law...is exasperating in life. Being the gladiator might be necessary, or even inspiring, but would you want to cuddle up to one?

Don't cross-examine your spouse when he or she disagrees with you. Don't berate your children for their inability to weigh the policy factors involving ownership versus usufructuary interests in toys. Don't be an asshole.

Why are we so hard on others...and on ourselves? Perhaps part of the reason lies in our reflexive genuflection before a false god of Logic.

Man is *not* a rational creature. We have the *capacity* for rational thought (...well, most of us), but that is a very different thing. Our actions and motivations are not known even to ourselves; it is the rare person who understands *why* he acts irrationally.

People are sometimes fools—present company included—who do foolish things. Recognize—and accept—that most do not judge the world in the cold, hard way that Lady Justice does. Most wander, instead, in a fog of mushy reality. Don't condescend: you do, too. You just cover it with a veil of logic fashioned during law school and painstakingly embroidered in practice.

Every once in a while, stop...and *listen* to yourself. If you'd smack you if you were you, lighten up. (The second you.)

Beware the Lawyer, just itching to consume the nice young person you once were. With competence comes a certain rigidity. Most lawyers suffer fools lightly. Trouble is, foolishness abounds. And, worse, those few who are excessively rational tend to be rather dull.

Either way, be careful whom you become.

Dear S.O.,

Ask your Significant Other[16] to read this book. Most honestly don't understand just *why* you're under such stress. Most are themselves frustrated by their powerlessness to help, which is only worsened by your emotional exclusion of them.

This, by the way, assumes that you're in the first of two schools of thought concerning appropriate SOs, and avoided an SO_L[17] like the plague. (In this scenario, the plague is the law.)

Having an SO_{NL}[18] helps maintain contact with the worlds outside law (...of which there are many), and lends balance. This can be more difficult to sustain, but it's worth it.

Others choose an SO_L to share the pain. If so, ask them to read this book, anyway. (Better yet, they should buy their own copy.) Okay, enough self-serving, selfishness-sanctioning sarcasm.

---

16 In keeping with the romantic theme of the law: "S.O." (or, if you prefer, the Beloved Significant Other ("B.S.O."), but not, for obvious reasons, "Beloved Other").

17 Significant Other $_{Lawyer}$

18 Significant Other $_{Non-Lawyer}$

Take some time to explain what you're going through. Here...I'll get the conversation started:

Dear S.O.,

My world is a very different one from yours. From the first day of law school, those many moons ago, I've spent nearly every waking moment reading, talking, or thinking about every mistake there is...and some we'd never have thought of. I've studied rules and rules and rules, and exceptions to exceptions. This has made me a little difficult at times, I know.

When I'm at work, I can't help but think of everyone who's depending on me. The client, the Seniors, my parents, you...everyone. Even me. Especially me.

Sometimes I have to do things for clients that I'd rather not do. But it's my responsibility to them, just as I have a responsibility to you.

Sometimes it's asking a lot, but have patience with me. I do see the world in terms of right and wrong, proper and improper, wise and foolish. I do expect more from you...and from myself. That makes me irritating, I know. Sometimes, I question everything, ad nause...er, on and on.

Here. I saw this most ~~excele~~ excellent book, and I thought it might be good for you to read it, too. Please don't crease it, though...I'd like to sell it back. Maybe they'll even gimme retail!

I had to catch myself just now. I was going to say that I'll try to lighten up if you'll try to understand me. But, unlike law, relationships aren't quite like that.

I'll try to lighten up.

— 3 —

Your Place in The Firm

Whatever you might think you'll be able to get away with in the law, you can't avoid dealing with Seniors. Most (indeed, nearly all) Seniors are not monsters; they are genuine Homo sapiens.

Do not expect to get away with what you see from them. You are a Junior, and are supposed to be an invisible profit center. You'll be surprised, however, to find out just how hard most Seniors *do* work. They lead lives almost as stressful as yours. They just have better kinds of stress, and their stress comes with better perks.

One purpose of this chapter is to give you a little insight into a universe beyond your limited world. Taking an honest look at your Seniors—and understanding where *they're* coming from—is a rare but worthy exercise. (It's useful with others, as well.) Most law offices are populated by Seniors who really *do* care. They'll usually try to point you in the right direction. Any shortcomings are often a result of their discomfort with their responsibility for you—or your mishandling of their shortcomings.

What's important is your *mindset*. It seems incredible to me, now, that, when I started, I had no idea not only what I should be doing, but *why*. The answer is in three parts:

First, relax. You're not expected to know everything, all at once.

Second, keep your eye on the ball: you *are* expected to figure it out, quickly. This includes both the lower-order tasks—completing high-quality work, on time—and the higher-order social graces. (Again, I was not kidding about this latter part of your learning. If you haven't grown up accustomed to formal settings, attend seminars on deportment, dining and social etiquette, and the like. These are *essential*.)

Third, keep your eye on the donut, not the hole. Success—in whichever form you wish—will come only after you figure out both the *what* and the *why*.

Along the way, you'll figure out as well what's best for *you*.

FIRST THINGS FIRST

Why were you hired?

Do you know? Do you care?

You'd better. Self-interest is fine. No, it is crucial. But, for just a moment, look beyond the benefit to yourself. Take a peek at the relationship, however uneven, from the *boss'* perspective: Seniors hire associates to improve their—the *Seniors'*—lives.

Think about it: Juniors are an unroyal pain in the posterior. Many a Senior has wondered (near midnight, while correcting the atrocious product of a legal neophyte's confused mind), whether it's all worth it. (For many firms, it really isn't, but Seniors look to a different model.) Regardless, you were hired for *their* greater glory. This glory takes two forms.

First, Money. *Ahhh...[sigh]...*money.

You = money. Or, more correctly, you equal *more* money. Your time is billed to clients at a certain multiple of your cost. (Usually it is by a factor of three or so). Money is nice. More money is nicer. Productive Juniors bring in more money.

Get it? Your efforts subsidize the overhead needed to support the lavish furnishings and ornate artwork in the lobby, conference rooms, and Seniors' offices. To the firm, you are Money.

This is so because of: *Time.* In law, time is more than just money. More than mere "billables". It is *everything.* All that is needed to practice law, and search for new clients, and run the firm, and...everything else...requires time. Once each unida de tiempo has slipped past—*Poof!*—it is gone. *Sed fugit interae, fugit irreparabile tempus.* Time flies, never to return.

Seniors make their money the same way that you will: by working their collective brains off. But, for Seniors, the problem is worsened. They don't want to do the legal particulars forever, and if they can make even more money by letting someone else do it, so much the better. Juniors, after they've learned, free most of that time for more interesting (and profitable) Senior work.

The trouble begins when Seniors realize that supervising others— particularly untrained others—is a serious managerial drain...and a sidetrack in *their* billables race. (Most new Seniors didn't think about this little caveat when they gratefully accepted the gift of Partnership from above.)

LAW AND ECONOMICS

Let's look at it another way: Investors can buy income-producing investments. These investments, once bought, will return profits, rent, or interest to the investor, usually with minimal maintenance effort. Law practice is unlike that. Indeed, economically, it is the opposite. It is, instead, labor-intensive...to the point of being labor-absolute. Rainmaking aside, an attorney is rewarded, with few exceptions, based solely on the work that that attorney does for clients. One unit of income for one unit of work.[19] If the attorney's work stops, then so

---

19 Even contingency-fee arrangements merely substitute the unit of income for a piece of the action, which, on average, provides a higher return...but which is still dependent upon work.

too does the income. Why?

Because the lawyer adds value (lawyer-bashers notwithstanding) through the fourth leg of the economic production quadrille: labor.

Businesses can make money in one (or both) of two ways: by making something or by serving someone. Businesses can expand to meet greater demand by buying machines or by renting people. Machines, generally, are easier to deal with, and, more importantly, enable an exponential rise in profit (assuming a strong demand).

Service businesses face more of a variable cost: people. This is problematic because businesses that *make* stuff can bring leverage to bear—making 10,050 widgets isn't much more difficult than making 10,005—greatly multiplying the productivity of corner-office folk.

Service businesses face a mushier world. As Seniors have found to their dismay, economic leverage is not quite so easy in the law. (And it's not all that easy elsewhere.) Okay, enough of economics?

Not quite, because most dream of escaping to Tahiti to drink piña coladas throughout the night (...and day). Unless willing to live the impecunious life of a hermit, this requires money.

The real problem comes in the clash between law as a profession and law as an industry/profession: Juniors aren't born as cash cows.[20] No...Juniors must be trained. What is taught in law school is, at best, only tangentially useful. It's not that law school is an utter waste in the world of practice (...although it might at times feel that way), but each has a different purpose. You're no longer there to understand the world. You're there to apply an *assumed* understanding to the frequently mundane legal problems brought before you.

Seniors must, therefore, make an investment in you. What is being invested, you might innocently ask? Is it money? No. It is something far more valuable to an attorney. It is *time*.

This investment of time will mark a difficult—and a potentially disastrous—stage for you. It represents an uncomfortable fact of law for those above you. Know this: If the necessary investment grows too large, relative to your expected future return, then your future return to the firm becomes relatively more expensive, and your worth to the Seniors correspondingly declines.

If the relationship is not seen *by* the Seniors as clearly beneficial *to* the Seniors and their firm, then *you're* in trouble.

THE APPRENTICE'S LAMENT

You might think to yourself—perhaps while reviewing the 32nd box of indistinguishable documents—"*Gee,* I'm being billed out at over a hundred bucks an hour, but by the hour I'm making minimum wage!"

---

20 Not a pejorative term: it merely means low-maintenance money-makers. My apologies to members of the Bovine Liberation Front.

Perhaps your indignation rises as you think: "Why should *they* get all of that surplus?"

But you forget: *You* don't have that work lined up. And, as you will come to appreciate, this is *at least* as important as actual knowledge of the law. A future responsibility for finding, courting, and satisfying clients will bestow a *profound* appreciation of a true value of Seniors.

Also, there are "hidden" costs. (Hidden because we rarely stop to consider them: bar fees, malpractice insurance, staffing, office space, furniture, social events, employee and retirement benefits—easily adding 50% to base salary—and so on.)

Sure, they make money. Be glad. If they didn't, neither would you.

A CHANGE OF PERSPECTIVE

To avoid some of the unpleasant by-products of frustrated Seniors, take a step back from your own travails, and try looking at the world through their eyes.

They're *busy*. They have clients to deal with, many of whom are less than pleasant. They have financial concerns, just as you do, but at a higher level. They have family pressures, social pressures, business pressures, and commitments of which you are, as yet, unaware.

Enter Junior, who knows next-to-nothing about *practicing* law. You have always been at the top, and, consequently, have gotten away with a thing or two. You wear a halo, and with that you've done pretty well...yet you're woefully unprepared for the real world.

Training Juniors is time-consuming, stressful work. Assigning a project to a Junior—only to have to rework most of it—will tax the patience of the most saintly Senior. This hurdle is raised several notches:

First, most legal projects are under moderate-to-severe time pressure, which makes delegation more difficult. Second, the nature of legal work tends to draw on bodies of law that are only barely understood by Juniors. (If truth be told, *Seniors* aren't comfortable outside their own specialties, if for no other reasons than the complexity of most fields, the rapid change of all law, and the limited number of hours in everyone's day.) This makes it more difficult to delegate all but the most simple of legal projects. Third, Seniors are just plain *tired*. They've worked hard to get where they are, having accumulated jumbo mortgages and such. They don't need the merry-go-round to spin any faster. Finally, lawyers are, generally, reluctant managers.

Dealing with Juniors is comparable[21] to flossing: Everyone knows you ought to do it, but boy is it easy to neglect.

---

21 Which, by the way, is pronounced "komp´ erebel", not "compare´ able". Just more snooty schoolmarmism for your phonetic enjoyment.

The flip side for you, unfortunately, is that your training will almost certainly be an exceedingly stressful, even depressing process. Notice that I used the word *training?* This word was not used lightly. You're not going to be *educated,* in the noble sense of that oft-misused word.

No. The bulk of legal practice requires two qualities: (1) an ability to look, sound, and act like a professional, and (2) a reasonably competent technical knowledge of the area of law in which you practice.

I hope you also noticed something about the preceding paragraph: You do not need a Holmesian mastery of the law to be successful. Indeed, such breadth of knowledge or even inclination would *harm* you, especially when you start. Few want their plumber to contemplate a revised General Theory of Relativity whilst repairing a kitchen sink. *They want the darned sink fixed.*

Your Seniors do not want you mulling over tertiary legal strategies in blasts of statutory brilliance. *It is not your place.* They want you instead to finish their projects—fast—so that *they* can mull over legal strategy.

What else seems a little funny about the above two factors?

Look at which is first. At the risk of excessive cynicism, the *style* of looking, sounding, and acting like a super-sharp lawyer is almost more important than the substance of actually being one.

Less cynically, the twin principles of substance and style—often set improperly in opposition—are, or should be, positively correlated. It *is* important for you to get comfortable with your new role as a professional. This comfort will be formed after you've acquainted yourself with the law (the substance) and its workings (a little style). Don't rush it, but do understand that much of the process is internal; no one can make you feel comfortable with yourself.

RUNNING FROM FEAR

Here's another managerial reality overlooked by Juniors (and other trainees) in their mad scramble for survival: Seniors, along with all employers, run scared. They want very much to not look the fools. Hiring people who don't work out—for whatever reason—makes them look foolish. This is one reason why the legal profession is obsessively (and wrongly, I think) credential-driven.

Yet we attorneys take such risk-aversion to new lows. If a top-ten law-review-editor nincompoop [22] shows his true colors, the Seniors can, with perplexed looks, cluck over the character defects of the personification of such a well-credentialed résumé. Far easier than an honest, if painful, look back to their own halting steps.

---

22   ...there *are* a few.

Sometimes, managerial inattention takes on a more sinister form. Some Seniors really *do* believe in sink-or-swim, either because they've survived similar torture and think it's good for the legal soul, or because they're bullies. Either way, you'd better brace yourself if you've got a live one.

To be fair, some degree of hardship, as opposed to none, does tend to give one a deeper perspective. The question is not, however, whether you will experience workplace hardships, but rather, how many... and what kind. And, more importantly, whether you learn from them. And still further, as a sign of higher maturity, whether you learn from the mistakes of *others*. (This is far wiser; you couldn't possibly live long enough to make them all yourself.) Learning from your *own* mistakes is the lesser option: it's only because your own blunders are so immediate and hurtful that the lessons stick so well. A keen observation will instruct almost equally, minus the pain.

Some Seniors—in all professions, trades, and walks of life—are immature. As a result of this personal insecurity, they are prone to abuse their positions of power. A certain percentage of hardened souls will be found in any calling. It so happens that law is one of those fields that tends to attract (and forge) this unpleasant bunch. Worse, the process of survival tends to weed out less-aggressive specimens. Social Darwinism in action.[23] As an issue of management and common sense, brutishness is an ineffective method, over the long-run, of getting things done.

Go tell it to the mountain.

(You do owe it to the generations to follow, however, to remember the pains you now feel, and endeavor to lessen them for those still innocent to the ways of the LSAT.)

Once your foot is in the door, you'll find that, while your law school glories reinforce you psychologically, professionally, and even socially, they're not enough. Once you have crossed the maturity Rubicon into the working world, different measures apply. If all goes (relatively) smoothly, you'll progress from legal novice to a reasonably independent billing machine.

Take advantage. Believe it or not, *this relationship is in your favor.* Seniors don't want to waste their time disciplining you, and they certainly don't want the expense (and lost revenues) of firing you. What they want, instead, is for you to mature into a prospective partner. Granted, many firms devote less energy in this process than they should—they expect *you* to *make yourself* into that prototypical partner—but that is neither here nor there: if *you* wish to *survive,* you'll have to see to your own path.

---

[23] It's *reverse* Darwinism, really: The smarter, better, *nicer* lawyers are less willing to put up with the daily hassles of the practitioner's life—which, for them, is no step up—and leave. Still, hassles await us everywhere.

They will help, but the greater burden is on you. Too, the process is cumulative. Once you've proved yourself competent on smaller projects, Seniors will feel assured, leading to bigger and better cases (and thus a bigger and brighter future). Occasionally, when you slip up, their confidence in you will be shaken, and you might find yourself set back more than a few paces. It's a rough road, but, for those suited to the finale, worth the trip. And, if you're particularly sharp (meaning practice-oriented), you might actually *enjoy* it. So much the better. And so much for Law Firm Economics 101.

A sports analogy (from a rather non-spectator-sports-minded guy): Given that everyone in this game seems to be terrified of failure, doesn't it make better sense for you to concentrate not on the miraculous long pass, goal, shot, putt, dive, or slam dunk—but, rather, on defense, defense, defense? The methodical, persevering, and moderately agile tortoise wins this race. The hare frequently gets skinned alive on the obstacle course.

TUNING INTO PERSONALITIES

As managers the world over know in their bones, distinct personalities resonate throughout every organization. Good managers try to accommodate most of their employees' personalities. Great managers take advantage of the benefits each personality offers. Given that lawyers are such reluctant personnel managers, don't expect them to understand—much less accommodate—you. And even if they *do* care, they probably won't change. The situation and its players militate against thoughtful, holistic relations among colleagues.

And now for a little forced categorization, which we lawyers—and humans—just love:

THE ACADEMIC. This personality is more common in the law than elsewhere because of the people who are attracted to law school, many of whom were too smart to be successful right out of college. Some even suppress their brilliance long enough to make it to Senior. Importantly, the Academic will recognize (and, usually, appreciate) *other* brilliance. Still, it remains far more important to do the little things well. My supervising Senior was (and is) an academic. She truly revels in the substance of the law, and pushes herself—hard—to excellence. It's as if she endlessly strives for the A+ and pat on the head from an imaginary teacher. She usually deserves it. All in all, a good star to which you might hitch your legal wagon.

THE BULLY. Sadly, the law also seems to have more than its fair share of this rather less hospitable breed. True, there are a few in every field—and there are lots of *nice* people in law, too. Nevertheless, members of this unpleasant group gravitate to power, which the law offers in abundance.

This primitive impulse is compounded by legal training, which serves as a clarifying lens, focusing the idiosyncrasies of each lawyer into an obsessive character trait. Worse, the process of thinking, acting, and *being* like a lawyer accentuates the power of lawyers to affect others with their personalities. If a janitor is insolent, he'll be ignored or fired (or, more likely, both...in rapid succession). If, however, a *Senior* is a royal jerk, take a number and force a smile.

In fairness to part-time brutes, though, the abundant stress under which we all labor—lawyers go to the head of the line—makes it inevitable that the fiend in each of us rises closer to the surface. (Oddly, there doesn't seem to be much correlation between assholism and intelligence. Overly intelligent people are more likely to be insufferable through too-high standards than by being assholic per se.)[24]

When confronted with a hostile environment, the relevant question is answered by a mantra of biology: You must adapt, migrate, or die.

Three choices. That's it. If you can tolerate abrasive behavior, your adaptation (or brutish-proclivity) will put you in good stead, relative to others with thinner skins. If you're a bully yourself (and a suck-up to boot) then—*Congratulations!*—you're almost home free under the boot of a brethren bully.

If, however, such abrasiveness is intolerable, you should recognize the two options remaining to any organism: you can leave, or you can suffer. In law, suffering will help no one, and will almost certainly result in your eventual removal, one way or another. A legal death is not too inappropriate an analogy. It doesn't take much brainpower to see where the advice is leading: If your situation is insufferable to you, then stop suffering. Leave. Yes, it might not be fair. Yes, it might not be easy. Good luck.

THE BUREAUCRAT. These are the folks who'd be perfectly happy if all of humanity were boiled down into neat little columns and rows, each fulfilling its Orwellian duty.

I once had an economics professor who was a similarly-minded mindless "quant". He dreamt of the quantification of *all* variables affecting econometric theory. What he didn't seem to realize was not only that the Nobel was beyond his grasp, but also that he was an idiot. The failure of economics is not that a large portion of human behavior is, by definition, unquantifiable, but that economists, in their lust for credibility, have resisted, denigrated, and perpetually assumed away this mushy reality, insisting instead upon a false precision.

---

24 My apologies for the sophomoric (attempt at) humor. Yet there is a serious reason for not editing this out: Many lawyers—far too many—*pride* themselves on being difficult. Don't be one of them. It's unnecessary to your clients' interests, it will hurt you, professionally, and it will cripple you, personally.

It's improving, but the prejudice is still very much there; just read a few academic journals. (Better yet...*don't.*)[25]

A Bureaucrat will be either agreeable or Hellish, depending mostly on you. Their demands upon you can vary widely, as can their pleasantness. The important point in dealing with them is that you will rarely get bonus points for brilliance, but will pay dearly for mistakes. Be *extra* careful and diligent.

THE FLY-BOY. These seat-of-the-pants barnstormers like to buzz each legal problem with the nonchalance and *joie de vivre* of their imaginary alter egos, *Flying Maestros Lex*. All too often, however, they've barely mastered the art of the taxi. Well, that's not quite fair. *Most* attorneys shoot from the hip. With experience, it's not (usually) dangerous and, after all, it's the only reasonable way to practice. (Would you pay *your* lawyer to double-check every thought?) Worse, barnstorming, hip-shooting law is *fun*.

The point for you: Get good at it, first. Practice makes perfect. But, before you've practiced to perfection, don't let a Fly-Boy sweet-talk you into lowering your standards.

THE INDUSTRIALIST. Not surprisingly, these colleagues are often the most helpful, and the most successful. They're there to get the job done, and they have the capacity to divorce work from play. (Or they think work *is* play.)

Seriously, this is a good model. Rather than resenting all that is expected of you throughout your long workdays, think instead how lucky you are to *have* a job, career, profession. Get to it.

THE PERFECTIONIST. This is where you'll learn to appreciate the Fly-Boys. The Perfectionist will part the seven seas in search of the uncrossed *t* or undotted *i*—and will expect you to do the same.

Now, now: a healthy dose of perfectionism is good—just keep your perspective: You need to be good, but you need also to be *fast*.

---

25 Sorry for the detour. Or was it a frolic? I never could keep those two straight. While we're here, though, we may as well figure out some moral to the digression: In law, don't make the same mistake. Personalities, emotions, gut feelings—all that subjective *stuff*—are more than just important to your successes as a lawyer. They often affect the outcome of cases that could as easily go the other way. Clients, juries, and opponents have *feelings,* and those feelings play a large part in the scene. Indeed, except for emotion and stubbornness, a good percentage of lawsuits wouldn't *exist*.

Unfortunately, the dichotomy is contrived—and constantly reinforced by thoughtless vested interests. The quantitative and qualitative are *both* necessary to complex systems. Learn which is appropriate...and when. Your tasks as a Junior will be primarily quantitative. You must learn the Law and apply the Rules to the Facts. Later, after you've mastered the law and your place in it, will the qualitative emerge.

The Perfectionist is often also an Academic—or a Bureaucrat. If the former, they're fascinated by the machinery of the law and how it operates to support a grand system of civilization. If the latter, they're obsessed with the nuts and bolts, either because they like the details of life, or because the grander machinery escapes them.

When working for a perfectionist: look, listen, learn...and make *darned* sure you've crossed and dotted all those loose letters. In the long run, working for a perfectionist is good—you really *do* need to do all of the little things right—if a bit overwhelming at first.

If *you* are a perfectionist, apply your inclination...but keep your wits about you, especially when Seniors show irritation at your time-consuming dalliances.

THE PINHEAD. These personality-challenged folk can cause the most headaches—and humor. They're usually junior Seniors with their heads so far up their respective *senior* Seniors' behinds they can't smell the...*well*, let's not get into the olfactory implications, here. More generously, they've mastered a field or two, and're feeling their oats...without the humility that comes with a little more seasoning. Add to that brew feelings of inadequacy, vis-à-vis *their* superiors, and you've got yourself a royally distasteful concoction. This affliction is often congenital, and, worse, they expect *others* to suck up to them.

Pucker up.

Surprising to some, but unsurprising to managers: junior Seniors can be (and often are) worse than senior Seniors, because the junior Senior is yet between two worlds. Too experienced to be treated as flunkies, they're not yet proven (or valuable) enough to be regarded as true equals among the *real* partners. Moreover, they're inwardly uncomfortable in their new role: they're Partners-in-Training. Growing comfortable with one's new station in law can be brief or indefinite. The factors affecting them as junior Seniors are the same ones that affect you as Junior: maturity, peers, personality, and whatever other emotional baggage is brought to the transformation.

Notably, the Pinhead is concerned primarily with success and standing, not substance. (Actually, to them, those *are* the substance.) Worse, non-Pinheads aren't aware how easily offended others—especially pinheaded-others—can be. Be aware.

Many of you might eventually empathize. For now, sympathize. Although it might not help too much in the short-run, understand that the louder the bark, the higher the level of insecurity. Help them along. Usually, this involves *deferential* courteousness.

Smile while you're at it.[26]

---

26 I assume, by the way, that *you* are less than a total pinhead. If my assumption is incorrect...fear not, for you probably won't need this book at all: you will do quite well in the law. Thank you for buying it, though.

THE POWER-LUSTEE. These are the ones who, for various reasons, crave the feeling of self-importance that comes with recognition—and deference—by others. Careful. They expect the full treatment.

THE SCHMOOZER. Schmoozers thrive on diving into the sea of humanity with an abandon that'd make the Ty-D-Bol Man® queasy. But, for these Captains of Life, pressing the flesh is a natural high, and law provides a nice (and reasonably clean) outlet for lots and lots of flesh. They're often also Power-Lustees. But not always. Surprisingly, some schmoozers have the social aptitude of an eggplant. (And that's not being too kind to eggplants, which, nutritional though they are, can be politely pushed aside at parties.) Schmoozers aren't so easily dismissed, especially for Juniors. If *you're* a Schmoozer, then you'll either get along famously, or hate each other's guts. Something about the alignment of the planets....

Whatever the alignment, yours is not to hate in your Junior years.

THE HUMAN. These categories are neither exclusively listed nor mutually exclusive. There's variety within, as well as among, each category. We are, after all, only human.

Occasionally, you'll be faced with a truly difficult Senior. In a sense, they're doing you a favor. This is part of your learning: some *clients* are difficult. It's better to learn—early—to deal with harsh personalities. Law seems to shorten everyone's fuse, including yours. Just ask your S.O. (...if you still have one).

One more thing: Although you're under lots of stress, and even though you feel (or actually are) treated unfairly, *don't get snippy.* First, it's a rather bad career move. Second, it's part of your job. Third, you're really not that special; everyone else has stress, too. Finally, it's a rather bad career move.

As a Junior...smile. Think of this all as a preparation for life, which will be filled with jerks, dorks, and evil-doers galore.

Okay, okay. A final note as long as we're here: Take a look in the mirror. You can get away with a fairly wide range of personality yourself, but *do* try to avoid the edges. If you're a condescending, bitter, humorless turd, order a new personality. Negative people drain energy faster than you can shout "matter/anti-matter containment-field breach". (Actually, if you're *that* bad, I'm not sure anything short of a lobotomy would help. Just stay away from *me*.)

You really should try not to make life so harsh, yes?

Now, some of you smart-alecks are thinking: *"Yeah, yeah...but after I make partner, what can anyone do?"*

A lot.

As maligned as juries are, they can sniff bullshit at fifteen paces—easily covering most courtrooms—and spotting the orifice responsible is even easier. (Don't even *think* about your nice-guy mask; it hides only your face, not your aroma.) And for you holdouts who laugh in the face of my hypothetical as you dream of that glorious tax practice awaiting you—think again of auditors, who can sniff the same substance from *one hundred* fifteen paces.

THE CHAMELEON

It's clichéd, I know, but all among us—non-schizophrenic hermits excepted—lead multiple lives. It's part of our design that we're different people to our bosses than we are to our friends than we are to our parents than we are to our teachers than we are to our lovers than we are to...everyone else. So it is in the law. You are a different person to your fellow Juniors than you are to your Seniors. It might seem obvious, but it's easy to forget that you're a different person to each Senior.

Remember the grand treatment you enjoyed during your summer clerkship, if you were lucky enough to land one? Few special Juniors (a.k.a. summer clerks) are treated to real law for the simple reason that they're not real lawyers. Instead, they're in a peculiar situation that prevents the real-life stresses of associateship to penetrate the artificial world of recruiting (which, in my opinion, is unfair to the majority of law students, unhelpful to the profession, and downright counterproductive for law firms). Regardless, you're treated specially because the relationship between you, as a *special* Junior, and the Seniors, as Seniors, is quite different than it is between you, as a *regular* Junior, and the Seniors, as Seniors.

Once you accept, they've *gotcha'*.

Less cynically, remember how you act around visitors (which is what special Juniors really are): You wouldn't dream of yelling at a guest for leaving the toilet seat up, even if you nearly hospitalized a sibling for the same thing. Sad but true: we're nicer to strangers than we are to family. (Perhaps it's because we don't *have* to be as nice to family.)[27]

What does all this have to do with you as a regular Junior? Well, think about each Senior for whom you toil, and those for whom you don't: you have a different relationship with each. To some, you're a reasonably familiar face, which they assume belongs to one of their underlings. To others, you're a straight-laced worker. To some you might even be a cool addition to the firm. Others perceive different variations on these themes.

The important point here is that, first, you must not piss off *any* Senior, no matter how remote he might be from your little hide-out in the firm. This is rarely a problem, but do try to figure out where each partner's Piss-Off button is...and avoid it. (It's best to find its location from others, rather than by hammering away at it yourself.)

---

27 Then again, by reverse corollary, few are heroes at home.

Second, you must treat each Senior with respect. This is also rarely a problem—and it's a good rule of thumb in any social event. The twist is that you really needn't worry too much about peripheral Seniors. Just be nice. (But don't be *too* nice. It's annoying.)

Now for the cynical part: Learn who the *important* Seniors are—there is *always* a big difference among the relative power bases of each Senior—and pucker up. Or, at the very least, be *extra* courteous. Just think of yourself as a chameleon. See beyond your own limited existence, and analyze the idiosyncrasies of the Seniors closest to you. Then, without completely losing yourself, maneuver into the most agreeable relationship with each Senior *on his or her terms*.

Beware the natural conceit that others must adapt to meet *you*. Though everyone has personal peeves, lawyers seem to specialize: we develop particular styles—and then become rigid in disrecognition of others' preferences.[28]

Oddly, *stylistic* differences tend to cause more, not less, discomfort that substantive ones. Find out what is expected, and…you can figure out the rest. Now isn't the time for you to grab your parents' love beads to realize your potential as an individual.

It really isn't all that sick. The best working relationships are built on mutual respect. Not surprisingly, the Senior/Junior relationship is uneven. Although it might not seem so, the hurdles really *are* lower when you first start. You must show through your behavior and attitude, however, that you're on your way to bigger and better things. *Whether you will ever actually achieve such glories is unknown and, more importantly, is irrelevant while you're still a Junior.* If you and your Senior share personalities and interests in common, so much the better, but that is not requisite to a successful relationship.

Learn what your Seniors are looking for and *give it to them* (within reason and without undue fuss).[29] Most want good legal puppies, intelligent and diligent enough to do their work and catch their mistakes (diplomatically, of course). The sooner housebroken, the better. (Not chewing on office furniture is another plus.)[30]

Lest you be offended by the implication that being the Yes-Person is the answer: You haven't been reading critically.[31] Many Seniors loath sycophancy. If this includes *your* Senior…*back off.* (You should not be overly fawning to *any* Senior. It'll be perceived as insincere, and worthy of contempt.)

---

28 I really like *disrecognition,* by the way. I don't think it's a word, but I do think it captures the attitude that professionals have after they burrow themselves into the conceit that their idiosyncracies are the axis around which the heavens—and all others thereunder—should revolve.

29 "Reason" and "undue" *are* rather pliable words, however.

30 …and try not to slobber too much on the papers you fetch.

31 *Gee*…are you offended *now?*

Some Seniors are willing to be corrected (and will even appreciate it, secretly)...if you're diplomatic about it. Be careful. You should be twice as sensitive in catching mistakes as you'd like them to be gentle in correcting yours: Make *darned* sure you're right, and present your case, dispassionately. I once heard a Senior in a minor (but 180°) misstatement of law. I double-checked, wrote a quick memo, and was told to call the client (which itself was unusual). Though my Senior was gracious (even so, it was a hassle), pay attention to the signs—verbal and other—posted by *your* Senior.

Adapt, migrate, or die.

You're dealing with your own species; use your head in adapting.

RESPECT

Offices—even large ones—are small places.

Just as you talk about Seniors, so too do they talk about you. (Actually, they're usually nicer about you than you are about them.) Beware. Seniors know that you and your cohort entertain a certain healthy disrespect—arising out of unavoidable frustrations—and harbor hidden dreams of retribution.

Keep it healthy...and hidden.

DANCING WITH SENIORS

Be a good assistant. It might sound demeaning (and, in a way, it is), but it's also a crucial part of the learning process—provided you assist with a higher purpose—and, happily, it makes your job a little easier. Rather than squandering your time in trying to maneuver into legal *tours de force,* all you need do initially is keep your nose to the billing grindstone, learn an area of law, and take care of your clients' problems. More on this later.

From the start, be *likable.* Your day will pass more speedily and easily, Seniors' tolerance of your errors will increase, and future clients will look to you more readily and approvingly.

Think ahead. I was indentured, at 12, to help renovate our family home. As a younger servant, my job was to have the proper tools ready for older siblings. I didn't appreciate the importance of this task until later, when I graduated to construction myself (which helped pay for college). Planning and preparation are 49% of a project. Any project.

Anticipate what will be needed next. (But don't anticipate too far, especially at first; you'll too likely race off in the wrong direction, before a Senior can correct you.)

Become indispensable. It goes against the grain of such talented folks as you, but it's part of the job. And it does count when it comes time to pass out the goodies. Sure, obsequious groveling has its place, but don't sell your Seniors short: they know what makes the firm run. If you're good, truly good, at law and with clients, you'll do just fine.

For you litigators—others too—don't rebel against your place as a glorified bench-warmer. Instead, be a *good* one. Second chair isn't wholly for appearances, so don't act like it. (If you're *that* anxious to genuflect before the legal altar, become an Assistant District Attorney, Public Defender, or JAG officer and get more trial experience in a year than most litigators get in a career...except that many top litigators have tried their hand with either).

You, like most Juniors, have an ardent need to impress others, and a correspondingly earnest need for approval from authority figures. *You will impress your Seniors most by doing the boring things well.* Perform well, but not extravagantly. Extravagance is unnecessary, and, worse, it will more likely than not trip you up.

It might also, following yet another of our human oddities, set you up for *higher* standards than would otherwise apply. Life as a Junior is life under a microscope. Don't turn up the magnification.

(Plus, if you start at the top, there's nowhere to go but down, and you might give the unintended signal that you're ready to be cut loose from normal supervision...before you're ready.)

Your extra effort ought to go into legwork, not one-upsmanship.[32] When your Senior gives you a project, spend a little extra time to take care of the loose ends. If that means taking thirty seconds to tell your secretary to confirm X, Y, and Z...*do so.* If your secretary is too busy, *do it yourself.* Even if you're timid, break out of your shell and *help* your Senior. As you gain experience, you'll learn more about just how you can help. For now, stay one step ahead of the "average" Junior. A helpful attitude that helps your Seniors will, in turn, help you. Mutual back-scratching, however out of fashion, works.

BATTLE OF THE TITANS

Now, here comes a predicament that happens with some frequency, and is almost as frequently handled poorly by Juniors, but needn't be: What happens when there is a conflict between—or among—Seniors?

More importantly, what should *you* do about it?

Well, one form of conflict is interoffice rivalries: If your office has a total of more than, say, *one* lawyer, odds are pretty good that there's some submariner movement astir. What should you do?

Stay the hell anchored. Even if you want to, *do not take sides.* Unless you're uniquely secure with your favorite Senior, who plans to

---

32 If, by the way, that legwork in your firm refers to anatomics, you have a rather different problem. More on that later. Being the naïve guy that I am, I'm using the word in a more naïve context.

elevate you after the *coup d'état*, and has written up a lovely, enforceable contract to that effect,[33] it's *your* derrière hanging out there.

Seniors can usually survive pretty well on their own; you can't. Just remember: the ax falls first on those whose necks are least valuable...and least loyal. You have little power over being the former. Don't willingly be the latter, too.

NUTS![34]

Another, relatively innocuous form of conflict occurs when too much is put on your legal plate. This is not unusual; it's the benchmark of modern law practice. The rub comes when you get too many assignments from *different* Seniors. Each does not know (...or usually care) about the work given to you by others. If you go from swamped to genuinely drowning, you'll get into trouble with everyone, and even sympathetic Seniors will frown on your immaturity.

The answer is simple: You must lay down a Rule.

That's right. You.

You *can* do it. And, in this limited context, it will actually make you look better. How'd you like to tell a disliked Senior to buzz off? Believe it or not, you can...and *should*.[35]

Here's how:

You're working on a project for Senior #1. Senior #2 pops his head in the door and asks if you're busy. If you're not *really* busy (meaning you're within a project or so of a clear plate), then you *must* smile and reply "Yes, but how can I help you?"[36]

---

33 *Yeah, right.* If he's anything close to a decent lawyer, he wouldn't do that, and if he would, he's probably too nice to flourish after the *coup*. Either way, contracts don't mean much in a Revolution, Karl.

34 Okay, for this heading I've gone too far. *"Nuts!"* was the response of Brigadier General Anthony Clement McAuliffe (who, as an acting commander during the Battle of the Bulge, led the vastly outnumbered soldiers of the 101st Airborne Division defending the beleaguered village of Bastogne against the German XLVII Panzer Corps) to the German commander's demand for surrender. McAuliffe's forces held their ground, and, best of all for our analogy, we won. Rumor has it that what he *really* said was "Fuck You!" (which makes a *whole* lot more sense under the circumstances). Apparently, censors cleaned it up for the virginal ears of the American public.

I always did think "Nuts!" *was* a little silly.

Perhaps I should've used my second caption choice: "THE JUNIOR THAT CAN SAY NO"—but *then* the footnote'd be about Shintaro Ishihara and Akio Morita.

Before you call in the Tangential Police, we return control of the main text to you.

35 The Fine Print: Under very limited circumstances.

36 If you're not *at all* busy: "Yes, but how can I help you?"

...Even if you hate this particular Senior's guts. (Chances are, if that's so, he's not so fond of you either.) In any case, do *not* lie about this. Few things will annoy a Senior more than to be brushed off by an *employee*, only to find that *that* Junior's billables were at or below the median (or, worse, below that particular *Senior's*—and some set a high standard). You're not an automaton, but you *are* an employee.[37] Keep that in mind.

If statistics are playing with that month's billables, explain that you are temporarily buried in work, but will be available to help in *x* days, with all your heart. Chances are he'll find someone else.

Do not lie.

If Senior #2 pops his head in the door and asks if you're busy, and you are, in fact, *very* busy, then say:

```
I am very sorry, Mr. Senior #2 [...use his real
name, though; it'll go over better], but I am in
the middle of a project for Mr. Senior #1. If you
would like to clear it with Mr. Senior #1, I will
be happy to assist you.
```

You must tell Senior #2 to take a number.

Most Juniors (and even senior Juniors) disbelieve, in their fright, that they have any control at all. The result is wrathful Seniors—and dysfunctionally frazzled Juniors—everywhere.

Senior #2 will respect you: (1) you're obviously an important team player, because you're busy; (2) you're obviously an important team player, because someone else wants you; and (3) you're obviously an important team player, because you're diplomatic yet strong. Not least, Senior #1 will appreciate that you put his needs first, which is as it should be. First in time, first in right.

Okay now...don't rush off thinking you've a license to be rude. You don't. Your attitude must be helpful, your demeanor cheerful. Even if you're secretly ecstatic that you're too busy to help Senior Satan, which lets you off the hook (...this time), don't let it show.

If Senior #2 gets huffy and declines to remove his then-deeply embedded hook, don't make a scene. Take down his project instructions, and contact Senior #1. If Senior #1 says okay, then you've got your marching orders. Even so, the pressure's still on (only moreso) for you to get *both* projects done as quickly as possible...and certainly before their (new) deadlines.

If they *both* get huffy, *then* you've got a problem. The answer is not to hide. Quite the opposite: You cannot ignore anyone...especially any *Senior* one. In a parallel universe, you can curse them for unjustly putting you in this Hobsonian predicament. In *this* universe, you

---

37 Okay, so maybe you *are* an automaton.

must work, quickly, toward a single goal: finishing the darn project. If you can go to a sympathetic, neutral senior Senior to mediate, *maybe*. This is risky; you'll win no friends whatever happens.

In any case, do *not* leave a voicemail for one of them saying, in essence, "Piss on your assignment"—unless that Senior is unavailable *and* you are darned sure the deadline is flexible. Better is to work as quickly and well and long as you can to help them both. It might work to approach Senior #1 or #2 and ask for the assistance of another Junior. So long as egos are stroked, the problem should abate. Or, ask for permission to delegate some of your work to summer associates (or, if you're feeling particularly cocky and the situation warrants, ask to hire a temp). It'll at least get their attention. The squeaky Junior gets the grease—and more respect, if it's a legitimate squeak. Remember, *you're* the one on the hook.

Some twists: be *very* careful about the relative position of each Senior. This plan won't work as neatly with a *senior* Senior #2. Also, the above Rule does not apply if Senior #2's project is an emergency rush, and you're working on a non-rush. Even so, if there's even the slightest hint that you'll miss Senior #1's deadline, you *must* contact him *immediately*, and clear the changed priority. Most times it won't be a big deal. At times, however, it can be. Seniors are like everyone else. They're inflated kindergartners, who want whatever toy someone else has. Sometimes, you're that toy.

Some Seniors, being spoiled brats, either aren't aware of their unpleasantness…or don't care. (Worse, they usually get what they want, because others are too timid.) This is a rare area where you can legitimately put your foot down.

What if you don't like Senior #1, but *adore* Senior #2? Unless you can tackle both projects without delay, stick with the plan. (It'd be worth an all-nighter or two to you, though.) They know the story, and besides, it's better to leave your maneuvering for other times.

If, by the way, your assertiveness causes apoplectic disbelief for a Senior, then you should take a long, hard look at your likely future in the same firm with that Senior. In the undiplomatic cadence of any drill sergeant: Shit rolls downhill.

And an outhouse is not the best kind in which to settle.[38]

TURBULENT WATERS

Friendly fire. There's a fair-to-good chance that your career will be torpedoed by a Senior. Maybe even a secretary. Maybe even an ally.

Why would someone *go out of their way* to *destroy* another's chance at a job, or appointment, or even career? Where are the members of this obviously evil caste? (If we can identify them, we can entertain

---

38   …and guess which floor *you* get?

visions of *their* destruction, or at least we'll know whom to avoid.) No such luck. Those who destroy others' lives, sometimes without a second thought, are...normal folks, just like you and me.

I once had to whittle a pile of résumés down to a manageable file—an odious process—and was somewhere in the second or third review. I received a call from an applicant. He had tracked me down, with little to go on. A good sign. He was pleasant, and obviously wanted—or needed—the job badly. Too, it was an international call, on his nickel. Impressed, I dug out his file, hoping for him. All was fine...except for the cover letter. Yes, it was well written. No, no errors. Why did I decide *not* to recommend that the justices interview him? [My decision not to recommendation a candidate was, as a practical matter, a death knell prior to the interviews.]

I debated for days. His qualifications were okay. His motivation—vastly more important, in my opinion, than the former—admirable. What he had written in his letter, however, doomed him...likely without his even knowing it. (A *needless* gaffe, moreover.) This was an appointment for a *court* position. In his letter, he displayed his ideology, proudly. It mattered not so much *which* ideology (...but, to be honest, this particular ideology busied itself with saving the world from all manner of human ill). An activist in a court! *Egads.* Sure, there's the still-raging debate about judicial activism versus conservativism. *Irrelevant!* This was a position as *advisor* to the justices; it is for *them* to be activist, if they so decide.

This was a *foreign* position; was his brand of activism appropriate? Sadly, no. Expatriates out to change the world usually end up on an early flight home. The world doesn't much care to be changed.

Maybe he was...*right*. Perhaps. But, in the end, it didn't matter. I killed his application, and perhaps much more.

I've been on the receiving end, too. On one occasion, once upon a time, I had applied for a position of some importance. I submitted the requisite paperwork and references. There were some at work with whom I didn't get along famously (...much as I like to think I'm an exceedingly easy guy to get along with).

I was stunned by what followed.

A message awaited me from a friend. His tone was odd. I called back, and he asked "What's going on? So-and-so [at the organization to which I was applying] said that you had said *x*." [*x* being a rather nasty untruth.] I was floored. Might it have been some errant miscommunication? Might it have been some innocent misunderstanding? No matter. The damage was done. *My* application was killed, and perhaps much more.

Why would someone have gone to some length to harm me? The reasoning is less important than the truth: someone *did*. I still am not sure who—I hadn't thought I'd made any blood enemies.

Blood enemies are not required.

Again, Seniors *will* talk about you. Among themselves, and among others. You will receive favors—choice assignments, parking stalls, and promotions—based, in the end, on the *subjective feelings* among that select group of Seniors. Few Seniors will cause you harm for the joy of it. Rather, they feel that they're doing right by a higher authority—the organization, perhaps. Sometimes they even feel they're doing you a favor. Perhaps they are. (...Though it won't feel that way at the time.)

Heed this lesson well: Splash not water in the faces of older ducks, or in anger at any of their favored ducklings, or anywhere else: you do not know yet the invisible allegiances that bind one duck to another and keep each in formation behind a Big Duck.

Objective measures are only part of the picture. Usually, they're the binary determinant that gets your foot in the door. It is something else—something along the lines of charisma and deportment—that makes the greater difference.

Beware and behave.

TURNING DOWN WORK

Don't. I was astounded to learn that some Juniors had the gall to turn down certain work that was, for them, just too *icky*.

Don't do that. It is not your prerogative. You might not enjoy some work, and, to the extent that you can, you should avoid it by being too busy on work that you *do* like. But don't turn up your nose. You are, after all, an *employee*. The likely Senior response is a raised eyebrow and a serious, negative mental note in your disfavor column.

If you don't like *any* of the work, then find a different firm, or start your own. And don't complain. Your employer don't *owe* you *nuthin'* besides what's in your contract.

"Lead, follow, or get the hell out of the way." That sharp advice is a double-edged, serrated sword, but the punchline is the same: If you think *you* can do better, shut up and try.

FINDING YOUR NIETZSCHE

From Law Day One, you should think, seriously, about which area of law most interests you. If you're among the lucky few who, seemingly since nursery school, knew that you wanted to be a star defense attorney, or civil-rights champion, or mortgage-foreclosure specialist, *Congratulations!* You'll save yourself the time and misspent energies of the ordinarily meandering search for a cozy niche. For everyone else, *now* is the time to focus. Not because that's the meaning of life, but because that's the path toward survival in the law. Only country lawyers, starving solos, and rainmaking gentle Seniors (with legions of specialist-minions on call) can claim generalist ways.

Don't chase after whatever happens to be the "in" specialty at the moment, unless you *truly* like it. First, as with everything else in life, "in" things *change*. For a decade or so, real estate was hot. Then mergers and acquisitions. Then bankruptcy. Environmental law is going strong, and intellectual property's looking pretty hot.

Get the picture?

Second, it's beside the point. Do you *like* it?

Choose your specialty; don't let it choose you. Many practitioners meander into an area and find themselves trapped by the sunk costs of expertise and an established practice. Although specialties aren't quite the La Brea tar pits, once you've focused your practice and acquired some depth, substantial effort is required to extricate yourself to journey elsewhere.

Look seriously to the attributes of various practices. It's amazing how lawyers fall into certain practices—or even into the main branches of either litigation or transactional work—without serious thought about what best suits *them*.

If you like people, then look to those practices that involve a lot of client contact, such as litigation, estate planning, family or criminal law, certain administrative work (...believe it or not!), public-interest work, and the like. If you like numbers, then look to commercial or tax practices. If you like being around wealthy people, go for the big firms. (If you *really* like being around wealthy people, get off on the estate-planning floor.) If you like, instead, being around poor people, there's *lots* of public-interest need out there.

If you lust after the fetal protection of a library, find a research position (most are in bureaus, which, by the way, can be exceptionally nice places to work). Or, contact one of the law book publishers; they're always looking for the spare pallid bookworm or two.

If you like big-picture stuff, courts or agencies can be the ticket. Don't worry about the money; you won't starve (and, by the hour, the pay's not at all bad). Appellate advocacy is tough to break into, but worth the trouble if you're a true law crafter.

If you want, instead, courtroom experience, run—don't walk—to your nearest District Attorney or Public Defender's office. At either, you'll be issued a front-stage pass to the best of courtroom drama, while your law-firm brethren will pine away the hours in their gilded offices, with only the rare excursion to court.

If you'd *really* like to be where the action is...join the Navy. Those guys are always getting into trouble. (I took the bar exam next to a Navy JAG officer, who commented that Air Force lawyers would call her on the rare times that those boys or girls in blue strayed. Somehow, Air Force lawyers never seemed to get as much trial experience.) Even better, Navy folks get into trouble all over the world.

It's not just a job....

Think also of *where* you'd like to practice. But don't assume too much. Sure, Bostonian firms tend to be more traditional than those in Reno...but not always. Notice what's missing? Do you *like* traditional? (If not, are you prepared to work *harder?*) There are cool firms in Boston, and stuffy ones in Reno. A statistical average is of little help in your single, solitary, stationary office.

If, after searching your soul, you're still unsure which trail you should follow, but you've a path to a big firm...go for the big firm. You might not like it, but it'll be easier to go elsewhere from there than vice versa. (Big-firm Seniors are more-than-moderately prejudiced against non-big-firm lawyers. They're positively aghast at their many former Juniors who have abandoned ship. Even non-big-firm Seniors carry the prejudice.) And you might just surprise yourself and like the big-firm dance.

If you like, instead, sleeping...*Beep! We're sorry. You have reached a career that has been discontinued. Please try again.*

SPECIALIZATION

To succeed in law, you must receive a constant, substantial stream of similar projects...immediately. Don't delude yourself into thinking that you'll just wander about the office until someone invites you into their comfy niche, or that the Seniors are going to tuck you in at day.

It might happen. But that's not the way to bet. It's kinda' like study groups in law school: They took effort, both to organize and to maintain, and required a large quantum of precociousness (or advice) and an unwavering faith in their worth. Yet most high achievers in law school were part of successful study groups, if only because the (hidden) structure of law rewards structured study.

Once you begin working for a Senior, you'll soon be pegged, both personally and practically through your new-found expertise, as their vassal. If you've done anything with some frequency and reasonable degree of non-incompetence—*Surprise!*—you're now an expert.

This might seem undeserved to you as you work through your first assignments, but it is cause for serious contemplation at your initial, hesitant requests for assignments (...and for steadfast completion of those tasks). When they can, Seniors will try to give you work in an area in which you express a preference, but most assume that Juniors have not the foggiest idea of their preferences (a good assumption, usually) and will make the choice for you.

If you were Second Assistant to the Auxiliary Stage Manager in your high school theater class, waltzed through a few memos for a pro bono community theater case, and laughed appropriately at the right Senior's jokes—*Presto!*—Entertainment Law. Hey, careers have been launched on less. (If truth be told, a certain level of bravado looms large in the success of any professional. *Shhh...*) The important point, again, is to decide whether you *like* entertainment law.

You should thus try, as much as possible, to do the early picking, rather than leaving it to fate. Again, you need to actively search for a niche from your very first day. You must pick a narrow area to start, even if you really want to be a generalist. First, it's easier to learn a narrow body of law. Second, it's easier to become comfortable practicing in a narrow body of law. Third, it's usually easier to sell your skills, at all but the highest levels, as a specialist. Fourth, it'll make your Senior's job easier, which will make *your* job less unpleasant. Finally, it will happen regardless of what you want. Far better for you to pick the subject and timing.

Many of you will even *prefer* specialties, if only because they give you something into which you can teethe. On a practical level, you must specialize fairly soon, because most simply cannot be proficient in more than a few areas, even in their prime. (The smaller the office, the more areas that you'll be called upon to learn. Still, the premise holds, generally.) Also on a practical level, your value—to clients and thus to the market—will depend largely on the knowledge, contacts, and people skills you pick up from those you meet while focusing as a specialist.

If you're one of the lucky ones who knows what you want, steer for that. Problem solved. If, however, you're like the rest of us and have no idea what you've been put on this planet to do other than consume resources, steer for your favorite Senior(s). Let them help with the choosing. Unless you find through a process of elimination that you *don't* like something, you'll probably find yourself quite happy, or at least satisfied, working with people you like. And if you like them, they'll likely like you.

This isn't an odd way to search for a calling: many Juniors—in all fields—are steered into niches not by the work, but by the people. Find out who the favored Seniors are...and seek them out. If you like one or more of them, or the work they do (especially if they're *not* one of the favored Seniors), *tell them so*. Don't be bashful. Make a joke of it and tell them you'll bug 'em to death until they load you up with work. The best way to ward off unwanted Seniors is to have lots of work from liked ones.

Now's not the time for you to be timid. Compliant, yes. Timid, no. Figure out, quickly, who and what you like. Then go for it. Don't be selfless; you're *pro se* on this one.

Be forceful, if necessary.

One colleague, who lusted after a specialized area in which one of the Seniors happened to be a highly respected expert, printed banners that commanded in exasperation: "GIVE ME WORK!", until, *finally*, he worked his way into the fold. It took him a solid year and a *lot* of self-teaching, but he *did* it. Now they're a happy (and *very* successful) semi-autonomous legal team within the firm. Ironically, she would now be up a fecal tributary without means of propulsion were it not for his (now) top-notch assistance. Yet it all happened because of *his* early and continued efforts as Junior, not hers as Senior.

Even if you have no idea what you like, pay attention to what you don't: the ever-trusty process of elimination. You'll likely get a variety of work from different Seniors. If nothing else, find something you're good at. Few are good at something they hate, and even fewer love something at which they're horrible.

Before you despair, look around. There really *are* decent Seniors floating about. If there are none around you, then you're probably miserable—and in the wrong place. Try to maneuver yourself elsewhere within the firm—or start looking outside—before your quiet misery sends *you* up the aforementioned tributary.

Making Partner

Ahhh...the finish line.

And the starting line for yet another race. The generous pay you expect as a Junior is just a warm-up to the lavish carrot patch that lies just inside the partnership castle. Don't assume that the world will stop spinning after you're coronated, however.

When—*Let's be ever the optimists!*—you do make partner, you will be assigned the organizational equivalent of poop-scooping: signing payroll checks, verifying expense accounts, law school interview trips, responding to unsolicited résumés, and so on. Whoopteedoo. Not that that's wrong...someone has to do it, and, like your Junior years, you still have ropes to climb.

You will then repeat your Junior-to-junior Senior process with a higher-order, junior Senior-to-senior Senior process. And miles to go before you sleep.

Just so you know.

— 4 —

GETTING THE WORK DONE

If you're just in it for the money, you're in the wrong business. Unless you're dripping with connections, you will work very, *very* hard for the big bucks in law.

If money's your temptress, bide your time, wait for a good opportunity, and get into commerce. *That's* where the money is. (Of course, unless you're dripping in *business* connections, you'll work pretty hard there too.) It's a tough lesson—and one that causes endless frustration—that the human compulsion for unearned riches is gratified only accidentally. More to the point, others will steadily intrude upon your dreams. Wake up. Seniors and judges expect real law out of you, and opposing counsel will take advantage of the fake variety.

OK. Everybody out of the pool. Back to work.

GETTING STARTED

When you strut (or slink) into your office on that first day, you should feel comfortable with the knowledge that, in the legal hierarchy, you are about two levels above amoebae. If you've spent a summer or two in the firm, then you're three levels higher.

Your first years in the law are a good opportunity to learn it. Take advantage. Glamorous though the Captain might be, it's more comfy as co-pilot. Enjoy your training wheels while you've got 'em.

When you first crank up your billing machine, you'll usually be given one of three assignments: (1) research; (2) document reviews; or (3) form-filling.

That's pretty much it. Sometimes you might need to pinch-hit (especially in a smaller firm), but that's the exception, not the rule.

So what to do when Señor Senior struts in with an assignment... and might as well be speaking Sanskrit for your comprehension of the expected task?[39]

The Answer? Four steps: First, take a deep breath. Second, don't panic. Third, go with what you know. Four, start your assignment.

Finished with the deep breath? Okay, then...

Don't Panic. If you do, you're dead. Panic kills the capacity to react. (You might *still* be dead *even if* you don't panic, but at least you will have a shot.) Thus, when you're handed a project that seems im-

---

39   If you happen to speak Sanskrit, you'll be particularly well suited in this cryptic hypothetical.

possible, spend a few minutes to sketch out, on paper, what you think the problem is. (Remember your law school exams?) If you're still lost, and your Senior doesn't shed some light, *sua sponte*, make a motion to that effect. Go back to your Senior for clarification, or go to another Senior if the question is innocuous enough and your embarrassment quota has been exceeded. (Be careful, however, not to exchange the well-intentioned but misdirected advice of another for your *delegating* Senior's instructions.)

Save yourself endless hours searching for complex answers to simple questions. Instead, ask Seniors, senior Juniors...even Staff (where appropriate for administrative stuff). They'll likely have an immediate answer or give you time-saving leads. Don't be a nuisance or give them reason to question your acumen, but do be an equal-opportunity inquirer.

Next: Go with what you know.

This is a lesson from flying. If you're on a heading of 270° and get lost, go with what you know. Spending a few minutes to check surroundings or instruments or beacons will usually solve the problem. If it doesn't (or you run into that bogeyman, weather beyond your handling), then...*go with what you know.*

Do most student pilots go with what they know?

Noooo...They wander about the countryside aimlessly, completely destroying the one certainty they originally had: that they were on a heading of 270° from...*their starting point.* All they need do in a real pinch is...*turn around.* Eventually they'll end up over familiar territory. Greatly preferable to corn fields and emergency low fuel.[40]

Go with what you know.

Take it one step at a time. If you gaze at an entire document at once, you'll be blinded by the enormity of it all, and gasp in terror at the overwhelming task.

If, instead, you take it section-by-section, it becomes child's play. (When I started this project, on a whim, I wondered whether I'd have enough to fill a pamphlet. Instead, it's been a constant battle to stop myself from digressing more than I have already.[41])

You know more than you think when you first start practicing. After all, unless you went into a van Winklian trance for three years, you do have *some* idea what *mens rea*, hearsay, and *ultra vires* mean. More importantly, you know where to start looking.

---

40 There's a saying in flying: The three most useless things to a pilot are altitude above you, runway behind you, and fuel you left behind. In the law, don't fight yourself over your inexperience and misspent energies: Get back on target and get on with the mission.

41 ...now look what I've done.

RESEARCH

Research will play a big role in your early work. It's the most Junior-accessible, and is viewed as (and is) a good tool for you to learn real law —on someone else's dime.

Think a moment from the perspective of a client, who has a legal problem: a zoning-variance appeal, a noisy neighbor, an injury, a new invention, or whatnot. They don't like to pay for attorneys any more than you like to pay for root canals. (And, at least with a root canal, you'll feel better (after a few ice cream sundaes).)

Remember your client, who goes to his lawyer—your Senior—who sums up the alternatives...and promises to take care of the problem. If the question is nebulous enough, or if the client likes reassurance, the Senior will ask for a memo from you. The client may or may not see this memo, but he *will* see the result: the bill. Every hour you spend adds up quickly to a sizable total, which will shock the client, who, in even his less cynical moments, wonders why lawyers (who he thinks already *know* the law) must pad their bills with endless and suspiciously unnecessary paperwork.

Remember your client, who doesn't know that lawyers—especially new ones—must wade through a morass of endless case law and the swamps of interpretation. The client would not appreciate paying for the (unrequiting) luxury of training *you*, as you spend half your time racing in the wrong direction, and twice as much time in serpentines when finally pointed correctly. It's a wonder clients are as complacent as they are. (Well, they're *not*...and they're becoming even less so. The centripetal pressures for law firms to justify their often exorbitant costs coil ever tighter, making *your* life all the more stressful.)

Remember the client as you bill your fortieth hour for research on whether *ex parte* motions must be filed on white paper.

Remember too your Senior, who doesn't like to write off your time —which is *his* money—and who likes even less receiving a phone call or letter from an irate client over *your* portion of the bill.

And now for the tricky part: actually doing the research.

Your Seniors delegate work, which they expect to see completed: (1) quickly, and (2) perfectly. Two rather important modifiers.

QUICKLY. This will seem impossible to you at first, because you have no [expletive deleted] idea what you're doing.[42] And in your uncertainty and desperation you go overboard, researching every

---

42 This is not an indictment of you; it's a result of legal education's lurch away from practical legal issues to ideological ones. For an interesting discussion of this transition—possibly the most important in the past two hundred years of American law—Mary Ann Glendon, a professor at Harvard Law, has written an excellent book: *A Nation Under Lawyers*. I don't, by the way, condemn this movement—it was undertaken with the best of intentions—but we have lost much that was good in our race against that which was not.

tangential legal topic within forty miles of the assignment. This is a no-no, and unnecessary. The answer? KISS—Keep It Simple, Silly.

Narrow the question. Focus like a laser on the result your Senior would like to see. Some Seniors are quite bad about this, in part because sometimes *they* don't know what they want...and they transfer this uncertainty onto you (which is the *last* thing you need more of). Yet it is *you* who will be the locus of discomfort when your memo is wildly off-course. *Framing the issue is 49% of the legal research battle.* (It's 49% of *every* legal battle.) When you start to wander, refocus, go back to your Senior, and refocus again.

Once you're in the jungle, don't stick to a path that leads deeper into the underbrush—without any hope for a shortcut to civilization.

It might seem embarrassing, but confirm with your Senior, in the narrowest terms, the "Question Presented". They won't hate you for this, and it's a good time to make sure you're not wildly astray. Confirm your position after you've started your journey. Five minutes here will save hours of wasted—and expensive—effort later.

You've a fine line to walk: You must examine the law—quickly, completely, and correctly. Yes, there *will* be false trails, but you must at least inspect them for their falsity. Yet you cannot tarry. And don't get clutched up: You will never be able to research an issue with nary a second wasted. Don't waste your time trying.

Still sitting there with no idea what you're doing? Draw that deep breath and think your problem through...from the beginning. Carefully. Dispassionately. Legally. *Visteme despacio que estoy de prisa.* Dress me slowly, for I am in a hurry.[43]

Now's not the time to race. I know, sometimes it's pretty hard. After a little practice, though, you'll feel comfortable enough to know where to spend your time; it'll be second nature. For now, try not to be the Junior equivalent of a spastic buffoon.

Part of the mandate for speed requires that you attend to matters immediately. If it sits on your desk long enough to collect even the slightest haze of dust, it has sat too long. Clients assume that their projects—which you may assume are rather important to them—are being handled with dispatch, and Seniors assume that Juniors would rather not face them after they receive a phone call from a client, who must be told either the truth (bad) or a white lie (worse...for you). Do not let any project slide, hoping against hope it will disappear.

You must become proficient at research, and you must become organized while *conducting* research. If you do not, you'll end up on the wrong end of your timesheet, which will expand to the point of Senior displeasure. There are a number of techniques, and a variety of aids, but the important point is to start and follow a logical model. For instance, to avoid spinning your wheels when reviewing cases, you'll

---

43   That's about a half-dozen years of high-school Spanish, by the way.

need to track the cases, with their holdings (and cross-references). A legal pad is usually the best way to accomplish this. Computers have modified this, but I doubt they will ever replace the psychic need of pen and paper. Whatever your preference, devote some energy to developing a good habit, here.

In a broader vein, take a look at your assignment. Here's a good opportunity to bring out your Crayons® and draw yourself a chart.[44] *Figure out who wants what, who represents whom, what needs to happen...and when.* (This is important not only initially—it'll reduce the likelihood of confused thought, later on.) With this chart, you can put some of the pieces together. (And, after the pieces are together but before the project is about to be forgotten, make a copy for your future reference. Organize your research, and—being ever the conservationist—*recycle* it. Also, make a copy of the *checklist* that you wisely created for this project—adapted from a form book—and start a separate file for your project checklists.)

A Streamlined Briefing Technique, by Clyde Emery, is a good nuts-and-bolts approach to tackling research. (Other guides are available. You might check the publisher's website, www.hits.net/~fpp/ , for the latest recommendations.) If you didn't spend much time in law school learning how to *do* research—to the point that you can find an answer to *any* legal question within *one hour*—find this booklet (or one like it) and *use* it.

PERFECTLY. This will also seem impossible to you, because (as was *almost* mentioned so indelicately before), you don't know what you're doing. The mandate for perfection only feeds this paradox. How can you give a glorious summation of law with only a few hours' research? The answer, again, is to narrow the research, and forget the glorious part. You're not there to ask *why*. You're there to figure out *what* and *how*. Answering broad—much less, philosophical—questions is both impossible and unnecessary.

Narrow the question. If it's interesting, it's probably too broad.

THE CASTES OF LAW

As we're instructed from the first day of law school, there is a hierarchy of authority in law. The irony in practice is: the *lower* you are in the hierarchy, the better.

The strongest cases are the ones that cite to the *lowest* level. Relying on an ordinance is better than a statute, which is *much* better than case law. Local is better than state, which is better than federal. And let's not even get into *penumbra*.

---

44 Close your office door if you do use Crayons, though. Ours is not a profession with a well-developed sense of humor.

It's not that "higher" law is no good, but reaching it necessarily removes your client's case from a cut-and-dry issue to a more amorphous one. Sure, you'll still need to double-check (and cite) higher authority. Just grab the lowest—and tastiest—legal apples first.

Regulations, rules, statutes. *Then* look afield to amber waves of precedent.

Beware the Grey.[45] Clients rely on you to solve their legal problems. Their needs are immediate, their patience limited. (They often come to you at the 11th hour, yes?) Worse, the world appears greyer when you start than it will a few years hence; not everything's as nebulous as Juniors perceive.

Beware the Grey. It's that great vacuum cleaner of your time and their money. Yes, it might help—in the short-run—in your billables race, but the result won't be pleasant if you've nothing to show for your antics.

Beware the Grey. If you even *think* of citing to the Constitution, you're *well* into it.

REAL LAW

At work, you're no longer a student striving to please a procession of teachers, who were often barely focused on the teaching job at hand. You're now playing with the big boys and girls. It might seem a little strange to you at first, but your Seniors expect you to provide them with solid legal answers—upon which they will likely base their legal advice to their—and *your*—clients. Seniors expect more than hesitant suggestions. They want *The Law*...answers as concrete as can be given this side of malpractice.

You're expected to provide legal *advice*. This is serious stuff. Don't clip together a few interesting articles from your local newspaper, or sketch a synopsis waltzing from the law of Medieval Europe through the Renaissance, brushing past the Reformation, then concluding with a few paste-ups of the Berlin Wall. You must provide *the law*.

Force yourself to give hard answers: You must begin making legal choices. Yes, this might require intuition that you have not yet honed. If you are uncertain—either as a policy choice for your Senior or as a business choice for the client—make a choice anyway and add a notation for your Senior's review. (If it's a major issue, confirm its importance, or draft a *finished* section in the alternative.)

When in doubt, *write it down*. Sure, you'll be uncertain—about almost everything. As long as your notations become less frequent and more insightful, you'll do just fine.

---

45 I know, I know. Here, it's supposed to be spelled "Gray". Forgive my Anglophile tendencies, but, to me, "Grey" just *looks* better.

MEMOS

You're not writing memos for the fun of it. Seniors need answers, and you're a good way to get them. But there's more to it: Research is an *investment*...in you. A significant, if secondary, goal of memo assignments is to increase your grasp of a field of law, so that when a client faces *you* instead of your Senior, you can handle most of what might be thrown at you. Thus, the more research you do in an area, the more likely will be subsequent assignments in that area. (Even more reason to choose your niche and Seniors carefully and quickly.)

Don't misinterpret the term *memo*. Lawyers have a horrible habit of convoluting the meaning of words beyond reasonable recognition. You already know that a "memo" is not what a normal, native English speaker would think it is; you're not to hand in scribbled notes of groovy cases you think might be of interest. It is to be a polished, thoroughly researched summation of the issue, suitable for framing. You're a *lawyer*. Your stratospheric hourly rate begs justification.

You may *not* turn in unfinished, or poorly finished, work. (The test applied isn't always an objective one.) I once handed in an unfinished draft (which required what I then thought were Senior-level choices) without explaining either my dilemmas or that I was pulled for another project in the aftermath of Hurricane Iniki. The Senior who reviewed my (unacceptable) work was not amused.

Do not skimp on *your* finished product, either substantively or stylistically. Even if it's a minor memo for a side issue in a modest case, it should look like a parchment worthy of the Founding Fathers, deserving of its own argon-containment vault. As you shall discover, your work has a most irritating habit of following you about.

By the same token, don't hand in a law-review-styled treatise. Your finished work should be a concise summary, written for the most restive of eleventh-graders.[46]

All of your memos must have a polished appearance, but the content of each should be proportionate to the question presented. It's best to follow a memo form. If your firm doesn't have one, ask to see a noteworthy memo...and *follow it*. (I like the model that starts with a "Question Presented", written to force a yes or no answer, followed by "Brief Answer", "Statement of the Facts", and "Discussion" sections. I usually skip the "Conclusion", because it's duplicative of the "Brief Answer" section. But, if your Seniors want it, give it to 'em.)

At the risk of repetition: Seniors want—and will demand—legal *commitment,* not a wimpy combination of hesitant, meaningless disclaimers. (*They* get to draft those.) Unless the issue is truly grey, you must figure out the law and give it to them straight. (Actually, *especially* if it's grey, give it to them straight.)

---

46 ...and *no* footnotes.

Sure, you'll be uncertain. Some assignments would've made Learn-ed Hand wince. If you can't figure it out upon a few dozen moments' reflection...*ask*. (Either a senior Junior or a Senior, depending upon the depth of your confusion and complication of issues. Before you *do* ask, though, run through what you have, and organize your thoughts. Nothing is more irritating—or common—than for Juniors to display ignorance of their embryonic research through a bald inability to discuss it intelligently with others.)

When assigned a project, ask what result is expected. A letter? A memo? (Most common.) A quick-and-dirty oral report? (If they say a "quick-and-dirty memo"...reread the preceding paragraphs.)

Ask how much time you should spend on the project. If you're approaching this limit with no end in sight, go back for guidance.

A final, crucial note: *know your purpose*. Not in life, but in the law. More specifically, in each memo: What does your reader *need*? Should you be the professor or the gunslinger? Generally, if it's internal, you should be the objective, informative guide; if it's external, you should be the less-objective, partisan proponent. The latter, if needed, follows the former, and the former, when written, informs the latter.

Write memos like you mean it, and in the expectation that they're stepping stones to *real* law practice, which they are.

CITATION

You *do* need to learn how to cite...properly. Law school is too frenetic, however, for most non-law-reviewers to worry about such ungraded extras as pretty Bluebook citation. Even if not among the most egregious of sins, citation faux pas *will* be noticed, and will be annoying to those—such as court folk—who *do* know better.

The law is a profession of intellectual snobs—some substantiated, many not. If you cite improperly—by ignorance or inattention—you will be—instantly and (all but) irreversibly—pegged as a dolt. Worse, each sloppy citation is an invitation to an overworked judge or clerk to question all that surrounds such slothful work. That's not a good start for you or for your client.

Do not use a system of citation (such as APA, MLA, or Turabian's) used in regular academic writing. Substantively, they're too sloppy for the demands of law, and much of what *is* cited is irrelevant.[47] Stylistically, they're not law.

If you happen to *like* Turabian's (or another) system, get over it. True, Turabian's was an improvement, decades ago, over the non-system that preceded it. Still, as anal as Bluebook form is, it *is* impressive when followed. Not only are assertions supported, but the reader

---

[47] I never could figure out the need for the publisher's name and home city. If a source cannot be found by author, title, or issue...it ain't worth finding.

knows, instantly, how *strongly* they're supported—and, though this duty is pooh-poohed in practice—*contrary* authority. Important stuff when we rely so heavily upon the goings-on of jurists past.

It's not that one way is right, and the other, evil. But, as with everything else in life, patterns are established...and woe be unto infidels. Though it might seem petty to you, do you *really* want to be on the front lines of *this* rebellion?

Hey, I dislike mindless convention as much as the next anarchist, but, if you're going to rebel, pick something worthwhile. Don't resent, just do. And, as with most of life's endeavors, learn it—*cold*—then relax a bit. To be further contrary, Bluebook citation is not mindless. It's an admirable and worthy system. Use it.

An effort's afoot to replace the Bluebook: first Chicago and now the Association of Legal Writing Directors, who are working on a simpler guide. Unless your firm *specifies* its use (which would be astonishing, at least for now)...*don't you follow it.* Yes, the Bluebook is geared toward academic writing, and yes, it takes some effort. But for whom do you think you are writing? Many court folk (especially clerks) *are* academically inclined. On a deeper level, it seems that the precision of the Bluebook is, well, just too much work for some.

Not-so-minor points: Don't use *see also,* unless it's *truly* closely related *and* an important addition. It's a flag for readers that you're bullshitting. (And it's usually flapping at just the right place.[48])

Absolutely no *cfs.* What's encouraged for tenure is a deadly sin when you're trying to get something *done.*

Include the *pinpoint* citation. (A pinpoint citation is one that cites to a specific page, or range of pages, from where you are (supposedly) drawing your reference. If it's a *range,* though, it'd better be limited, or your reader will, rightly, draw an unflattering conclusion.)

Give pinpoint cites. *Dammit...*you're *there.* It doesn't take any extra effort, and, though it (probably) won't be a deciding factor, it'll be appreciated by court folk...and it'll more strongly convince them that you're not full of crap. (It's the first thing to go when you *are.*)

Think for a moment from the judge's (and clerk's) perspective. Vague citations force them to read through unrelated material to find support for what you're asserting. That's not fair. More importantly, it's not unlikely that they'll read around what *you* intended to cite— finding either contrary authority or distinguishing facts—to your client's severe detriment if you *were* playing with the passages.

Pinpoint citations look professional because they are.

Okay, enough citation ranting. Take some time, preferably while you're still in law school, to learn the Bluebook. Follow it, in practice, as closely as you can without being overly irritating...and focus your efforts on substance.

---

48 *See also* SHERWOOD SCHWARTZ, INSIDE GILLIGAN'S ISLAND (2d ed. 1994).

READING

There are two things you must do in law. They're quite simple, really. Sadly, few bother to do them correctly, even though we all know we should. Are you ready? You must: (1) Read; and (2) Read On.

You must *Read*.

All right. You're thinking, *"Well, duhh...!"*

Yet, time after time, you'll realize—afterwards—that you could have, and *should* have, looked up—or double-checked—*The Rule*.

When you start into a new area, find the applicable statute...and *read it*. Every word.

When you've a question, grab the statute *first*...and read it. *Every word*.

As you gain experience, you'll be able to rely on memory for much of the basic stuff. But even then, you must be careful: legislatures and courts have the bothersome habit of changing the rules. Until you do have experience, you should cross-check yourself. Confirm that what you think is true is, in law, actually true. Occasionally, you'll find you weren't so sagacious, after all. It might take a little extra time (...not too much, mind you), but it's your job.

The second part of your job is a little harder: You must *Read On*. *Huh...?*

You start reading a case or statute or text, find something that looks close to what you're looking for, and shout (...or at least think, loudly)...*Eureka!*

You stop. You've got The Answer.

No.

You must *Read On*. The answer might still be the same, but, then again, it might not. Drafters do not draft with you in mind. They don't put all the magic words up front, in the kind spirit of helping out fresh new cadets. There's nothing quite so embarrassing as citing a rule, only to learn—publicly—that something a few sub-sections later is the exception that fits your client's case.

If the material cites to a different source, read that too (unless it's not relevant). If the material doesn't make sense, go to a secondary source (or to a tertiary source, your Senior), figure it out, then reread the original.

Read. Read on.

LEARNING THE LAW

Master Seniors know, and you are yet to learn, that most cases are won not on theatrics or impassioned brilliance, but, rather, on careful, even obsessive, attention to detail.

Quiet brilliance. Your job is an especially quiet part. Leave the shimmering brilliance, for now, to your Senior.

Law is not *supposed* to be sexy. It's the blueprint for society. And blueprints aren't centerfolds.

Sure, if you happen to have a spark, and the moment presents itself, let your Senior in on it. You might get the Junior equivalent of the Pulitzer *and* Nobel: a grin and a pat on the back.[49] But keep in mind the object of the game: getting the work done.

Before you begin to write about the law, spend the time to make sure you're fully in command of the *facts,* and that you're looking for the *right* law. If you do the opposite—as many do—and begin instead to search the law and try to fit whichever facts fit, you may well manipulate the facts incorrectly, and you might miss a *better* legal theory. This is when you should *not* hurry. Keep an open mind when you start: your first job is to spot the issues. *After* you've spotted them all, discarded a few, and discussed the case with colleagues (a key step), is in-depth legal research appropriate.

Your work—both transactional and litigation—must show clear, linear (if multivariate) thinking: A, therefore B, therefore C, and not X, Y, or Z; consequently, Q.

Alternative arguments, well constructed, are particularly effective: We win because D; even if not D, we win because E; even if not E, we win because F.

The final result should make *moral,* as well as legal, sense. If it does not, go back to your office, figure out why, and figure out a better approach. This is not only to preserve your soul: if an argument flies against what is "right"—even if you really *should* win on a technical point of law—you will quite likely lose in front of a court that prefers to do what is right.

Memos, briefs, and motions should be short, sweet, and packed with powerful, on-point authority. String cite the rest.

Simple generally wins its day in court. Much as you like to think a snappy smile and rapier wit will overcome any weakness...in law, logic wins. Really. Judges and their clerks can smell puffery almost as well as a veteran German shepherd can sniff out your average cargo hold full of contraband.

Force yourself to cut the tangential crap. Yes, there's a natural inclination to throw in everything, hoping that *something* will catch the judge's attention (and justify to your client those many billed hours). *Resist.* You might indeed catch the judge's attention...but it won't be the kind you like. Blustering will only annoy a judge. (Yes, you might win some extra points with your client—assuming he reads what you forward to him—but as the lawyer you have to draw the professional line somewhere...and you *really* shouldn't annoy a judge.)

---

49 It's kinda' funny. After years of practice, *those* are the moments you'll remember. Plus, they're a useful counterbalance to the dreadful times when you'll want to slide under the desk in shame.

More to the point, the court does not have the time to search for the nugget of wisdom hidden deep within your rambling commentary. Lead the court instead past a careful, dispassionate recitation of the facts, through a brief and clear explanation of the relevant law, beyond the arguments of the opposition, to a logical and common sense conclusion favorable to your client.

Don't repeat your arguments. Saying the same thing twice—or, hell, why not three times—is not going to transform a bad argument into a good one. It will, however, annoy your reader...and you *really* shouldn't annoy a Judge.

Don't repeat your arguments. Saying the same thing twice—or, hell, why not three times—is *not* going to transform a bad argument into a good one. It will, however, annoy your reader.

Do not cheat. Don't make an assertion without proper foundation, or force a conclusion that's not supported—without mirrors—by *law*. You might think you can slide one by. *Think again.*

When you write to a Court—which is what you do every time you file a motion, brief, memorandum, or anything else—substantiate *every* sentence that begs a question in the mind of your reader.

`"The general rule is x."`

Says who? *You?* Your next-door neighbor? The Supreme Court?

`"Mr. Sixpack entered the store at 5:03 p.m."`

Says who? *You?* Your next-door neighbor? Some witness down the street whose glasses slipped off at 5:02 P.M.? The anal-retentive proprietor of this particular store, *The Clock Shoppe?*

Yes, it might seem a little silly at first, but it's an important part of your job. Majestic as "Learning the Law" sounds, if you're doing it right it should happen right under your nose. Each research project you complete, each form you fill, and every deposition you take adds to your treasure chest of knowledge. With a little seasoning from your Seniors, from handy reference books, and from experience, you'll soon be on your way to lawyerhood.

THE KNOW-IT-ALL

Don't act so smart. It's natural, especially among such talented folk, to showcase your knowledge. This isn't a good idea for (at least) a few reasons: First, it's rather likely that your Senior, perhaps, knows more. Second, if you act as if you *already* know everything, you might just be treated that way. There's no happy ending if you *don't*. Third, it forecloses an important learning tool. Spend this time, when you're not *expected* to know everything...to *learn* everything. There's no need to act stupid, but there is an advantage in not cutting someone off—someone who might just teach you something you will later be able to use, when it really counts. Fourth, there's a natural dislike of know-it-alls.

And, of course, it's not impossible that you know less than it all.

THE LIBRARY

Your exposure to law school libraries provides only a vague reference to the working world of the law, and will prove only peripherally useful to the needs of your clients. Unlike student time, your work in the firm's library must be both purposeful and pragmatic. When you first start work (or, better yet, during the preceding summers), you should take some time to find out what's available. But after that, it's work, work, work.

When the time comes to actually break open the books for a client, understand that, eventually, you'll have little need to do "research". You'll instead zero in on a source or two to confirm your suspicions. This is a skill honed by experience. Start working toward that goal.

As long as we're in the library, though, we may as well stop by a few of the shelves.

SECONDARY SOURCES. When you first begin in a new legal territory, go to the secondary sources (you know...topical binders, digests, local law services, Am. Jur. 2d, *Corpus Juris Secundum, American Law Reports,* law reviews, and the like) for a fast overview...and for quick cites to get you going. Again, narrow your search to discrete topics; *cherish* the indices, tables of contents, and digests.

Secondary sources provide a useful overview and starting point, but be careful. Don't spend an afternoon drifting though a tangential, if fascinating, article on Admiralty Law as Applied Extraterrestrially if your assignment is limited to Starship Alien Anti-Discrimination Liabilities while Exploring Strange New Worlds. Let others explore for five-year missions. Yours should be finished sooner.

LIBRARIANS. Don't overlook this most consistently overlooked of research resources: *librarians.* Your time should be spent reviewing sources, not looking for them. Don't be shy; ask for help. They won't mind. Indeed, they'll relish the challenge. Not that you can abdicate, mind you. Many law librarians are not lawyers, and although they can work wonders in finding a source, it is *you* who must learn of that source in the first place. Still, it never hurts to ask what's available.

COMPUTERS. Ya' gotta love 'em. *What!?* You're *scared* of 'em? Get over it. Seniors can get away with their holier-than-silicon attitudes (less and less true, nowadays), but you won't. True, computers are often misused, and thus aren't as helpful as they could be. Understand what they do best. In a sense, it's analogous to you...when you're cookin'. They do the simple things very well. And very, very fast.

Want to search three zillion cases for the term *retrolental fibroplasia?* No problem. If you get into the computer's mindset,[50] your job will be made all the easier, and—here's the good part—*you'll* get the credit. Make your computer *work*. Let it do the boring searches, sortings, and whatnot.

If you don't adore Messieurs Lexis and Westlaw, shame on you. They're the greatest pair since legal-sized paper and subpoenas. One caveat, though: Don't meander on-line. This isn't law school, where you could log on, break for lunch, head off to Spring Break, then realize you hadn't logged off...without worrying about it. No more.

In a polite variation of bait-and-switch, computer searches in law practice are expensive, and, more importantly, are *added* to your time charges. They're only valuable because they can be so much faster and more exhaustive than manual searches. Note the words *can be*. You need to treat computer searches seriously, and put some thought into them *before* the meter's running. Idling in a Lamborghini isn't too bright, is it?[51]

Before going on-line, get a solid grasp of what you're looking for. *Thoughtfully* formulate search and alternate words. This is crucial: computers are only as good the user. Don't rely on just a single set of search words or Boolean connectors. Be imaginative: when searching, for example, for an issue involving Trusts, consider that exactly the same issue might arise under Contracts or Agency. Prepare multiple searches, as variations on the case theme, before you start. If you've a more-than-modestly complicated search, then take advantage of the services' reference attorneys. You can talk to real attorneys, who're available to help you use their databases. They're quite good at finding on-point authority. That's the prize: somewhere in legal heaven a bell chimes for each case found on point. (The uppermost bells are reserved for the Supreme finds.)

These searches can save you lots of time, give a better result, and save your clients money, which should make you happy because it will make your Seniors happy.

CD- and DVD-ROMs. Get acquainted with the latest technological offspring. These blocks off the ol' chip present a significant improvement over on-line research in that you *can* spend a little time meandering—without racking up fees of biblical proportions.

Take advantage. (If you have the burning desire to quest for one of the Lost Tribes of the Law, however, you'll have to summon otherworldly strength—of either altitude—to restrain yourself. You don't have the spare time.)

---

50 Oxymorons, anyone? (...Then again, maybe not for long.)

51 Unless, of course, the object is to keep your license—and spleen. Computer research does tend to be safer, though.

GET THE NET. Your firm probably has, or will get, access to the internet for everyday use. As if CD-ROMs weren't good enough, the Net can be a joyously fascinating tool. But it's still in its infancy, for legal research. And, as anyone who pays on-line charges (or hourly billings) will attest, Net time flies. Be careful out there.

DOCUMENT REVIEWS

This is the second of three likely tasks that await in your first years. This category, however, is generally reserved for those associates in the largest firms, whose corporate clients wish to purchase (or sell) divisions worth billions. Or, an estate worth many millions might require extensive (and expensive) review of box upon musty box.

Thus begins perhaps the most dreaded of all Junior assignments: the document review. Hour after hour, day after day, sometimes week after week—looking for something. Something bad. Something good. Sometimes you're not sure what.

If this falls to you: rather than resent it, turn the lens around. First, thank your stars that you're earning the money that you'll earn while you're doing your duty. Second, it *is* a duty. Third, enjoy the relatively mindless task as a break from Categories One and Three. Finally, beware if assigned these jobs too often: everyone in a big firm gets them, but they *are* mindless, and are thus reserved for junior Juniors and those not on their way up.

FORM-FILLING

And now for the fun stuff: Form-filling.

Think again from your clients' perspective. They want their deed, permit, loan, will, divorce, or whatever...without waiting months and without paying twice the annual income of your nearest tycoon. The secret to winning clients' hearts and influencing Seniors' minds—two things that you should very much wish to do—is that form-filling is pretty much what its name implies.

Let's stop for a moment. Most projects, although they might seem unmanageable or downright esoteric at first, fall into predictable categories. Regardless how fancy the building, a transfer from one owner to another is pretty much like any other transfer. Sure, you must watch out for the occasional exception...which only proves the rule: the law loves plagiarism. Lawyers—even Senior ones—are too risk-averse (and logical) to create new forms for each new case. Instead, they copy their old ones...and other good ones they run across. This isn't wrong; it's smart lawyering.

I once had to review a lease drafted for a prospective borrower of our client, a lender. The more I read, the madder I got. The lease—to put not too fine a point on it—sucked. It would have been worse than useless had a dispute (over the fairly simple loan) arisen; it would have *created* problems. Even worse, a vastly superior form already existed...for a dollar.[52] Instead, the loan applicant had paid hundreds of (...if not a thousand) dollars to a lawyer to draft a crappy one—and then, indirectly, hundreds more to our firm for me to review it.

But that's not all! I asked my Senior for permission to recommend simply that our client require the standard form. Not quite so easy. She—rightly—reminded me that such a straightforward ultimatum would—human psychology being what it is—more than likely poison the deal. So I had to spend hours to critique the lease, prepare a long letter detailing the numerous necessary changes, and offhandedly offer the option of the standard form. (The result? A new lease...using the standard form.)

It wasn't fair. The prospective borrowers, innocent to the ways of law practice, were cheated, with neither reason nor benefit, by thoughtless and inferior replication of legal effort. A thousand-dollar non-lesson, with neither honor nor glory.

Don't do that. Rely on the expertise and wisdom of those who have trodden the path before you. For your first year—at least—you'll be given projects that require some degree of extrapolation from conventional forms, using client-specific information. Keep in mind the object of the game: your client needs some papers—forms—*done*.

Keep in mind the practical workings of law; you're not the first to have run across whatever the client needs; your firm probably has a stack of similar stuff done by last year's cohort of Juniors. It's all a sophisticated version of pin the tail on the (legal) donkey.

Keep in mind, too, that different forms are drafted for different perspectives. You'll eventually read, for example, commercial lease forms drafted for lessors, and ones drafted for lessees. The difference is startling. Before you become indignant, think about what's going on: Clients pay attorneys their hard-earned money to put, in writing, the best deal possible for *them*. Whether it takes them a step closer to the Pearly Gates is not your concern, as a Junior.

They're not children. If they want to kick out a commercial lessee that is six hours late with the rent, and the lessee agrees, and the law says it's okay, then...there you go. If they're a big lessee and they insist that the punishment for being six months late with the rent is an apology and a promise to pay within the next six years, and the lessor agrees, and the law says it's okay, then...there you go.

True, the fairness of the deal—or blatant lack thereof—arises from the relative bargaining power and sophistication of each party. So be it. You cannot change the former, and the latter is your job.

---

52 A near-perfect standard lease form is almost always available—usually from the local board of Realtors®—and does the job, nicely, for just about every (impartial) lease one could think of entering.

We can argue that perhaps the law shouldn't allow such lopsided contracts. Before you shout *"Hear, hear!"*—consider that a lopsided deal might be better than none at all. (Keep in mind that most deals hum along just fine without us.) And consider too your position in the game. Many, many people have lost in the cause of trying to change this little part of human nature. Don't be another, uncounted loser.

If that's your passion, seek out those little people—there're lots around—and fight for *them*. Still, it's the same game.

PERSPECTIVES

Some assume that a document drafted for a client should be drafted wholly and immoderately to that client's benefit. This is a short-sighted approach. It's unlikely that you'll deal with a client who insists on an entirely one-sided deal, but if your client does so wish, explain the reasons that being fair is being smart:

One, it's better business. Profits that extend into the future are more important than a short-term benefit. Even with one-time deals, your client's *reputation* has a value. Often, it's as important as the day-to-day business, because it *creates* that business. (Beware, too, the client who is happy to short-change a business partner: he likely has as few qualms about doing the same to you.) Granted, this veers into a discussion of enlightened business practices, but businesses that thrive are not businesses that cheat. Don't hide behind the *"Oh,* that's a *business,* not a *legal* question" cop-out. It *is* a legal question if it will come back to haunt your client. And better attorneys, like better chess players, think several moves ahead.

Two, does your client *really* want to fight, later? That's the option, as a practical matter. If the other side wants to back out of a bad deal, there's not a whole lot your client can do, absent an interest secured by law and diligence, and wise termination language. Think *now* about the calculus, *then*. What will be worth fighting over, and what will not? Once the future battle lines are distinct, preemptive drafting is relatively easy. This applies not only to issues of bad dealing, but also of *fair* dealing; many clients would rather not focus on the negative possibilities, and an even larger percentage do not consider even innocent contingencies, such as delays, *force majeure,* changes of market and other circumstances, and the like. It is your job to think through these contingencies, for them. (One of the worst feelings is knowing that a client's problem was caused by *your* failure to guard against a contingency that was staring you in the face.)

Three, if a fight *is* on...how will a court view your one-sided, poison-hearted document? (Do you suppose the courts *really* genuflect before *contra proferentum* disclaimer provisions?)

Fourth, which is more important: the last legal inch...or the deal? Especially with a proposal draft, angering the other side with overly aggressive lawyering will likely provoke the same, to no one's (but the lawyers') advantage. (And even the immediate billable advantage will wear thin after you've killed a few deals.)

Fifth, *your* reputation is on the line too. And—a bit of self-interest, here—sometimes it pays to impress the *other side* as well. I've been in conferences where the opposing side sat in open admiration at the principled protection of *our* client's interests. Even where it was a point against *their* interest, a constructive, gentle, yet firm stance is a sharp relief from many practitioners—and almost always results in a better, faster, more agreeable result. Conflicts aside, to whom do you suppose that other person might turn, in the future?

In any case—unless there's a substantive issue for your client to decide—follow the more moderate path. That's the trail to a speedy victory, with the minimum of cuts and scrapes. If the client insists on a more hazardous path, and is heedless of your warnings, beware of your professional responsibilities: you remain bound to your broader duties as well. For example, drafting an agreement that you know (or *should* know) violates the law is an invitation to a malpractice suit, especially if the other side gets burned. This is more likely, the more extreme the deal. (Granted, this is an issue on the cutting edge, but do *you* want to be the one testing the grammatical implications of that phrase?)

INSTRUCTION?

Do not make the mistake of assuming you'll be told what to do. *Nope.* You will, instead, be handed a stack of papers beneath a Post-it™ and scribbled note to...*huh?* If you can even read it, you'll sit there and wonder when the J.D. Police will burst in to take you away for impersonating a lawyer.[53]

You're operating outside your envelope of proficiency, which is a major reason your first years are so stressful. It might feel as though you've been thrown to the lions, but that sound is the scream of inexperience, not the growl of hungry felines.

As mentioned before, what's expected of you is the ability to look at previous versions of similar projects, and extrapolate the variables to your new one. This usually isn't too hard, because most law work, once you get the hang of it, is deadly boring. (You can be assured that you won't be handling cutting-edge work; that's the interesting stuff that Seniors like and deserve.)

Important point, here: Most (say, ninety-two-point-six percent) of legal work well done is not—I repeat, *not*—a function of intelligence. Sure, you need to know enough to separate the motions from the

---

[53] You might first remove the plaque in your office: "I'm not an expert, but I play one at work."

memoranda, but that's only enough to get you to first base. More important is the ability to take a case, recognize its shape, and mold a legal response to fit.

Some Juniors expect hand-holding. A few (*very* lucky) ones actually get it. Don't hold your breath. First, Seniors don't remember all the nitty-gritty you're now expected to learn. Either the rules have changed, or their attention is diverted to too many other, higher-order demands. They know what to look for when reviewing your work, but they might not know, for example, how many copies to send to XYZ Bureau. You will instead need to rely on senior Juniors, paralegals, your secretary, and other staff for these answers. Really, it's not fair to expect more of Seniors; they've got enough to worry about without wiping your ears dry every few minutes.

Learn how to (1) recognize that some detail needs attention, and (2) figure out how to attend. Without so much as a whisper, you're responsible for the small stuff. If you're unsure after a few moments, ask or flag it...and move on. This will cause headaches when you're first getting into it, but it'll start to make sense once you become familiar with what the finished papers *should* look like; a large part of the answer for practitioners is to create, and use, form files.

More on that, later.

One technical point: You must be *very* careful not to corrupt revisions with earlier drafts. Establish and follow a clear procedure. It's a good idea to throw correction (typographical) drafts immediately into the trash, *er*...recycle bin...so as not to accidentally switch the wrong papers. (Your firm might prefer that you file substantive revisions for later reference.) Follow the routines of your secretary and Seniors.

One more point. Don't do too much of the scut work. It's useful to know, but you *are* getting paid quite a lot of money—and costing even more—for, supposedly, real talent. Automate your work as soon as you learn what you're doing, and delegate as soon as you're allowed. (You won't be worried about delegation for a while, though.)

For now, understand the demand on you. When presented with a simple motion, you cannot diagram and reinvent each sentence. You must assume that the structure of the previous form—the *Seniors'* form—is correct, and make the changes unique to your assignment. You must, particularly the first few times, read the entire document, and note anything that seems astray. This is especially frustrating in transactional work, where constant additions to each edition make for a jumbled mess that a Junior almost never comprehends. Litigation presents its own problems, because each case has its own facts, which change the dance, however slightly.

Thus, a fine, if slightly unfair, balance between obsessive care... and getting those darned documents out before you retire.

DEADLINES

Deadlines are *good*. Always ask for a deadline. If a Senior is too nice
and comments *"Oh* ... don't worry about it."—don't believe 'em. Unless
you're *sure* it's a bona fide low-priority make-work *especiál*, assume
that it needs to be done ... *pronto.*

    ¿Comprende, muchachos?

You *do* need a few swift kicks to quicken your pace. It's an unpleasant necessity of practice (and it's better to do your own kicking).
If the project looks like a recurring one, then ask, when it's finished,
how long it *should have* taken. Your Senior will usually lean back,
smile, and reply that, when you're "up to speed",[54] you should be able
to complete a similar project in about a zillionth as much time as you
think it should take to read the first page of the cover letter.

    Not to worry, for now: Just keep this information in mind as a
cross-check to your later meandering efforts. The point is to meander
less and less. A reminder of your Seniors' unspoken expectations will
prove a powerful focusing device. And the faster you learn, the faster
(and more easily) you climb.

HOCUS FOCUS

In law school, in the profession, in life—with exceptions rare to the
point of non-existence—the world doesn't care what you think. Perhaps that's a bit harsh, but, especially as a Junior, keep your wits
about you. Go light on the philosophy. Even lighter on the *should be*s.

    Just the facts, ma'am.

PERSPECTIVES II

You'll get some projects that, to you, look hopeless. You're not looking
hard enough. If it seems as if you'd be sanctioned for even *opposing* a
motion for summary judgment, look again. After you've sifted through
the facts and law awhile, you'll find a legal theory that puts your case
in a different, more pleasing light.

    If you're assigned a case and honestly feel that there's no possible
legal maneuvering room, and, after some thought, still think so, go to
your Senior for a little perspective. Juniors easily become frustrated
because they feel instantly that they're on the wrong side of an issue.
That's inexperience ... and bad lawyering.

    True, you might actually *be* on the wrong side of an issue, but that,
for now, is for your Senior to decide. Until you've gained some per-

---

54 Lawyers (and military folk) exhibit a special fondness for this expression.
Kinda' gives the impression of daredevil agility, eh?

spective of your own, be dispassionate when reviewing cases assigned to you...and get on with your job.[55]

CALLING DR. RORSCHACH

No matter how simple the issue, or how clear the facts, it is truly amazing how different people will look at the same set of facts... and come up with completely different answers. What's even more amazing is that *lawyers* will look at the same set of facts, and derive radically different *analyses*. This is only partially forgivable. Law is supposed to be unified; different lawyers should come up with roughly the same answer, based in law, for the same set of facts.

Ah...were it that simple.

In real life, our predispositions, well...*predispose* us to certain results. Even science succumbs to the human ego. We speak mightily of the "scientific method". Is that how science *really* works? Do we really observe, *first*? Do we absorb with a reverent impartiality all facts, wherever they lead? Or do we instead screen, however innocently, for favored facts? In civics, are we *really* satisfied with mere equal opportunity? Do we search for Truth, wherever it leads, or, to paraphrase Nicholson, are there some Truths we can't handle?

In practice, there's an incentive, both pragmatic and emotional, for clients to see the world differently. This, at least, is understandable; most clients look at their problems through their own eyes, while Lady Justice's are blindfolded.

This leeway should not extend to her assistants—you and your counterpart—who are supposed to navigate a known legal field in battle (or in reaching an honorable treaty) for your clients. Although they might not understand their respective legal positions on the field, you, as a lawyer, should. On most minor points, you should see eye-to-eye with your adversary. Unless it's to your tactical advantage

---

55 A digression for future reflection: One criticism of modern law practice is an ethical "race to the bottom" in which each attorney risks losing a client if standing too firm—when ethical push comes to unethical shove—for what is right. This is only partially true. First, business clients now face their own ethical training...and *real* liability. (Environmental constraints and the Foreign Corrupt Practices Act are two examples.) Second, most folks really *want* to do right. Third, clients *do* look to attorneys, in part, as keepers of their conscience. Fourth, they want your respect, both professional and personal. Fifth, if you do falter, their respect of *you* vanishes. Finally, in the long run, it's better for business.

If you've apprenticed under honorable Seniors, this will be second nature, and your dilemmas will be of a different, better kind. If not, you'll need to think this through, before the request arises for a walk on the shady side. Yes, this can be a difficult ethical hurdle in any difficult case.

Consider the consequences.

to delay (and, unfortunately, it's almost always to *someone's* advantage to delay), you won't need to worry about uncontested issues. Just don't contest issues without some thought.

Part of your job, as a bearer-of-legal-knowledge, is to fulfill your role as the wise counselor, guiding your charge to the legal position best for them. Part of your job, as the rational lawyer, is to not race off on too far a legal tangent in attempting to outflank your opponent; your client rides with you. And part of your responsibility, as a human, is to prepare the both of you in following—or rejecting—such tangents...even if they cut across your client's path.

MAKING IT SO

As Jean Luc glibly commands, and as Riker trustworthily complies, when assigned a task you must "Make It So". That curt command is pregnant with assumption. Your client (or your Senior) shouldn't even *know* how much work went into it: they merely nod in satisfaction at the result. (Of course, ever wise, you're sure to make your work and efficiency known in other ways.)

This is a corollary to the military expression—to force an appreciation of duty—of the three acceptable responses: "Yes, sir. No, sir. No excuse, sir." The point is important there as here: the middle option is unavailable to you, and the last is most unwise.

COURT GESTERING

Unless you're an ADA or PD or First Lieutenant or small-firm Junior, your initial exposure to the exotic world of the courtroom will be light. Most of your assignments will be either standard hearings for minor cases, or minor hearings for standard cases. You might occasionally get something bigger, but that'll be the exception that proves the rule: You're still very much in training.

Play it cool. When in doubt, *ask*.

No one, judges included, expects Darrowesque oratory from you. (You will discover that some *Seniors* are less-than-composed in court.) Everyone expects, instead, to see bumbling, confused puppies wandering about aimlessly, whimpering to whoever'll listen. You can be a *little* confused, but you shouldn't be bumbling.

No. That's too flippant. Everyone expects you to know enough to get the job done (albeit without the polish that comes with experience). You should not appear to be even a little confused.

Play it cool. Don't pretentiously hide your inexperience—but don't flaunt it, either. Learn from the Seniors in your firm, and, less attractively, from others in court. (But don't rely too heavily on the good graces of your more experienced adversary; most will honestly help, but some will not. And even if they *will*, it puts them in an awkward position, and it is unprofessional.) Otherwise, don't be shy. If you're uncertain, *ask*. Don't forget that accessible, if oddly camouflaged, resource: secretaries, clerks, and so on. Ask. And be *friendly*.

Finally, try to learn as quickly as you can, as *early* as you can. Don't wait until the morning of your first trial to learn that you should have requested subpoenas for your witnesses ... *the day before*.

Or that no court reporter will show up unless *you* ask for one.

Or....

At the risk of repetition, look at those reference books. Most of the information you'll need is right there: Rules. Procedures. Timetables. You were in Kansas all along, Dorothy.

DRAFTING

[If you're a litigator, don't assume that you can merrily skip this section. The law is generous; *everyone* gets to draft. Moreover, as courts become increasingly reluctant to grant time for oral argument, and as computers level the playing field for research skills, so do your *writing* skills move ever more sharply to the fore.]

Few are given serious help in learning the mechanics—and art—of legal drafting. That's unfortunate, because it's so central to our craft. Instead, you are expected to pick up, by review osmosis, your Seniors' drafting skills and preferences. Do what you can to keep your antennae so attuned.

Before you start a project, ask: (1) for whom am I writing; (2) what *should* they learn; and (3) how best should I tell them? The first two are *crucial*. The last—on which most focus—is almost ministerial.

A few quick pointers: You must be *precise*. In choosing words, you must consider not only their legal meaning, but also other meanings and *possible* connotations. *That's* where ambiguities arise. And you must consider the *reach* of your terms and phrases, especially within the context of *other* terms and phrases in the document. This is the technical side of drafting, and it is *crucial:* you must include everything your clients need, but you cannot include anything they don't. *Over*inclusion is as much a sin as *under*inclusion, and, worse, it is much more seductive.

You must also consider your *tone,* especially when writing to non-lawyers. Before sending a nasty letter, let it sit for a day. Before drafting an onerous provision, let it sit for a day. What are the consequences, and does your client *really* want you to do that?

You must be *concise*. Organize your thoughts before you write, and write at a brisk pace. Rely on logical abbreviations, without needless puffery. (A simple parenthetical, in quotes ("Quotes"), is better than a *hereinafter to be referred to as "Whatever".*) Absolutely no "Party of the First Part" nonsense. Not only are such contortions silly, they will likely trip *you* up; if *you're* confused, how can you expect to persuade anyone else of the just cause you represent?

You must be *deliberate*. Make a conscious effort—in writing—to cover all angles, parties, and extras. Make a conscious effort, with outlines, to draft all forms, exhibits, and extras. Make a conscious effort, with checklists, not to forget anything. Again, much of your work is done for you. Just make sure that your final product is complete and *thoroughly* proofread.

The more creative part of drafting is, first, looking ahead for the pitfalls and crafting anticipatory solutions, and—when you get good—crafting the best deal in the first place. For now, though, your efforts should focus on the technical. Here's one way to start: Keep it simple, then play a game...think of all the permutations you can:

```
"Anthea will give Hilary all of her shares
in XYZ Corp."
```

To whom does *her* refer? Is *XYZ Corp.* the correct one? (Maybe it's its subsidiary, XYZ Co., Inc.) Must *Hilary* give something to *Anthea*, too? (If so, does she have to give it *before*, at the *same time*, or *after* Anthea gives the shares to Hilary?) *When* does Anthea give Hilary the shares? Have *all* shares been accounted for? Are there different *classes* of shares? Are there *restrictions* on the transfer of the shares? Could *will* be interpreted as less-than-mandatory; is *shall* better? Do they *intend* it to be less-than-mandatory?

Ask the "what if" questions: What happens (to the stock and to the parties) if Anthea won't—or can't—give the shares to Hilary? What if someone—or something—else interferes? What if the shares become worthless...or golden? What about dividends, options, calls, voting....

Just as in *Indecent Proposal*, you must ask the questions that others never consider (or don't want to think about): What if performance is rendered impossible? What if the Offeror changes his mind? What if he dies during performance?

A large part of your job is to *think ahead*. Clients pay you to get (or keep) them out of trouble. They might not like what it takes, but you've still got your duties. Drafting is one of the more obvious—and perpetual—of those duties.

You *can* go overboard, though. If it is a fairly small transaction, you really shouldn't draft a fifty-page masterpiece that covers every conceivable possibility (many of which the law already takes care of, thank you very much), and costs nearly as much as the case is worth. Especially for smaller cases, use the size of the project as a rough guide to the proper depth of your scrutiny. (As a Junior, though, rely more directly on your Senior's answer to the question: "How much time should I spend on this?")

Don't look at your projects as billable notches on your timesheet pistol—they're also your Seniors' and clients' projects. *Get 'em done.*

(Don't worry—there are *plenty* more billable hours where *those* came from.)

Keep in mind, too, the needs of the parties. Anthea and Hilary might not care about all this extra...*stuff*. Perhaps they're happy sisters, and would just like to take care of a pesky detail. It might be better for Anthea to short-circuit these issues, and just indorse the stock certificate.

Then again, it might not.

Also, you cannot spend more than minimal time cleaning up a bad document. For some documents (or clients), everyone expects to see "magic words"—whether they're useful or not. (An unfortunate by-product of risk-aversion is the longevity of incrementally bad forms.) Even if not, your client should not pay for your grammatical or stylis-tic sensitivities.

A bundle of contradictions at every turn. That's yet another reason why your first years in law practice are so frustrating: you *know* these conflicting interests are floating about, but you're not quite sure what they look like, where they lead, and which way *you* should bend.

Patience. It'll all start to make more sense.

Still, for now...

Do the little things well. Be methodical, attentive to detail, quick, responsive, and mature. Sure, this requires intelligence, but of a different, and lower-order, kind. If you use your natural abilities and earnest motivation to fulfill the relatively mundane duties assigned, you'll outshine others with uncommon competence. Later, after you've grown a bit into your new role, will your horizons expand.

DETAILS IN DRAFTING

As amazing as it might sound, it's quite likely that you will be given projects requirine specific knowledge...about which you'll be clueless. Amazing, but probable.

You might, for example, be given the task of assembling convey-ances, which requires *scrupulous* adherence to property law dictates. You will stare at the pages-long real property descriptions, and you might even be shown old, finished documents. Guess what? From the two, you must fashion a new document *and* learn the inner workings of the old. Before you complete the former and master the latter, you must take the time to absorb the operation of the discipline. Again, this is not rocket science. (Real property, for example, was designed for surveyors and land claims offices, not doe-eyed young attorneys.) But it *does* take discipline. Consult your reference books. Ask a senior Junior, or paralegal, for questions you have arising from the books.

Learn. Absorb. Master.

...Then move on to grander tasks.

DRAFTING IN DETAIL

Whether you work in litigation or transactions, a large chunk of your working day will involve drafting, revising, or interpreting contracts.

It is essential that you focus on mastering this skill. (A CLE course is a good idea, although the technical end of drafting is rarely offered as an entrée. Moreover, this is an area in which you will receive surprisingly little line-by-line help. Thus, it's up to you to look for good drafting, and emulate—and spot bad drafting, to transcend.)

A few tips: Be consistent, in words, phrases, and organization. Choose *one* term to describe an important thing...and use it *consistently* throughout the document. Close your thesaurus; now's not the time to invite your poetic side. A Golden Rule of Drafting: Never change your language unless you wish to change your meaning, and always change your language if you wish to change your meaning. Also, pay attention to the *class* of words used: general, specific, or a usage of trade. Meaning follows, wanted or not. Careful with phrasing: Even minor changes, however inadvertent, might later be seen as having an import never intended. Repetitive phrases can usually be consolidated to better (...and less conflicting) effect. (Numbered sub-groups, similar to outlining, are often the answer.) Finally, think through the document: how should it best be organized? Which issues are most important; which rely on something else; which should be treated together, and which separately?

A logical numbering system is useful, but be careful about internal cross-referencing. It's helpful to refer to other sections within a document, but the danger is that changes—during editing or for a later edition—will render the cross-reference incorrect. Thus, as a rule, do not re-number when deleting provisions. Instead, change the section to "[Reserved.]" or "[Deleted.]". This preserves the structure, and leaves room for additional provisions as the need arises.

Be especially careful about such cross-references. (Thus, it's a good idea to keep them to a minimum.) Use a separate checklist to make sure that you forget none.

When referring to another document, be careful not to cast a new interpretation on it. (You should probably attach a copy of the other document to the referring one; if not, make sure a copy is in the *file* for future reference.[56])

Be *exact* on time. "This option shall expire at 5:00 p.m. EST on Dec. 31, 20xx" is better than an expiration "...on Jan. 14th, 20xx".

If it involves a foreign party, "...at 5:00 p.m. [17:00], U.S. Eastern Standard Time, on January 31, 20xx". [I prefer the European system of dates, which would be written "...on 31 January 20xx," but again, it's best to keep your heresies to a minimum.]

---

[56] Never, never, *never* give away an original or your only copy of *anything*.

On the other hand...be careful when fixing times for performance. Only if time is *truly* of the essence should it be specified precisely (and, if so, it should be stated conspicuously, along with the consequences for failure of performance). You *should* specify an end to *any* guaranty: don't let them float indefinitely. (It needn't be only a date, but can be the earlier of a date or other occurrence.)

When you can, avoid the musty, useless verbiage[57] so common in stuffy documents, such as the consideration recitals: "...in consideration of the sum of [blah, blah, blah]...and other good and valuable [blah, blah, blah]...the receipt of which is hereby [blah, blah, blah]...." *Utterly superfluous.* If consideration is there, it's there. If not, all the pretty declarations in the world won't make it so.

Short. Simple. Legal.

"Jones shall *x*. Smith shall *y*." *Done.*

Be particularly attentive when creating conditions. They're noble creatures, serving weighty duty—excusing or creating all manner of accountability. If a party is to be relieved of a duty upon some occurrence, say so. If concurrent performance is a condition, say so. If complete and exact performance is a condition, say so. If substantial performance is not acceptable, say so. But think before you so say.

Define terms with care. Unless you have a *strong* reason not to, follow the conventions of the trade. For example, "net profit" has meanings in both economics and accounting. Your client might want a definition different from either. First be certain that the test should be *net* profit (it almost never should), then be *very* clear about how it is to be calculated. (If you're unfamiliar with accounting, by the way, you should enroll in a CLE course that is offered in most places to impart the basics. This is *essential* knowledge.)

Pay special attention to termination provisions. In general, avoid automatic termination; difficulties arise, and it's usually best for the parties to deal with them in good faith. Also, anticipate the damages that might arise under the many termination scenarios. Don't try to divine them all, but do draft clear standards. Finally, what happens if performance is impossible? Impracticable? Unprofitable?

Are there third-parties floating about? If so, how should they be handled (if at all) in the document?

Even with a form, double-check your document with...*the statute.* Do this your first time, and spot check every once in a while thereafter. You should, of course, follow the developments in your field—through advance sheets, bar journals, and the like (it doesn't take that long)—and incorporate them in your practice. Why so picky? Well, for one thing...*bureaus* are. For another... Care to explain to a client why his request isn't satisfied, because the Secretary of State

---

57   "Verbiage" refers to *excess* wording. I had one client who loved the word, and used it often in his legal requests, as in "Throw some verbiage in here."

rejected your document, because you filled it out incorrectly, because you insisted that the statute was—and here I'll quote—"goofy"?

It's not enough to advise on merely the law; you're expected to protect your client's broader interests, as well. A narrow construction of your duties might fulfill those interests, in a narrow sense, but it won't win you any medals ... or lasting loyalty.

When, for example, a client comes to you to set up a corporation, it's not unlikely that he *assumes* that that's the form his business *should* take. If you comply without inquiring further, you will be doing a disservice, in many cases. *Why* a corporation? Limited liability? Capital aggregation? Perpetuity? Taxes? Prestige? (In the real world, the answers are: not really, not without some other hook, not a major consideration, nope, and hardly.) *Where* should the company be incorporated? When? In what overarching structure? For a closely held corp, what about agreements among shareholders? (A necessity.) Between shareholders and the corporation? (A good idea.) Third parties? (Always a few out there: Who must be accommodated, and how?) Contingent liabilities? (Not *if*...which are the concern?) Non-cash consideration? (KLAXTON BLARING. *Danger!!*) Capital structure? Debt instruments? Promoter novation(s)?

Beware also the tendency to overcomplicate things. A Senior once walked in my door, and asked me to write up a quick memo: a Japanese client was concerned about whether a thinly capitalized corporation was exposed to liability. The legal answer was easy—*yup,* if the insolvency works a fraud on a third party—but what amazed me was the bizarre structure (not uncommon among Asian clients). It took me *hours* to figure out the connections among the *dozens* of corporations and limited partnerships. (And it didn't make much sense, even then. Fraud wasn't the intent; culture was. Even so, there're better ways to protect a client's assets.) And, though I knew I shouldn't—you know me by now—I added a line in the memo's conclusion about avoiding the "liability tail wagging the corporate family dog."

Mr. Senior removed the surplus clause.

In all of these questions—in just this one area of practice—the *real* answer is to *situate* your clients in the most appropriate position for each.

This requires more than a cursory "Thanks for last month's check."

FOR LITIGATORS

There is far too much by way of technical advice to relay (as if *I* were the right one to relay it), and this is more appropriately gathered in *your* jurisdiction. One quick note: don't be so quick to do your opponents' job for them.

Think in terms of chess: what follows not from the *next* move, but from two or three moves hence. Learn *when* to corner your opponent.

(Fun though mating is, it pales without the proper check.) If you respond too forcefully, too soon, you might well serve only to disclose to him his weaknesses...*which can be strengthened* in due course. *His* course. Raising issues is only part of a legal battle; stage the battle not only for your advantage, but also against the other's failings. As with damning grist for cross-examination impeachment, it's wiser to *hold* the *coup* for better use, at the right time...*de grâce*.

As with comedy, timing is (almost) everything.

THE PAPER CHASE

Before any document leave your office, stop for a moment...and start thinking in terms of the proper flow of information. Who needs what, how many copies, who else needs what else, who else should receive copies, and, almost more importantly, who should *not* get copies. Seniors are horrible about telling you this *real* information, and it's crucial that you do this right.

Usually, you can look in the file of a previous, similar project, but be careful...*you* need to spot the issue. When in doubt, confirm it with someone. (If you're never in doubt you must be cataleptic, because there's *always* this sort of stuff you won't understand.)

FORMS

Most firms maintain some semblance of form files (though the depth of disorganization can be frightful). Forms—ranging from barebones, fill-in-the-blank sheets to complicated, pre-fab documents drafted for real-life case alternatives—are a logical way to systematize the creation of documents. Moreover, if you try to create a form from scratch, and then compare it to an nth generation form, you'll be *stunned* at how much you've missed...and how much longer it took you to miss those many issues.

On the other hand...don't let a pre-fab form replace your mind. (Isn't a mind a terrible thing to waste?) Think through each issue, especially the first time around, and make sure your client is protected. I still remember the first time I ran across a "cross-indemnity" clause. It happened to be a particularly gawd-awful version, and it took me a few cases after that one before I figured out the *substance* of the provision, much less its proper workings. Now, it's child's play. Before it's playful for *you,* take the time figure it out, for real, without leaning so heavily on the crutch of a *pro forma* form file form.

This is often knowledge that cannot be explained to you. You must, instead, figure it out on your own: Retrace the law to as basic a source as you need, keeping in mind that the most exotic permutations in the most esoteric areas of the law are almost always variations on basic legal themes. Child's play.

YOUR WORK PRODUCT

One client never seemed to realize, or care about, the importance of his signature. He repeatedly signed papers (prepared in-house, by non-lawyers) incorrectly, which potentially (and once, *actually*) exposed him to personal liability.

There's a related lesson there for you: When *you* sign papers going out—or memos going up—*take it seriously*.

Take a moment to make sure you've done what the Senior requested, and done it well. If not, correct (or improve) it, *before* it goes out. You can't take back a bad impression. Months and years hence, someone will look at your work, and, from it alone, will draw conclusions about you. The fact that you were rushed like crazy and hadn't slept in two days won't be reflected, except in sub-par writing (and an even less favorable evaluation). Worse, some Seniors will hold grudges for unfocused or poorly written memos, which can be a problem come annual review time. Odd things stick in our minds. Be careful. Don't sign anything you wouldn't want a committee of Seniors to pore over.

(And, since you don't really have a choice whether to sign or not, make sure that what you *do* sign is worthy of such scrutiny.)

The good news: depending upon your firm (and you), research projects will quickly wane once you prove your reasonable proficiency and have become more useful than as a minor paper-pusher. You didn't actually think you'd get to spend your entire career in the rarefied air of the library, did you? *No.* You will spend your time cleaning up the piddles of real law.

IN PRAISE OF ALL THAT IS BORING

I commented, some pages back, about nine-tenths of litigation success being in outpreparing your opponent. To be blunt, being the flashy litigator might help *occasionally* (especially if you golf with the judge), but, nine times out of ten, you'll come across not daring, but dull.

If it has become clichéd that preparation is so important, why is it such a constant issue? Well, it *is* more exciting to dance in the courtroom than in the library. And courtroom dancers *do* seem to get more attention, and attention of a better kind. And preparation *is* a lot of...*work*.

Think you're the first, or only, one to have confronted this devil? The following words were spoken [in 1930!] by a New York trial legend (at the time), Emory Buckner:

One of the most boring topics which I want to discuss I shall take up first; and I can anticipate a spirit of disappointment when I take it up. I can just see you sink in your chairs. I am not going to talk very long about it. It is an old subject. Everybody who speaks on the trial of cases talks about it, but as Mark Twain said about the weather, everybody complains about it, but nobody does anything about it. That is the subject of preparation.

Now, I can hear you say to yourselves, 'Rotary Club! Chautauqua speech! Copybook maxim! Everybody should prepare his case.' And yet the more I am engaged in this work—and it just happens by accident that I have ever since I got out of law school done nothing else at all; I am so frightfully lopsided I practically have only one leg professionally—the longer I live the more I become impressed with the importance of the preparation of a lawsuit.

None of us prepares a case as well as he should. We do not have any time. We are driven and driven and driven. The calendars are behind. And that rather chloroforms us and puts us to sleep, and we wait a year or wait two years before the case comes up, and then the preparation is difficult and more and more catch-as-catch-can.

But in my judgment that is a very great mistake. If I were a client and knew as much about the trial of cases as I have learned as a lawyer, I would rather have a wholly inconspicuous and utterly unknown man of only mediocre ability who would prepare the case, who would exhaust every possibility of finding out all the facts that are relevant, than to have some very well known and very astute and clever and capable forensic orator, who went in as so many of our specialists and celebrities do, with no particular preparation except to pick things up as they develop.

I could make a whole speech...to recall some of the very conspicuous cases [determined by] preparation [alone].

He went on to discuss "the greatest difference" between successful and unsuccessful lawyers—a sense of *proportion*:

I have spoken of preparation; you should have, of course, the utmost preparation, but you should not use it except as you need it. It is like the Texas man with the gun, who said, "I don't use her very often, but when I need her I need her awful bad."

[S]ome lawyers believe in the democracy of facts; that every fact is free and equal before the law; no aristocracy; no classes; no hierarchy. Every fact is a fact, and therefore it ought to be asserted. That is the thing that ruins so many law suits.

Keep a sense of proportion...Visualize your case as a backbone, with certain supporting ribs...Don't get off the backbone...If the thing is unimportant, don't bother about it...Let the trifles go.

A sense of proportion! That is where we fall down. I have tried several cases, both public and private, where I have had fifteen hundred to twenty-five hundred documents, but almost every single case can be resolved into simple elements, and if it cannot be, it cannot be won.

A man after my own Texas heart. And, as you might tell from his language and tone, true greatness requires both adherence to the minutiae, and aspiration to the magnificent.

Finally, ever the contrarian: even the boring isn't *really* boring, if you're doing it right. Every fact you confirm, every document you peruse, every witness you interview and re-interview...can be but a piece in a grander, vibrant puzzle, if you so see it.

MISTAKES[58]

You *will* make them. Lots of 'em.

Don't cover them up. As soon as you figure out you've done something wrong, take a moment to confirm what happened. This is not to assuage your guilt before you rationalize burying it. It is, instead, to figure out what *should have* happened. Sometimes—no, *often*times—you'll get spooked where the problem really isn't as severe as its ghost would suggest. Even so, you should not be the judge of that, unless, upon reflection, you really did see shadows.

Not all mistakes are created equal. Learn to distinguish embarrassing gaffes from true legal dangers. You should also appreciate that careful drafting, and careful lawyering, will reduce the risks.

When you make a serious error, see first if you can fix it. If so, problem solved, quietly. (Make sure, however, that you're not just burying your head in the sand...or putting the finishing touches on a time bomb.) If the mistake is serious, go to the assigning Senior (or, if it's not *too* serious, to a senior Junior) and tell 'em up front: "I think I made a mistake here. What should I do to fix it?" Unless you've just assigned all of the Firm's assets to a recently indicted embezzler (...who's mysteriously unavailable), your Senior should be pleasantly surprised at your candor, and will sit down with you to help fix the problem. Most of your mistakes will be silly little bumps on your journey. As long as it doesn't happen every hour, you'll be fine.

This has another benefit. If your Seniors see that: (1) you know how to identify mistakes, and (2) you're not too egotistical to hide them, they'll likely be more trusting of your judgment in the future.

Even if this scenario is a little optimistic for your firm (which, unfortunately, it probably is), you *still* cannot hide your mistakes. Yes, it is human nature to try, and even more human to react badly to subordinates' gaffes (particularly when they create more trouble, which

---

58 The first edition used a rather more indelicate header. I spent three years searching for a better one that might carry the humor without the affront... and drew a blank. The lesson: I risked offense to a minority of readers for the benefit of a *different* minority. Although the latter minority is, to me, more important, I was wrong. As morally equivocal as self-censorship is, it is a necessary reality in life: You will always be at risk of offending *some* minority. Choose wisely.

they do), but take heart. Even if your Senior becomes visibly upset, it will likely be forgotten (by him), or at least forgiven...*as long as it doesn't happen again*.

For the Senior who is truly unforgiving of your inevitable mistakes —find yourself a better mentor. As will become apparent (hopefully) before you collect social security, life is too short.[59]

THE OTHER HAND

I've gone back and forth on this advice, ever since the first edition was still a few stray electrons. Part of me wants to bellow, in recognition of the wry ironies of life, *"Yeah, sure...if you can get away with it, cover it so deep the FBI'd never find it."* That is the natural inclination, and many times you'd be better off, as a practical matter.

I dislike being cynical, at the expense of a greater good, but this is, after all, one of the lessons of life. Use your judgment: how serious the mistake, how likely you'll be able to get away with it, how forgiving your Senior, how much credit you'll get for maturity. Not an easy set of questions, to be sure.

Still, let's focus on a more positive issue: how to *avoid* the problem in the first place.

ANATOMY OF A MISTAKE. Here's how it usually happens:

1. Senior gives a new project to Junior.
2. Junior does a horrible job.
3. Senior, expecting this, corrects the work, and, sometime the following month, sits down with Junior to explain the many mistakes.
4. Junior understands the first and final two words: "Don't worry..." and "...don't worry."
5. Junior worries.
6. Weeks, or even months, pass.
7. Senior assigns a similar project to Junior.
8. Junior, even more confused, does *another* horrible job.
9. **Now**... Senior, who is forced to skip a rerun of his favorite episode of *Gomer Pyle, U.S.M.C.* [don't laugh: yours'll be *Laverne & Shirley,* with a *Dukes of Hazzard* chaser] ... is **pissed**.

---

[59] I'm not sure who, exactly, came up with the notion that *hopefully*—in the sense "it is to be hoped that"—is a akin to some cataclysmic literary faux pas, but they might want to loosen their straightjackets a bit. It's a perfectly decent use of the word, it fills a colloquial void, and I'll be darned if I couldn't rework the passage without risking a hernia. This seems to be one of those common usages—where it's sometimes useful to exploit a vague referent— that makes more sense than the "rule" to the contrary.

Break the cycle at Numbers Two and Three. Rather than doing a horrible job, make sure that you have all of the resources that are available to help you produce a less-than-dreadful result. Your first source is the fileroom. There you (or, more appropriately, your secretary) will find real documents, some of which have already done what you're supposed to learn how to do.

Upon being given an assignment, one of your questions to your Senior is: "Which files should I look to as models?"

Sometimes, they'll point you in the right direction, without being asked. Shamefully, they might just as often not. Yet once you have a previous example, most of your job is pretty simple: just apply the facts of your client's case to the previous form.

Careful. You *do* have a brain, which is, supposedly, modified for legal activities. *Use it.* Pay attention to what might be client-specific provisions. When your trusty proboscis sniffs one, and your trustier brain can't figure it out, go ask: (1) the person who did the previous document; or (2) your Senior.

Your goal is to do a better job than someone in your situation *should* be able to do. You're not (usually) expected to know what you cannot know, but you *are* expected to catch on quickly (...or faster). If you're still uncertain on your second or third try, *scour* your previous work, search additional references, keep asking, and *figure it out*. Making *new* mistakes won't sink you, but repeating an *old* one is a torpedo to the munitions hold.

When you get your draft back with corrections, *take a look*. (If you don't get your draft back, go find it.) It ain't over until you know not only *how* to draft it, but *why*. And this you won't know as a Junior.

Figure out why your Senior made those corrections, and, if you can't...*ask*. If you're embarrassed, ask someone who works on similar projects. They won't bite. (...well, most of 'em.) If you've spent a few minutes studying the question, they'll be impressed with your diligence and critical thinking. (But don't ask just to show off. It's annoying, and it'll likely backfire because you're more concerned with looking good than with the question.)

You'll often look back on your work, hidden beneath a sea of red ink...and *cringe*. You'll instantly recognize that you should have figured this or that point out on your own. Such errors should decrease, rapidly, during your first years. In years past, apprentice lawyers could pick this stuff up more gradually. (Mostly because they started at an earlier age.) There's no such luxury of time, now: Seniors are as pressed for time as you'll be. Thus, there's much less leeway for late or fumbling starts.

When your Senior sits down with you to discuss your mistakes, don't get defensive. Repeat: *Don't get defensive.* Seniors *hate* that— with good reason. If they're going to the trouble of trying to help you, the least you can do is...*sit up and shut up*. Your mistakes are as much a hassle for them as they are heartrending for you.

If you know that you'll be going to lunch to discuss a certain case that you worked on, *go read the file*. Refamiliarize yourself with the particulars of the forms and the client's situation. If you've been given back your draft, look it over, *painstakingly,* and try to figure out why and where you went wrong. Sometimes you won't have the draft—or some time will have passed—and you'll be pretty much in the dark. If you don't even have the file, don't give up: Read the basic reference that you asked your Senior about when you started.

The point of all this is to give yourself some basis to be able to converse—or at least *listen*—intelligently. Most times, Seniors don't want to berate. They just want to improve...*you*. Take advantage. Show through your attitude and courtesy that you appreciate their effort and time (...as well you should). Don't be afraid—or worse, resentful—of supervision. Accept it, instead, with genuine gratitude.

You may ask questions, but *govern your tongue*. Remember what some professors said: "There's no such thing as a stupid question"? They obviously never practiced law.

You *do* need to screen your questions. You should not ask, for example, whether the cross-complainant is also the appellee. Figure that out for yourself.

You should ask, for example, whether, given facts A, B, and C, the client shouldn't do X, Y, or Z. In most cases, Senior will already have thought of X, Y, and Z. Occasionally though, you can in your legal infancy spout wisdom. And, even if not, your Senior will appreciate that you're thinking legally and creatively for the client's interest. That's good.

(Yes, you *should* ask questions—and not just as a Junior: *Qui tacet, consentire videtur.* He who is silent is understood to consent.)

CLEMENCY

Every firm has a different tolerance for mistakes, varying from moderate to none, and often depending upon other, unrelated factors.

Likewise, each Senior within each firm has a unique level of tolerance for error. Wise managers know that mistakes are an important reality of training—and an inevitable by-product of work life (especially *effective* work lives)—but, in the conceit of law practice, are tolerated not. Unfortunately, you won't know how little leeway exists, and, in any event, you should strive to avoid testing the limit. Moreover, any mistakes you make will significantly decrease tolerance for *future* mistakes.

True, some are unavoidable, even in hindsight. Still, do what you can to minimize your exposure to the minefields. This is accomplished best through reliance on the experience of others, particularly those who previously handled the projects you will be expected to assume. Again, be careful that you don't substitute vague directives of your supervising Senior with the well-intentioned but different advice of another Senior, senior Junior, or—*heaven forbid*—another Junior; be sure you're running in the direction the *assigning* Senior wants.

It will be no use to complain that someone else advised you otherwise. Indeed, it'll make things worse, because it will emphasize both the deficiency of the assigning Senior's directions, and your perceived lack of ability to follow instructions.

It will also make you look disloyal...and unworthy of that Senior's future patronage.

CUMULATION

Most accidents are caused not by a casual (or even grossly negligent) mistake, but, rather, by *combinations* of errors that, together, build to catastrophe. Back to planes: If a pilot takes off with an overloaded plane...no problem.

What?! Aviation heresy!

Stand by.

The *real* problem is twofold: First, any pilot who would knowingly take off with an overloaded plane—there's no credit for *un*knowingly taking off—is no doubt foolish enough to overlook other dangers, such as that odd tail-dragger configuration on the tricycle-gear plane, that puddle of funny-smelling liquid forming underneath the engine, the thermostat, which had just exploded in a puff of boiling mercury, the hydrometer, still dripping from a recent downpour, or the lightning thundering off in the distance.

Second, an overloaded plane, though sluggish, will (probably) do just fine *if nothing else bad happens*. Sadly, when investigators peer into the wreckage, the tale unfolds: additional weight aggravated the pilot's inability to compensate for a center-of-gravity too far aft, engine failure, and hot, humid, foul weather.

Any two of these factors would, quite likely, cause an accident. Add inexperience, and you're just begging for one.

In law, don't compound your errors. They don't need the help.

PUTTING IT ALL TOGETHER

Becoming an attorney can be a kinder and gentler process than many make it.

Lower your standards.

In the beginning, law work is not brain surgery. Come to think of it, for a new surgeon, *brain surgery* is not brain surgery; the process of becoming even a general surgeon is lengthy in the extreme.

Don't think too much. Thinking is just too hard. Less cynically, it's unnecessary. The Law is designed for the lowest common denominators. Whatever rule is promulgated, someone will break it, ignore it, or subvert it. Out of necessity and timidity, we look to precedent. So should you. You needn't reinvent the wheel for each assignment. You're not expected to, and doing so is counterproductive…and highly irritating.

This maturation process is not, by the way, just a matter of time. True, experience is measured by time, but measurement does not equal maturity. Mere existence is not enough. Punching the clock of the space-time continuum will only give you sore knuckles. Age (or experience) does not equal wisdom (or competence). Part of your job is to mix, with time, a sense of purpose and an active curiosity…with one eye fixed on constant improvement.

Here's one more way to look at it: Most of you are rather highly intelligent. You've always done well. Only now, the competition is real; everyone *else* is smart, too. But wait a second…how is it that everyone else seems to survive, while you wallow in this morass?

Part of the problem is that you cannot see beyond your limited Junior world. I remember when I was first assigned a mortgage project. No one explained to me that the process, from a paper-pushing standpoint, is pretty cut-and-dry, particularly at the entry level. Anyway, there I was, reading every word in a horrific, 17th-century-styled, half-inch thick treatise, replete with *heretofores* following *notwithstandings*. No one told me that all I should have done was change a few pieces, double-check to make sure no chunks were missing…and pass it on. What should have taken minutes took *hours*. The fear of making a mistake overshadowed the common sense (…in hindsight) that I was taking *far* too long. Worse, my preoccupation with the forest made me lose sight of some trees: applying client-specific information to the form.

The dilemma is inherent to the position: You cannot get sloppy, but you needn't—and cannot afford to—waste time.

Escape the horns of this dilemma. Figure out which are the variables, and—quickly—double-check the rest. Be careful. Omissions will haunt you, and no one will care that finding the proverbial misprinted needle in the dissertation-length haystack is something the client is unwilling to pay for.

A Final, Editorial Note

Your work will be changed. No matter how diligent your research, no matter how careful your draft, no matter how wonderful your prose, Seniors *will* edit your work. This can be more difficult for some to accept than it should be. Sometimes it's a difference of styles. Sometimes it's a difference of opinions. Either way, you lose.

More often, though, it's a healthy process by which you render a raw product for the finer touches of a better craftsman.

And the process never stops. As part of our egocentric instinct, we just can't help but add our own two cents' worth to *others'* work. (Sometimes for the better, sometimes not.) Still, two pairs of eyes *are* better than one. Take advantage of those many eyes, connected to those many brains.

Don't rebel. Don't fight. Don't resent.

Instead, appreciate your Seniors' greater experience and insights, and endeavor to do better…in the hope that red-pen purchases on *your* account shrink.

— 5 —

DETAILS, DETAILS

GRAMMAR AND FRIENDS

It should go without saying—but it does not—that punctuation, spelling, and grammar *count*.

In the past, no one would have expected—or been permitted—to even attend college without a decent-to-chokehold grasp of English. Especially for future law students, who were usually the non-science majors without a chance in the job market or a clue to the meaning of their incipient lives, basic command of English, at least, was a given.

Sadly, grammar has been devalued over the past few decades by otherwise well-intentioned nonconformists. New Age parents didn't help. It seemed so much easier, and *nicer,* to let things slide.

The result, distressingly, is not a generation of enlightened, freed thinkers, but, rather, a crop of undereducated young adults who must cope (or not) with ever-higher demands on their talents...and an incomplete set of tools to rise to the challenge. (There's a reason it used to be called "grammar school". Sadly, attempts at egalitarian niceness have *worsened* the lot of promising, poor students.)

The law is not exempt; a depressingly significant percentage of law graduates have a dismal command of language.

English is our—and now *your*—currency. You will either master (or at least understand) it, or you shall forever linger in its shadow. And there's no need to be lingocentric; but for the odd historic fluke or two, we could as easily be practicing civil law in French, Spanish, or—no kidding—maybe even Chinese.

Yet English it is.

And, with all due respect to Professor Higgins,[60] it *is* possible to admire, or even *adore,* our language...and not be boorish about it. Rules of grammar are not cast in stone. (Many were borrowed arbitrarily from Latin.) Still, there's yet another lesson here: Grammar has rules, but law *is* rules.

You must double-check, or learn, grammar *promptly*. If you don't know grammar, *er*...joins the club.

C'mon...don't be ashamed. Grammar causes confusion for everyone. (*Anyone* who's paying attention will be confused, regularly.) What is unacceptable is not confusion, but carelessness.

---

60 Which isn't much; his conceit and pretensions—diseases infecting many pedants—rendered him unworthy of admiration, as a human.

If you've noticed, for example, that I've veered from the American model concerning quotation marks and follow instead the more logical English model, you'll do just fine on the technical side of the law.[61] In the practicing world, however, wait until you're a Senior to be likewise contrary. (Even then....)

There is a serious point to my grammatical liberties: Much of law practice is a matter of paying attention to detail. *It doesn't really matter what the particular details are, just that you pay attention to them.* You must learn the Rule before you can master it. And you should master it before you subvert it. This should not imply, parenthetically, that subversion is necessarily the way to go. Fun, yes. But what stops most subversion is the wisdom gained in the process of mastery.

Granted, the Great Quotation Mark Caper is notable mostly for its unimportance. Still, the lesson's there: pay attention. You must carefully proofread your work...as you write, as you edit, and before you sign. You cannot abdicate this responsibility: *You're* the one whose salary all but begs for challenge.

You needn't go overboard, however. Many lawyers act as if they *invented* grammar, and are God's gift to the Queen and her English. If that's your Senior, tread lightly. If that's you, *lighten up.*

Hey, we all catch mistakes after a document is on its way. Aside from embarrassing and annoying you, it should alert you to avoid similar mistakes in the future. As was ironed onto one of my favorite T-shirts decades ago: *"Be alert!* The world needs more Lerts."

Insist that your secretary spell-check every document before you sign. (Insist that the *signature* copy be checked, even if previous versions were checked, so that errant revisions don't slide by unnoticed.) Moreover, do not rely on others—or on computer spell- or grammar-checks—*you* must proofread whatever goes over *your* signature. Few things will cause as much embarrassment as overlooked misspellings in a document that (naturally) becomes central to litigation. You can't go back to change it...unless you like spending a little time with your neighborly Sheriff for tampering with evidence.

Part of the answer is: *learn.* We expect, with nary a pause, that coal miners be "retrained". Well, get off your high horse; don't you dare expect a double standard. If *your* education was deficient—and

---

61 I've pondered this one for a while. (Now you know how much fun *I* am on Saturday nights.) I've finally decided in favor of the east side of the Atlantic, because, otherwise, it's too easy to mistake the importance of quotation marks, which stop the world and alert the reader that something unique is contained within. Unless it's part of the original—*verbatim*—it has no business within those marks. This might be going overboard, I admit, but unless the comma or period is an *exact* part of the quoted material, writing it that way adds an imperfection for no benefit other than, very arguably, aesthetics.

most of ours were—pick up a reference book and retrain yourself both as a matter of personal pride...and before *you're* embarrassed professionally.

Get a style manual, and *use* it.[62] I unabashedly recommend the *Texas Law Review Manual on Usage and Style,* which, not surprisingly, is geared toward legal writing. It's available for—crowbar-to-wallet time—four dollars.[63] Pocket-size, helpful, and, believe it or not, easy to use. Recommended by four out of five dentists who chew gum.

EMAIL ETIQUETTE

The advent of the internet offers a new excuse: many believe that words conveyed by electrons rather than ink are immune from those bothersome rules of literary etiquette. Surely, the thought goes, speed forgives deficiency.

It doesn't. Nor does anonymity forgive discourtesy. The same standards that apply to regular mail apply as well to its newborn electronic cousin. *Any* document that goes out over *your* name—even if it's a quick message over an internet handle—reflects on *you.*

It is *not* informal; it is *written.* It can be copied and distributed, without notice or control, to anyone and everyone: You never know before whose eyes those stray electrons will eventually stop. Too, it may well be used against you in a court of law.

Sending an email that's filled with typographical or grammatical errors isn't cute. Nor is it excusable, even if it's a personal note.

It's an insult to your reader, and to yourself.

Sloppiness should *bother* you. If not, you're not a good lawyer. This isn't (just) about mental snobbery: proofreading should become second nature. Neither is it mere style; it's substance as well. And it's part of that pesky attention to detail that attends all successful careers.

Should *anal retentive* be hyphenated?

$\approx$:)

---

62 This is not the same as the feared Bluebook, which concerns rules of legal citation. *See* CITATION section, *supra.* Rather, a manual on style is a reference for proper usage, grammar, punctuation, and the like. You know...*style.*

63 Add $2.00 for mailing (or pick one up while you're in Austin). Order from:

> The University of Texas at Austin
> School of Law Publications, Inc.
> Post Office Box 149084
> Austin, Texas 78714-9084

I don't think I get a kickba...*uh*...incentive payment. Want me to check?

THE OPPOSITE PROBLEM

Then there's the opposite problem (...which, oddly enough, is usually related to the ignorant first): Pompous writing.

Those who are self-confident generally have less need to show off. Those who feel inadequate must compensate, in the hope that others will be cowed by impressive-sounding rhetoric.

Unfortunately, many lawyers—including most Juniors—are in the same group, and, consequently, are cowed.

I once corresponded with an attorney who seemed to put nearly as much effort dredging up archaic phrases as he put into his client's case. His letters were amusing in their stilted display of 𝕺𝖑𝖉𝖊 𝕰𝖓𝖌𝖑𝖎𝖘𝖍, but his legal threats lost much of their punch in the translation.

Don't be a peacock. Don't be a putz.

Write simply, clearly, and quickly. Judges and Seniors don't want to be impressed. They want to be informed. Opposing counsel doesn't want to be grandstanded; they will likely respond better to a lighter touch. (How would *you* respond to a long letter with words like "liar" and "unethical" and "grievance complaint"? Better to send a one-paragraph letter: "Enclosed is a copy of the letter I sent to you two months ago. I have not yet received a reply. Please let me know when you will respond.") Short, simple, sweet. (And it makes the *other* side look bad, while making *you* look chivalrously above reproach.)

Use ~~hyperpolysyllabic~~ big words as needed, but, unless you have to, not to impress. This is a tough one; how can everyone see how brilliant you are unless you *show* them? Show them in other ways. To restate, brilliance is not the answer. Proficiency is. And, to state it a bit differently: graceful proficiency *is* brilliance.

Avoid the common assumption that real attorneys must use words mere commoners never would. (This disease has metastasized to business, where dull people feel compelled to use terms like "paradigm" and "polycentrical matrix systematization".)

Likewise, take it easy on the superlatives (both grammatical and argumentative); power needn't shout, it need only whisper.

Minimize the *hereinbefores, whereinsoevers,* and other abominations. Yes, occasionally they do simplify sentences. But not often.

Also, get out of the habit of writing mindless clichés.[64]

Don't use *utilize*. Can you explain the difference between *use* and *utilize?* [65]

Don't use *which* when you really mean *that*.[66]

Don't use *irregardless* when you really mean *regardless*.

---

[64] That's redundant, isn't it?

[65] Yes, there is a difference, but it's not one often intended (or known).

[66] Here's an easy shortcut:

If it needs a preceding comma, it's a *which*. If not, it's a *that*.

A writer or speaker *implies*; a reader or listener *infers*.

What did you mean when you used *and/or*?

Appreciate the comma,[67] and adore the period.[68] Pity the semicolon, which though elegant remains woefully misunderstood.

capitalize Carefully.

Figure out, once and for all, those irritating homonyms.[69] And, every once in a while, double-check your understanding of them. I once received a letter from an otherwise quite intelligent attorney, who proclaimed that his client "*bares* no liability." (My emphasis, obviously, and another example of the importance of proofreading.) I held my tongue, of course; my client wanted *his* client's money, not clothes.

Define key words, in the text, with simple quotation marks inside parentheses. Skip the *hereinafter to be referred to as*. Then stick with that abbreviation throughout the document. (Some documents create short-hand abbreviations—only to revert, oddly, to the full nouns.)

---

67 Regardless of your grammar teacher's bias: *use a comma at the end of a series*. Omissions of commas are sometimes syntactically ambiguous (especially with disjunctives), often awkward, and nearly always stylistically abhorrent. Style aside, law's needs are too precise for such silliness. Ambiguity is the fifth Horseman of the Legal Apocalypse. I know, no one's told you of him, but what's the benefit anyway... saving ink? We spill plenty enough as it is. More ominously, an omission can, sometimes, affirmatively *change* meaning:

Jeannie said Tim is the murderer.

Jeannie, said Tim, is the murderer.

I once read a draft of a contract where an omission of a comma *reversed* the intent of the parties. For our client, it would have been a $200,000 comma. For the firm, it might have been a $200,000 malpractice suit.

Lesson Number One: Intent shouldn't ride on a comma; *reword the provision*.

Lesson Number Two: Even in less extreme cases, the meaning of a sentence with poorly used punctuation *is* changed, if only in nuance. But, when litigators are forced into the Grey, nuance becomes the legal weapon of last resort. And, when money's at stake, last resort is better than none at all.

68 This pun really *was* unintended. A particularly sharp (or perhaps merely warped) editor picked up on it, though, thinking it a sly reference to unwanted pregnancies. I suppose waiting month after month for revised drafts to flow'll do that to ya'.

69 The simple ones seem to cause the most trouble (and, if you miss one more than once, are the most embarrassing). Here's another clue: An apostrophe is shorthand for some missing character(s) that we lazy writers omit. Thus, "its" *without* an apostrophe is its own word, indicating possession, but "it's" *with* an apostrophe is *two* words ("it is") joined together. Two very different meanings, using the same three characters. Odd etymologies give rise to other homonyms. "There" refers to location. "Their" is a form of "they" modified to show possession: remove the "y" and add the "ir". If you know that you're talking about *them*—as opposed to *that place*—you can't miss this one.

Separate sections for definitions are appropriate only for truly un-wieldy documents (...and they never seem to carry the weight in court that they imply).

Avoid those double negatives: "Tenant shall not act in a manner inconsistent with the Rules and Regulations of...." Ugh.

"Tenant shall act in a manner consistent with...." *Ah,* better. (Be careful; sometimes there *is* a difference. First, confirm the need. Then doubly confirm that the meaning your client needs isn't lost or confused in those grammatical loops.)

And now, some of my favorite puffery:

LEGALISH	ENGLISH
at the time	when
at that particular time	then
at this particular time	now
during such time as	while
for the duration of	during
for the reason that	because
in order to	to
in the event that / in case of	if
in the interest of	for
it is the duty of / it is directed that	shall
it shall be lawful to / is authorized to	may
notwithstanding	despite
on the part of / by means of	by
shall be construed to mean	means
under the provisions of	under
until such time as	until
with reference to	for

Beware too those omnipresent legal redundancies. As with critical systems in engineering, redundancies can perform a valued, if ineffi-cient, service. But you can't make this claim to drafting excellence unless you first recognize that a redundancy redundancy exists.

Does the other side really need to cease *and* desist? As with many clichéd phrases in the law, this was an attempt, originating in the complication of the common and civil law systems in England and the Continent—long before we wiped our runny noses on the skirt of Lady Justice—to cover all the bases. Thus, we have English and French phrases galore, all mere repetitions of the other. Property law is particularly bad, since much of it derives from those very dead white guys. (On that other, ubiquitous hand, some of these phrases *do* sound pretty cool.)

Some marvels span *even more* than two words: assign, transfer, and set over (or, in the alternative, "bargain, sell, assign, transfer, set over, and convey"); free, gratis, and without consideration; give, devise, and bequeath; hold, perform, observe, fulfill, and keep; null and void and of no force or effect; ordered, adjudged, and decreed; remise, release, and forever quitclaim; revoked, annulled, and held for nought. *Whew*.[70] (Well, I do kinda' like that last one.)

As to these various rules: If you choose to ignore them (...or don't even bother to think about it), you might scrape along just fine. Then again, you might not. Law and craps are like that. Ninety-plus times out of a hundred, it's no big deal. No one actually *reads* those documents, anyway. (Except, of course, when something goes awry; then that unloved instrument will take on a whole new interest.)[71]

Still, why worry? If professionalism doesn't grab you, how about a brief image of you sitting in a conference room with your (then) partners, explaining your grade-school mistake that will cost each of them a shiny new car?

Most of these remarks are mere quibbles. But that's not the point: *Bad grammar is a symptom, not a disease.* The more attention you pay, the less likely you fail. The danger in these many literary vices lies not so much in a misuse of ink, but in unintended ambiguities, which tend to grow like Hydraic heads in unanticipated, and often unwarranted, ways. It's ironic to our profession, but the simpler the words, the more enforceable the document.

This, by the way, is another of the benefits of a clerkship, where you'll read a steady procession of badly written briefs and memoranda drowning a few clear gems, and quickly come to the conclusion that most lawyers *harm* their cases by failing to simplify their writing— and thinking. The flashier the language, the more it looks as though you're trying to hide a weakness.

Even where you're not, sloppy writing follows sloppy thinking.

> A Final Note in this Rather Condescending Discussion: Attempt Ye Not to Single-Handedly Battle the Raging Anachronisms of the Law. Thy Noble Efforts will Not be Appreciated. Moreover, if *Your* Senior is a Big-Word Olde English Blockhead, follow *His* Lead, not Mine. I Don't Sign Your Paycheck.

---

70 For more additional information on this debilitating affliction, please contact or write the Committee on Redundancy Committee, Washington, D.C., District of Columbia.

71 In school, you (reasonably) assumed that everything you wrote would be read with care. In practice, much of what you write will never be read, at all. Your writing skills are thus, perversely, all the more important.

MATH AND FOES

A visiting law professor once remarked—in the middle of a discussion to which the concept of a standard deviation was crucial—"*Aw,* I hate math. That's why I went to law school." Although summary dismissal might have been a *little* extreme (...but not by much), this attitude among lawyers is offensive—and disgracefully common.

It's offensive because mathematical concepts are both majestic and profound. Like a shadow consciousness, they underlie all that exists. Math is abstract...*it* doesn't exist, except as a symbolic expression of the relationships among all else, and as a self-contained, *wondrous* system of logic unblemished by words.

On a more practical level—and as a sweet, if belated, rebuttal to your mournful appeals in school ("Why do we *have* to study *this?* We'll *never* use it! *Neaahh...*)—you *will* use it.

If you think you can get away without math, well...you're right. You can. But you won't be a very good lawyer.

When your client is to give (...or get) money, how do you structure the transfer? Are you sure the numbers are accurate? Are you calculating percentages correctly? If there's a time factor (and there almost always is), then what about interest, security, remedies? If a portfolio of values is involved, are you handling the individual and collective values wisely? If non-cash valuables (or foreign parties) are involved, what about unexpected changes in value?

Even non-commercial litigators face the math monolith. If you're suing for damages, how are they calculated? If you're suing on a debt, how do you set up the repayment schedule? If you're *defending* a client, how do you set up the payments to reduce your client's loss?

If...

It's common because many of you really *did* go to law school because you hate math. An early hesitancy easily blossoms into a full-fledged phobia. Worse, harbored deep inside many is a paranoid illusion that math hates *you*.

Don't flatter yourself.

But don't be scared, either. True, math is easily intimidating—the harder the science, the less susceptible it is to bullshit—and boring (especially the way it's usually taught).

Step back a bit and look at what frightens you: Is it the tedium or the transcendence? If the former, don't be lazy.

If the latter, don't be overwhelmed.

At the peak of every discipline is...art. Quantum physics, chaos theory, econometrics: each relies on creative, playful inspiration—an ability to look at the world as does a child—for expansion into new directions and for a grasp of what's truly important. It is no accident that many of the great discoveries were...accidents. But it took perception to see each accident for more than a mere mistake. And it takes the same perception to appreciate what others—great minds that have gone before—have seen.

Thus do we stand on the shoulders of giants.

Conversely, *every* discipline is, at its base...*science*. Even Picasso was a slave to pigment, just as Mozart spent his energies manipulating soundwaves, not changing them.

As a Junior, you learn the science of law. Later, you learn the art.

And now for the good news: What's important is not an ability to memorize formulae. This, in my opinion, is one of the greatest sins of our schools. What *everyone* needs to know are mathematical, statistical, economic, and scientific *concepts*. But, unless you're going to be a mathematician, statistician, economist, or scientist, delving into the nitty-gritty is more than frustrating—it's a waste of time. No one remembers all that stuff. And even if one did, there's a word for relying on memory for the details: *malpractice*. (Besides, that's why we went to the trouble of inventing books.) Instead, we spend mind-numbing hour after cerebral-hemorrhaging semester learning the quantitative innards of the beast, in the faint—and wrong—hope that the big picture will appear, as if by magic. An interminable, infantile game of Hide-the-Ball. The only magic is the reemergence of the space-time continuum...the bell finally rings.

And now for even better news: Much as some "experts" mislead you otherwise, these concepts are pretty darned easy. Compared to the limitless labyrinth of the law, they're downright agreeable. Best of all, once you've figured them out, the world is a smaller—and more inviting—place. The only trouble is...you won't be able to stop.

If you're doing it right, within every answer lies the next question.

And now, back to work...

IT'S A BIRD! IT'S A PLANE!! IT'S *SUPERLAWYER!!!*

It's hard to predict the volume of work that awaits you. Most Juniors are swamped from day one. (And even if you're not *really* swamped, it sure *feels* that way.) A lucky few are fed just the right amount. Still others languish in a patchwork of assignments without coherence.

In the long-run, both workload extremes are bad. But here's something for you sweat-shop bottom-feeders[72] to mull over: in the short-run, too much work is *far* preferable to too little. Too much work gives you valuable experience, and a sense of camaraderie with your trial-by-fire compatriots (which is one reason that many Seniors assume it ought to be this way, even though they've long since forgotten the hardships). Too much work is also an implied expression of the value the firm places in you, which builds esteem...for those who survive.

---

72 How's *that* for a mixed metaphor?

Conversely, a dearth of projects is a not-so-subtle insult as to your professional worth, regardless of the reasons (...or mere inattention) behind such leniency. Some Seniors cannot delegate. If you want to work for them, the burden's on you to pry work from their desks.

So...if you're buried under paper, take *some* comfort in your unhappy predicament. If you're one of those lucky few whose Seniors actually give a thought or two to proper scheduling, take a moment to appreciate them.

THE CHAIN GANG

As an abrupt reversal of the gradually declining workweek over the past century or so, office folks—led by those eager yuppies—are expected to warm their office chairs ever so generously. Get used to it.

(This, by the way, is your defense against cries of evil yuppiedom: Rarely has it been possible to rise so quickly to positions of responsibility and reward, which irritates those who've been forced to wait longer. The flip side, unfortunately, is the accelerated responsibility—and stress—that go with the accelerated rewards.)

If your work is backing up with no letup in sight, change your routine. Rather than dragging into the office at 8:30, only to drag the rest of the day 'til midnight, get to the office at 5:00—yes, *a.m.*—and enjoy a little productivity. Then take a nap later, and work through the evenings if you have to.

I know, I know...(much) easier said than done. Those of us who were meant to guard the cave at night must now suffer under the social tyrannies of the anti-insomniatic Morning Regime. Well, like it or not, the five o'clock club does offer serious productive time without the distractions of office goings-on. (And it does avoid rush-hour.) For a few lucky ones, it's natural. For the rest of us, it ranks right down there with used diapers. (Of course, you can always have a kid—as a dual-purpose alarm.)

If you're continually buried in work, and you seriously doubt your ability to withstand it, consider a less stressful path, either within the law or without. Beware the fate of one Yale law graduate and associate with a high-powered Wall Street firm, whose life ended far differently from the indomitable ideal of a promising young attorney. The lawsuit brought by his father—a wrongful death action against the firm for working him to death—was dismissed.

What is manageable—or even thrilling—to one might be crippling to another. (Don't be misled into believing that vocational Darwinism is at work along with you. An ability to handle stress varies not only among individuals, but also over time, in relation to other life-stress events, and in relation to self-confidence.) That last variable should be one of your first priorities: Take care of—or ignore, for now—your other problems, get comfortable with yourself as a lawyer, and you're halfway home...no matter what they throw at you.

LAWYER VAGRANCY

You might actually find yourself with the opposite problem: *no* work. Pleasant though that might at first sound, it is *dangerous*. If you're luxuriating for an afternoon with a clean desk, no problem. That's a good time to catch up on low-priority stuff,[73] which you should have waiting in the wings for just such an occasion.

If your desk *remains* clean, however, *then* you have a problem.

Or, more emphatically, then *you* have a problem.

You should never, as a Junior, have to worry about where your next billable hour will come from. That's the Seniors' implied part of the bargain (...and it's rarely withheld). A lack of work is not only destructive to your self-esteem, it is a self-fulfilling disaster-in-waiting. Unfair or not, your billings will suffer, which will only compound your troubles. You will be more likely to do too much on those projects you *do* get...to the displeasure of clients and Seniors alike. And you will flounder. The Seniors may be managerially foolish, but it is not they who will bear the heaviest burden.

If you're being bandied about by Seniors...stop and take notice. Something's wrong. Valued Juniors are coveted, not ignored. Don't wait. First, ask for work. Go to your favorite Seniors, in order, and tell 'em you're available.[74] If that doesn't fix the problem—*fast*—then sit down with a trusted Senior to find out what the problem is. (Most likely, it's *you*.) Explain that you feel something's going wrong and you don't know how to get back on track. Usually, this is the awareness they're looking for, and they'll bend over backwards to help.

Don't be embarrassed. Or, more realistically, don't allow your embarrassment to interfere with this necessary part of the learning process. Your Seniors are not your peers. Nor are they your parents. Most will forgive your youthful stumbles...as long as you show the promise of a long-distance runner. (And, once you've crossed the Junior finish-line, you'll be better able to look back and laugh at your earlier shuffles.)

If they truly don't have enough work (...which is unlikely), then they're foolish to keep you, and you're foolish to stay. More likely, however, is a loss of confidence in your ability to finish their assignments, quickly and well. If so, you need to redouble your efforts, and, depending upon how far gone the situation, you might consider looking elsewhere, where others are not similarly burdened by negative preconceptions of you. (Once you lose someone's trust, it is virtually

---

73 ...or a visit to that museum exhibit, *The Lighter Side of the Dark Ages,* you've been promising yourself.

74 Don't go to senior Juniors unless they've been authorized to assign work; it will get *them* into trouble. Clients don't like to pay for unknown lawyers. Would you?

impossible ever to get it back.) Keep in mind, too, the correlation between substance and success. Though far from perfect, it *is* positive.

PRO BONO

Well, call me Mr. Capitalist Cro-Magnon, but I just don't get this.
Volunteering is one of civilization's more honorable and worthy tradi-
tions. Yet students and firms alike dwell on this non-issue for new
associates.

Law firms tout their pro bono programs to star law students like
most-favored-sons. A few actually live up to their billing.

Most, however, do not. Not only are total hours routinely exaggerated, but the expansive definition of "pro bono" can stretch even an
astrophysicist's capacity for imagination.

Aside from larger questions of how society, the bar, and individual
attorneys ought best ease access to legal representation among those
less likely to have access through normal channels (i.e., money), I still
don't get it. True, pro bono can satisfy inner desires, and sometimes
offers interesting work one otherwise might never get. Still, for both
firm and new associate, pro bono ought not be an issue.

First, unless you're either masochistic or utterly irresponsible, *you
don't have time*. (You'll be expected to feed the billables beast just as
heartily.) Second, you're not ready for most pro bono work. Unless
you're a CPA and're going to help taxpayers before the Ides of April,[75]
you simply haven't yet had the grounding to directly counsel clients,
paying or not. Third, when you do work on pro bono cases, you need to
disabuse yourself of the notion, as many maintain subconsciously
(or not-so-subconsciously), that pro bono means sans diligence. You'll
be held to the same standard—paid or not. That oughta' wake you up.
(Rest assured that your Seniors lie awake at night thinking about
your *billable* doozies.) Fourth, what's the rush? There will be plenty
of time—and need—for civic contribution later; for now the best thing
you can do is to prepare for future generosity. Finally, as a Junior,
you'll likely be limited to reminding your Great Uncle Sonny that, no,
pets aren't tax deductible.[76]

In most firms, you'll eventually have plenty of opportunity to help.
Your Junior years are no time though. Unless a Senior drags you into
something (or unless you have a passion for something that a Senior
shares), just keep your nose to the billing grindstone. More often than
not, *firms* are pleading with fashionable charities for the opportunity

---

[75] Yes, in ancient Rome the Ides of *April* would have fallen on the 13th, not
the 15th. A little poetic license, per chance?

[76] *But cf.* I.R.C. § 1231(b)(3).

to help. In any case, you'll likely do for a pro bono client the same routine work that you do for paying ones.

Now, for those of you with a particular interest and exceptionally copious quantities of chutzpah, fine. Find a Senior who's interested and see what happens. But if you're conspiring for some angle, you'd better hope it'll turn into a paying position elsewhere, because few firms can be more than modestly generous with your time, which, for the seventy-third time, is *their* money.

More cynically, many firms use pro bono to lead to *pro moneta*. It's a big world out there; don't let naïveté spoil the unwelcome realization that utopia is rarely compatible with being a grown-up.

If, by the way, you feel *entitled* to a generous allowance of your pro bono interests, and think of regular work as a necessary—or even oppressive—evil, *stop.* You're wrong.

This isn't the venue for a discussion, pro and con, of bono, but, as a Junior, you're way, *way* out of your element in this debate.

Seniors are, generally, generous with their time, and equally generous with *senior* Juniors' pro bono interests. This is no small compliment; pro bono is *expensive*. Show a little consideration in your demands on partners' generosity.

For now, do *not* feel at liberty to accept pro bono cases on your own. Even if Sonny does call, confirm any true representation with a Senior. (Don't be surprised if the answer is *No,* particularly if the case lies outside an area of the firm's expertise.) Serious responsibilities attach to lawyering. Pro bono is no exception.

EXTRACURRICULAR DUTIES

You might be asked (...or want) to do extra work outside the office: pro bono, boards, writing, or whatnot.

First, find out if your firm expects you to meet extra obligations, which will make it all the harder to meet your billables quota. (A few firms even add "client development" to *everyone's* plate, which adds an extra portion for Junior's smaller plate. In fairness to firms, it *is* a good idea, in theory, to prepare future partners for this most important part of practice. In practice, however, this is rarely coupled with serious, one-on-one training. Instead, you're expected to pick up these business graces on your own. More on this topic, later.)

Pro bono's been covered.

BOARDS. You will likely be asked, after you've been out a few years, to sit on the Board of Directors of one or more of a variety of institutions; charities are in constant need of professional guidance.

If anything in particular attracts your interest, you have only to contact whoever's running the show. (You likely will already have made a contact, through your job.)

day wears on, add descriptions and time. Many lawyers now use computerized tracking software, which makes the process marginally less tedious.

Describing your activities is almost an art form. (If it weren't such an unproductive irritant, we'd hold monthly exhibitions of our most impressive timesheets.) In describing your work, you need to explain, clearly and in reasonable detail, what you did. Don't go overboard, but *do* do one thing that few do: look at it from the *client's* perspective. If *you* were being asked to pay the bill that you will be partly responsible for sending, what would you expect to see by way of explanation? (There's another benefit: not only are normal client dealings eased, detailed billing decreases the likelihood of disputes...and malpractice suits.) It's a regressive exercise, true: you'll feel just as you did in front of your grade-school teacher, pleading that the dog did, in fact, eat your homework.

Take a moment to describe, in concise but clear detail, the papers you drafted, the law you reviewed, the research you did, etcetera. Yes, it's a pain. But it's also part of the job. Take it seriously.

Different firms have different policies about keeping track of such things as proofreading, Continuing Legal Education, officekeeping, file-putzing, and the like. If you're uncertain (which you will be), *ask*. Ask also about preferred terminology for the various duties you'll be performing: clients don't like to pay for "proofreading"—regardless of how important that is to their case. Also, be sensitive to the *context* of descriptive words. This isn't puffery, exactly; it *is* wise packaging. (*Hmm*...mere "puffery" isn't actionable under contract law.) Complain as you might about the superficiality of self-promotion, this complaint is best lodged against our own human nature. Put on your better face.

Now onto less-neutral ground: calculating time. In theory, no discussion would be needed, because (physics aside) time is time is time.

Well...welcome to humanity.

You will feel awkward writing down the *actual* time spent in your fledgling efforts. To avoid looking like a klutz, you'll be tempted to shorten the time reported. Not only does this *seriously* undermine your race against the billable-hours pacer, it presents distorted data to your Seniors. They need to know how much time you're spending on each project; in part, it's a rough guide to your progress.

You must record every minute legitimately spent on every case. Let *them* write off your time.

Then there's the opposite problem: *over*stating your time.

As a mathematical truism, it's vastly more difficult to be precise than to err either way. In reality, it might be an innocent miscalculation, or forgetfulness of that excursion to the newsstand. It might be a not-so-innocent addition of a few tenths here and a few more there. It might also be a concerted, if *very* unwritten, policy of the firm.

Careful. Children and matches.

Don't fudge your time. First, it is stealing—either from the firm, if you undercount, or from your client, if you, *well...*you know. Second, it's against the law and rules of professional responsibility. Third, it's a dangerous game; like Skywalker, Jr., you must avoid the powers of the Dark Side. Yes, Darth might have gotten the goodies, but what goes around does tend to come around. And, as the real insult, only *mala fide* evil emperors seem to get away with it. (If that's you, rehabilitative theories aside, nothing will dissuade you...least of all a book from Pollyanna's cousin.) Finally, if your firm *does* play on the rougher, darker side, let the *Seniors* play.

As much as possible, let the Force be with you.

PACING ON THE TREADMILL

As you truddle along, you might notice some unfortunate economics stoking the treadmill. Seniors now expect annual draws in the multi-hundreds of thousands of dollars. Such income is, by economic and historic standards, rather high. The impact on you? These draws are supported by ever-higher billable hour requirements...and guess who gets an extra helping? Were everyone content with a nice house and mid-powered boat...*well,* those days are long gone (for now, at least).

Why do you think firms pay new associates such ridiculously high salaries? Niceness? *Yeah, right.* Because you're worth it? *Get real.* Well...you *are* worth it, in a technical sense: you are valuable because your services are salable. The rub is that your cost to the firm is fixed, but your potential revenue is limited only by the hours in your day.

Thus the never-relenting push for ever-higher billables. Strangely, Seniors aren't the only ones stoking. Juniors, in an innocence to life beyond competition, too often delight in the unrefined art of extra-temporal one-upsmanship. This is a bonus for Seniors, and sustainable for the youth, but it'll get old, quickly (...and so will you).

A little balance. Don't shoot for billable superstardom. Sure, you might add a golden pat on the back to your mental trophy shelf, but you'll probably also add an ulcer or two to your personal collection.[77]

Instead, shoot for—and hit—a target slightly to moderately above the median. Unless you're in the Tour de Rat, *moderated* exhaustion will be enough to get you the crown of partnership.

Whatever your caseload input, and no matter the expected output, you must work steadily on your throughput. (See what technology has done to our language?) Although it might be against your excellence-prone mentality, the steadfast marathoner usually wins this race.

You can do the math. If your firm requires 2,000 billable hours per year, you'll have to *bill* eight hours per day, five days per week, fifty weeks per year. No small feat. If you (still) have a reasonably intact

---

[77] ...and a divorce decree to your document collection.

sense of integrity, this will take an extra twenty percent—or more—of your raw time (not counting CLE, vacation, or sick leave).

Time drains lurk everywhere. Scanning the *National Law Journal* to see which of your classmates jumped ahead of you in the race. Being regaled with a Senior's war story (...real or imagined). Calls home to assure your S.O. that a missing-persons report is unnecessary. Wandering over to make sure your floormates haven't left you out of their afterwork plans. A mid-afternoon expedition to the espresso bar for another *Triple-Mocha-Gotcha!* to ward off the sandman. And you never just stare into space, do you?[78]

Ten-to-twelve hour days are the *minimum* norm to meet "average" billable requirements. To be realistic, throw in the spare weekend. If you're in a real pressure cooker, quite a few weekends (...and midnights). For larger firms, these billable frenzies are an *assumed* part of the job. If you're doing less, beware.

There's perennial movement afoot to replace the billable hour with ...something else. Clients are more insistent on getting a better legal return for their checks, despite the unfortunate reality that legal productivity—from their view, an oxymoron—is such a difficult button to push. The punchline for you is that, even if the invoices change, the pressure on you will only *increase,* yet again. This is so because those same economic realities continue to grease the treadmill; most alternative billing methods stress the "value" rendered to clients. That's the whole point, from the clients' perspective: making you more worth the expense and trouble. Unfortunately, sustainable productivity improvements are best made by *eliminating* legal steps. We don't want *that*, do we?

Okay, enough sarcasm. Your work comes first, and other, personal wants come later. Learn it and live it.

If your Senior is an early riser, so are you. If your Senior is a midnight-oil burner, so are you. (If your Senior is *both*, save your salary to order a new life...'cause you ain't gonna have much of one.)

Do not let other *Juniors* interrupt your work. This can be difficult, especially with wildly different work habits and social needs. Still, you *do* need to put your foot down. If an officemate likes to drop by in the late afternoons, just as you're hitting your stride, *kick 'm out.* Diplomatically, of course. (Unless his personality and hint-taking acumen rival the densities of lead and thorium, respectively, in which case you should change your schedule...or install a trapdoor.)

You have *work* to do.

Whatever your quantitative obligation, you must work up to a brisk, high-quality pace...*quickly.* The student mindset will harm you, here. You should think, instead, of the law-exam mindset, where you were rewarded for getting it down, however jumbled...and

---

[78] ...after that much caffeine, you might be hovering just above coma.

moving on. In practice, however, you must get it down quickly and *without error* before you move on. No easy task. Your time is on-line, similar to an air traffic controller's. Miss a beat and nasty things can happen…fast. That's why they pay you the big bucks.

Your goal is to finish a project in not much more time than it takes to scan the file and draft a response. Seriously. Anything more is, usually, superfluous to the needs of your client. Get into a *practice* mindset. Fast, fast, *fast* turnaround, based on *practical* solutions.

Practice. Practical. Spot the issue…and *solve* it. You really *can* get a lot done, *fast,* when you put your mind to it. Clients will love you. Seniors will love you. Stray pets will love you.

ZZZ*zzzzzz*…

Here's another macroeconomic analogy for you: a surprisingly subtle relationship exists in the economic-development recipe. Slight differences—of mere *tenths* of a percentage point—between changes in productivity and population growth rates will, over time, make the difference between economic prosperity…or stagnation. Such is the glory of cumulation, so easily lost in the drear of numbers.

It's striking that such important consequences depend upon such mundane variables. So it is with you. Your productive abilities must steadily increase, which requires that your mistakes correspondingly decline. You need not, and cannot, change from law student to legal superstar overnight—*just make sure you improve apace.* Granted, this must occur within the frenetic constraints of practice, and, unfortunately, in competition with others on the treadmill. Still, worry less about the competition than about yourself.

This doesn't always require that you dedicate your life to the Firm, to the exclusion of all else…but it's close. Your life is not your own, and you must take the needs of your clients and Seniors *seriously*. Occasionally, and perhaps frequently, this will require shelving your personal life. *Planning* will eliminate many time vacuums; smoother will be the result, and easier will be your life.

You can't account for all—or even most—contingencies, but you can take advantage of some basic management techniques to make your efforts more efficient, and, consequently, your life more pleasant.

INTEGRATED PROJECT MANAGEMENT TECHNIQUES

Here's where a little thanks to those guys in industry, the Navy, and dweeb-central—academia—are due. You see, lots of folks have been worried about *real* logistical problems—long before our little assignments—and have devised useful scheduling tools to help. Going by exciting acronyms like PERT (Program Evaluation and Review Technique), CPM (Critical Path Method), LOB (Line of Balance), and the ever-popular Gantt charts, these techniques are used to coordinate and smooth the flow of work in a series of component subprojects leading to a finished whole.

As applied to legal work, the techniques are pretty simple. (If you think not, appreciate for a moment the engineers who designed your vehicle's fuel pump, which works busily and unobtrusively along with counted thousands of other subcomponents to bring your legal butt to your fancy legal chair six days a week.)

Much as we might like to think otherwise, legal work is like any other process: it can be reduced to discrete components. Client walks into office. Problem disscussed. (Thirty minutes and thoughtful nods.) Case commenced. Retainer retained. (Don't forget *this* step.) File opened. Lots of papers back and forth. You know (...or will figure out) the rest. Sure, exceptions arise, but they only prove the rule that planning for the knowns speeds the process and increases your ability to deal with the unknowns.

Law *is* process. Exceptions can be disorienting, and the more you can fit exceptions into the big picture, the less disoriented you'll be. The real concern is in setting priorities. Rarely are your projects complicated and plentiful enough for serious conflicts to arise. More often, you need simply to put each project into its proper place in your (relatively) finite working day. If it's more important, or has an earlier (or stricter) deadline, then that sounds like a good candidate for early attention. If it's significantly shorter than other projects, maybe you should get it done first, then turn to longer ones. If the case, facts, and melodrama are fresh in your mind, strike while the iron is hot. If you need a little think time on a research project, don't waste time billing on it—work on something else while the first simmers.

One hazard merits special mention: Have you ever been in a store, waiting for someone to take your money, only to notice that *very same* someone...piddling behind the counter, doing something that looks suspiciously unimportant? We often work on what we like, and avoid what we don't. In stores, *customers* are too often in the latter category. (Such indolence is a sure sign of bad management.) In law, do not force a customer—your client or your Senior—to wait.

Back to setting priorities: Events are linked to a time-line. From beginning to end, the user knows which projects are finished, which are underway, and which are waiting in the wings...and for how long. Engineers ordinarily track events to a projected time of completion, but law more realistically tracks in terms of time to future critical events (for example, how many days until *Paper A* must be filed). These, too, are backtracked from later events. For instance, certain pre-trial motions might need to be filed x days before the pre-trial conference is scheduled. Unless you think first about the conference, and then (carefully) subtract the days to arrive at a pre-trial motions deadline, you're in serious trouble...before the real fun even begins.

Confirm the rules for *your* jurisdiction. Every place has its own quirks—most written, some not. Still, you're responsible for them all. The sooner you learn, the sooner you win.

This is basic, basic stuff...but it's easy to mess up.

It happens all the time. (Why do you think there's so much fuss about statutes of limitation?[79])

The important point for you is to not miss easily-missed deadlines. No...more than that. You need enough time to do a good job *before* the deadline passes. Once something's filed it's a permanent record, fixed for all to see, of the sum of your legal acumen...or sloth. Though you might not yet have the former, don't be guilty of the latter.

Develop good habits, early. Your desk should never look as if a nearby typhoon recently blew out your windows. Even if *you* know where everything is, that's not the point. Soon enough, you'll have too many cases to keep track of by seat-of-the-pants lawyering, and it won't help if your secretary can't find anything, either.

You must become organized...and *stay* organized. Do not let *any* project fall through a crack. Keep track of each with a status report, updated weekly (...at least). Happily, your job is substantially done for you, in the form of numerous case management software packages (derived and simplified from these techniques) available off-the-shelf. If your firm has one, learn it and use it.

Transactional work is somewhat different, but still amenable to helpful organization. At the start of each project, take out a clean sheet of paper and figure out what must happen for the client to be happy—and when. Nothing fancy. Just something to refer to when you start to wander.

In *all* offices, create **To Do** lists *at least weekly*.

Don't be a stacker. Keep each project in its own pile, and keep each pile distinct from all others. If you must stack, keep the pyramid formation clear. Out-of-sight might be out-of-mind, but it could also lead you out-of-a-job.

Another notable technique is the scheduling of slack time, which is almost as important as knowing the critical events. Letting a project sit will almost always improve it, because you will more easily pick out mistakes on a fresh review that your eyes have glossed over after numerous readings.

Later, when you're in control (as much as any practitioner can be), it'll become second nature to stagger projects so that your work load is somewhat smoother. Sure, that's what everyone *says* they've been doing, but why make your life any harder than it has to be?

Work hard *and* smart.

---

[79] ...which, by the way, are among the sharpest pegs upon which to nail an attorney to the malpractice board (...or so I've heard).

Feed Back

Now for one of the main problems Juniors—and you—will face: a void of information about how well (or poorly) you're doing. Unlike school, where steady feedback is the (indirect) *raison d'être* of classroom life, you will now labor in darkness. Law school was a taste, though: no feedback until the end of your first year.

THE ANNUAL REVIEW

In continuation of tradition, the primary feedback for many Juniors is the annual review. At some firms these yearly rites are prompt affairs, conducted with the solemnity of 𝔄𝔫𝔠𝔦𝔢𝔫𝔱 𝔊𝔬𝔱𝔥𝔦𝔠 𝔕𝔦𝔱𝔲𝔞𝔩𝔰, leading to no small rush of adrenaline and a nearly uncontrollable urge to race for the nearest restroom. (*Gee*…good thing you swiped the barf bag from that last trip.) At many firms, however, the approach is more haphazard. Either way, treat this annual event seriously, for you can be fairly certain that your Seniors will…even if they think it's a royal pain, which it is.

Seniors are human: perceptions and memories fade. True, it might not be fair to be judged according to your behavior over only the most recent few months of the previous year, particularly when it comes to your mistakes, but…what was that Rule? Life's not fair. Get over it. (Come to think of it, we always have been—and always will be—judged according to artificial slices of our lives. It's inherent to the process of measurement. Remember the LSAT?)

The solution, when annual review season is approaching, is to do what others have done: pucker up. Don't be obvious, but do be *extra* careful a month or so before. Produce mountains of paperwork, and be particularly sharp. Prepare a (restrained) memo listing your projects and accomplishments, great and small. Let *them* speak for you.

Also, let your significant other (…if you still have one) know what's going on, and why you're becoming even more tense than usual. (Kinda' like law exams, *eh?*) Don't plan your vacation within ninety kilometers of this time; it'll skew your billables tally, and it'll mess up others' plans…no matter how early you've notified everyone.

Still, the annual review is mere window dressing. (Much criticism is of the fill-in-the-blank variety, more for the file than for you.)

No, not quite. It's more like a sideshow. It is important, but understand in which arena: The main event is your emerging legal talent and professional maturity (…or blatant lack thereof).

Keep your eye on the ball.

THE OCCASIONAL, QUASI-REVIEW

Then there are firms in which annual reviews are barely observed, if at all. If you're in this category, you can relax a bit, because the annual review is not their measuring tool of choice. (Instead, you're being evaluated *all the time*.[80]) Pay attention: if you are having problems, go to your favorite Senior, and ask for help.

CRITICISM

Our species has an almost overriding aversion to losing face: It is the rare person who purposely seeks out criticism. The learning process is thus marked by delicate dancing around problems, unkind bursts of pent-up frustrations, and vague mysticism surrounding the deciphering of responses—good, bad, and indifferent—of Seniors. Worse, many Seniors aren't even *aware* that they are constantly being scrutinized for the slightest hints of (dis)approval.

They're not there for that Mentor-of-the-Year plaque. Like you, they're there for the money. (...And because *they* didn't know the meaning of their incipient lives.)

Disabuse yourself of the notion that it's up to *them* to understand that you're open to change, but it is they who must tell you how. No. Instead you will generally receive only subtle hints. Like anyone else, Seniors don't like to tell others their breaths smell, and are singular masters at beating around the bush...or ignoring the problem completely when it comes to Juniors. Remember, they're looking for cash cows, not problem children.[81]

Be thick-skinned about criticism. Seniors don't like giving it any more than you like getting it. But...get it out of the way.

Do not talk back. Do not get defensive. Do *not* get argumentative. Lawyers seem particularly susceptible to this human phenomenon. We've been taught to fight for the faintest glimmer of an argument, no matter how dark the side. We thus too easily forget—or reject—that sometimes things really aren't that complicated. When it comes to us, *personally,* we seem incapable of admitting defeat, ignorance... or wrongness. Parents call this process growing up. Show, through serious consideration, that you *are* taking them seriously, and that improvement will follow. And that you're worth the trouble.

Here I go again, but look at it from *their* perspective: They have stresses, too. They don't need to add to those the severe demands of wet-nursing you to maturity. Managing people is probably *the* most difficult managerial skill to hone and exercise well. Not all lawyers have the natural humanistic bent. *Very* few have the time. Do not try

---

80 Actually, you're being evaluated all the time, in *all* firms.

81 And, unlike parents of problem children, Seniors are not under the same moral—or legal—constraint to keep you.

their patience. More often than not, they'll take the natural human course and ignore the problem...until it's too late, for both practical and psychological reasons, to fix.

Beware also the too-nice Senior, who will kill you with kindness. You *do* need guidance, and sometimes (as here) that guidance is less than pleasant. (As an extra bit of caution: don't believe your Seniors when they disclaim a problem. Assume that they're just being polite, and endeavor to correct it anyway.)

FRIENDLY ADVICE

While you're being thick-skinned about criticism, be specially attuned to friendly advice and off-hand remarks. Step back a bit and analyze the emotions going on here.

It's akin to sex, really.

You know what you want. Your partner knows what he or she wants. But how often are we uninhibited enough to *tell* the other?

We're too embarrassed. We're too ashamed. We're too repressed.

So what happens? We grow frustrated. Our frustration grows.

Eventually, the situation resolves itself...usually by despondency. In law, Junior will either catch on, or not. If not, the odds are pretty good that that particular Junior will soon be pounding the pavement, and will carry the same harmful idiosyncrasies into a new position. Perhaps a new halo shimmers, but why sully it immediately (and irretrievably) with chronic dysfunctions?

Most times, it's a matter of pet peeves. (Even so, *you* must adjust to each Senior, not vice versa.) Other times, more serious matters are involved. Pick up on the subtle comments, particularly from junior Seniors. They're the ones with the unofficial role of bringing up Junior. Don't brush them off. They see and know, and usually are honestly trying to help. But they can only hint. They cannot, or will not, command. And it's unfair for you to expect them to.

Usually these subtle hints will take the form of compliments when something is done right. If, for example, you're having trouble focusing your research projects, and you accidentally focus on one because you were so completely lost that you did it step-by-step, and you are complimented on the job you did...then figure out how you did that assignment, and follow that model in the future.

The more of a *self*-correcting Junior you are, the more likely you won't be one for long.

THE BLIND LEADING

Do not follow the lead of other Juniors: By definition, they are not leaders. (Even if they act as if they are.) Most are just as lost, even if they *don't* act like it. Even as you gasp in wonder at their seeming familiarity with it all, recognize that that's your own insecurity, not reality. (Those few who truly *are* on the ball usually are for different reasons: A parent who's managing partner, perhaps. It's unlikely that those same circumstances apply to you.)

Pace yourself, judge yourself only partially by external clocks, and get on with the tasks at hand.

LET THE SUNSHINE IN

A few years from now, when the chairs are reversed, adopt a habit my father, ever the teacher, wisely used. Before any task was begun, he cleared the decks with a little *Sunshine*—pardon the mixed topside metaphor—to shed some light on what was expected. Spending a few moments to put yourself in the shoes of a subordinate is well worth it, for both master and servant. For servant, it makes clear that which is unknown or confusing. For master, it reduces the complications arising from ignorant and confused servants.

Add something else my father, ever the navigator, insisted upon. After a task was underway, he came by again for a *Base Fix,* which in navigation refers to an initial check to assure that the traveler is on course in a journey. Don't wait for a nervous Junior to screw up. Stop by his office after he's started one of your projects, and, friendly-like, nudge him back onto course. When all is done, this will take *less* of your time (and produce fewer grey hairs) than to correct the mistakes that are bound to occur, repeatedly, otherwise.

And when you're head honcho, add an *Anonymous Advice* tradition to your office. *Officially* encourage anonymous notes from everyone to anyone—Seniors included—over whatever peeves. Provide an outlet for constructive criticism, like the Japanese custom of getting smashed with your boss and then letting him have it, (supposedly) without fear of retribution. Be confident enough to allow good-natured, helpful ribbing. Most importantly, *Sunshine, Base Fixes,* and *Anonymous Advice* keep the relationship on a friendly keel. This is an infinitely more pleasant way—for the both of you—to guide Junior along the path to legal maturity.

Why so hard on Seniors? Messinger Rule No. 3,419.7: The elder is responsible. For it is he who knows—or should know—better.

As a Senior, sparkle with uncommon excellence. Manage proactively, rather than riding shotgun on the vagaries of life. If you want your firm to be big, fine. If you want your firm to be small, fine. But don't accept whatever happens to happen. You'll be greatly rewarded with the satisfaction (and power) that competence in these business (and life) skills brings.

As a Junior, sparkle with uncommon proficiency.

— 7 —

FITTING IN

Pull out your trusty tricorder and probe the atmosphere in *your* firm. A big, blue-blooded 𝕱𝔦𝔯𝔪 in an old-money capital is rather different from a young boutique firm in SILICON CITY. (But not always in the ways one might assume.) Firms are as different as the people within them. Use your senses to consciously determine what's appropriate for your firm, and what's not: Many problems that Juniors face are social, not legal, and are the result of foolish indifference, not subversion.

GETTING ALONG

A perverse psychology pervades law (...and every other walk of life). When you enter this world unto itself, your Commandment is simple: Be Thou a Good Puppy. This means, in part, playing the diplomat with others ... particularly Senior others.

Don't "talk stink" (...a handy phrase in Hawaii) about anyone.[82] You can listen. You can laugh, within reason. But remember, part of being a lawyer is the ability to keep secrets. Few are good at it under the social pressure of providing dirt to the rumor mills. Get good at it.

It's akin to sex, really.[83]

No matter how open your relationship, no matter how honest you think you should be, no matter how vociferously your partner insists it's okay...never, never, *never* recount your sexual adventures past. It's a no-win game. In law, what goes around comes around. Bet on it.

Be discreet.

MODESTY

Were we to go back in time and interview a young Eisenhower or Earhart or Einstein or...other eventual big name, we would probably be quite put off by an *honest* conversation with each of an estimate of him (or her) -self. Although they probably *were,* even early on, better than their then-superiors—both technically and cerebrally—their relative modesty was likely a big factor in their success.

No one—particularly the mediocre—wants to be reminded of his relative inferiority, especially from a subordinate. Immodesty breeds

---

82 Except pinheads. (But never to *other* pinheads, or to pinheads substantially senior to you.) In truth, this is just more satire for your reading pleasure. Don't talk stink about anyone.

83 *Gee,* is *everything* akin to sex? Perhaps not, but it's more fun to read, yes?

hostility. Even where arrogance might be justified, those who don't learn to hide it all but beg for higher standards ... and lower tolerance for mistakes. It is deeply ingrained in even our individualistic culture that modesty (but not the false kind) is the best policy. Try it.

Plus, your Seniors might just surprise you.

RULE NO. 1,438

Rule No. 1,438: *Do Not Criticize.*

Anything. Ever. Even if asked. Regardless of how correct you think you are—or might actually be—it is *their* firm. They are entitled to mess up on their own. If you're concerned about the impact on you, sharpen your Machiavellian reflexes, and cover your posterior. If the fit is truly uncomfortable, find a different employer. Be forewarned, however, that the weeds are usually just as plentiful, if of a different genus, on the other side.

Do Not Criticize. There are practical reasons behind this Rule:

First, you almost certainly don't know the whole story. The life of a Junior is marked by the paucity and poor quality of facts, while the grapevine sprouts a cornucopia of aphid-infested, hybrid, and downright bizarre anecdotal varieties.[84]

Second, wise or not, Kings do not like bearers of bad tidings. Not too long ago, in kingdoms not too far away, such bad news bearers were beheaded. Now they're only belittled.[85]

Third, criticizing will rarely help, but almost certainly will hurt. If you voice dissatisfaction—or worse, offer advice—you're a troublemaker. *Not Part of the Team.* The most saintly of Seniors would be hard-pressed to not feel irritated at such presumptuousness; it's not your place. In short, it is seen as discourteous in the extreme for you to offer any serious contribution until at least several years have passed. (In stuffier firms, even new *partners* face an extended waiting period before serious input is acceptable.)

It is the rare leader who overcomes the near-instinctual defensive response to criticism, and instead endeavors to shift organizational momentum ... which, after all, is an extension of that leader's ego. Think about it. Seniors have a vested interest, both financially and emotionally, in *their* firm. Would *you* like it if someone came into your home and criticized your taste in furniture? Even if your taste sucks? And even if you know it?

---

84 Don't disparage this viticultural reality: grapevines *exist*. They thrive in darkness, and mutate in suspicion. As a Senior, *cultivate* them to your taste.

85 I hope you enjoyed both the alliteration and (exceedingly) obscure reference to Ms. O'Neil. If, as a practical matter, you *do* need to give bad news about a legal assignment, then tell your Senior up front, propose alternatives, and ask for guidance. Seniors, and wise humans, appreciate this.

Fourth, it's *easy* to criticize. It's a bit harder to *do*.

Fifth, the practicalities of life make it impossible to know that each firm has its frailties. You can guess, though. *Hey,* if you think they're being foolish...so be it. It's their money. It's their firm. If it's serious enough that you can't stand it, then don't stand it. Leave. Or find a new career altogether, because there aren't too many perfect firms out there.

Finally, you might just be wrong. It happens.

LEARNING FROM WAR

You've little to be critical of. Time for another digression: Armies win because they're stronger, smarter, or luckier. On those rare occasions when they're *all,* empires are built (...and, until entropy takes hold, are they sustained).

Darned few organizations—of any kind—are immune from the common, rhythmic curses of spotty management, miscommunication, and fluctuating morale. Indeed, this is common to all professions—save, ironically, the military, which has recognized the importance of morale, and (usually) does a creditable job in at least considering the personal needs of its charges. The military is not gushy out of kindness. No. It is a killing machine, and incorporates institutional mechanisms to maintain the sharpness of that unkind machine. Personal problems interfere with the machinery. That the military is regularly derided for its workings is ironic. SNAFUs and bureaucratic bumbling are endemic to *all* large organizations. Most law firms have trouble at predictable stages: a dozen lawyers, as the firm shifts from a start-up to a solid firm, then again at a hundred or so, as the firm shifts from a solid firm to an established institution. Try two million.

RULE NO. 1,438.1

A corollary to Rule Number 1,438: Do Not *Whine*.

No one likes a whiner. It spreads like the cancerous by-product of a foul personality that it is. If this is you, change your personality.

Someday, a court will recognize co-worker whining as a legitimate (and complete) defense to premeditated vocational homicide. Whatever the jurisprudential fallout, keep your whining in the cellar, where it belongs.

BROWN-NOSING DONE RIGHT

Brown-nosing is *good*. Far from being contemptible, it is in the time-honored tradition of successful career ladder-climbers all. The danger lies in its abuse, not its existence.

The trouble with brown-nosing is that it's all too easy to forget the object of the game. It's healthiest if you have a true respect for your Senior brown-nosee, and, consequently, feel that brown-nosing is a proper form of courtesy. In most cases, your Senior will truly deserve it. (In which case, it isn't *really* brown-nosing, is it?)

Trouble arrives twice: first are the overdoers, whose brown-nosing is so complete they often plunge in entirely, and might be lost for days on end. Aside from being rather uncomfortable for the Senior, this requires extensive spelunking gear...and it isn't a good way to conduct oneself professionally. You are, after all, supposed to be a fully sentient being, with a reasonably intact ego, capable of distinguishing diplomacy from overbearing sycophancy. Seniors worthy of respect are looking for top-notch, right-hand *attorneys,* not lap dogs.[86]

Brown-nosing is frequently worsened because it is often congenital as well as immature. The King—*any* King—can indeed do no wrong. For any member of this obsequious coterie, all Seniors—by virtue of their status alone—are just below God. Barely.

These people we call *pinheads.* We should all feel great sorrow and pity (...when not sharpening our letter-openers), for some terrible tragedy bestruck them during their pin-headed youths (perhaps during their tenures as Hall Monitor), resulting in an utter inability to commit their lives to anything other than pleasing authority figures.

The second, related problem is more nettlesome: when these Juniors climb the legal ladder (which they do with irritating frequency), they then expect *others* to climb in. Take a flashlight.

SPENDING THE PART

Money. A Junior is expected to make the transition from starving student to affluent attorney. This transition is supposed to occur invisibly, outside the realm of the work world, except that denims are replaced by sharper woolens. Some handle this transition more easily than others. Part of your job is to understand what will happen, and minimize potential troubles.

Be neither the spendthrift nor the miser, but do tie up your loose ends. You're no longer a starving student. Don't act like it. But don't take your newfound affluence for granted, either.

Fun though spendthriftiness might be, it's immature...and foolish. This is because, for most of you, even where lawyering gives you a tidy paycheck, you're *not* wealthy. *Oh, no.* As many, *many* people discover as their lawyers guide them through bankruptcy, income is not the same as capital. Easily confused, true, but not the same at all.

---

86 Yes, I know I said "be a good puppy" earlier, but that referred to eager assistance, not unthinking—or obsessive—adulation.

Worse, we often realize—too late—that what we thought we wanted doesn't please as advertised. Don't wait until *after* you've accumulated those plentiful student loans, mountains of credit card debt, a hefty mortgage, and luxury-car payments...only to learn that you'd prefer to get off the (well-paying) merry-go-round.

(And if you find yourself expelled from the amusement park for excessive merriment—not unlikely in today's unamusing market—your lofty expenses, unconcerned with your incidental life, will take on a whole new meaning.)

For those who move to a new city for your first job, the process is somewhat forced. Take this chance to get rid of your dormroom debris, and *slowly* assemble whatever accouterments you desire. Note that that word usually applies to the outfitting of military equipment and accessories. There's a lesson there: Go light on your early purchases, even though you're feeling flush. It's far, far better to concentrate on your job for at least your first year...and gather money jingling in your pockets, rather than things and bills jingling you.

All in good time, my pretty. All in good time.

COMMITTING TO THE PART

In life, you cannot succeed—*really* succeed—at more than one thing at one time. This is a truth that goes against the grain for many, who dream of escaping the daily grind for something a bit more glamorous (and less exhausting).

If *you* suffer from visions of sugar plums, fairies, and grand book contracts (reserving the lead in the movie to yourself, of course) for your best-selling thrillers...wake up. Sure, follow your flights of fancy. But, while still on the ground, don't forget the art of the taxi.

Life as a Junior is difficult enough without extras: You don't have the time to worry about leaky faucets, radiators, or mothers-in-law. *Ahem*...perhaps I should try that again: You don't have the time to worry about leaky faucets, blown radiators, or sweet mothers-in-law. *Whew.* You also don't have time to keep up your commodities trading, which, lucrative though it was, ain't the same since Hillary.

Lighten your load. If you've spent each weekend for the past three years feeding the homeless, you'll have to stop. You don't have time. (Give food or money, instead.) If you're addicted to computer games, give them away or burn them. You don't have time.

Beware also the allure of false economy. If your car is unreliable, sell it or junk it. I remember my search for a car when my wife and I were first in Hawaii. It took four weeks (a speedy record for me), and in my impatience we bought—by my fault—a piece of junk. I spent lunch hours at junkyards getting alternators and other parts, ruining clothing, and, well, not much was pleasant about the experience.

That was the *last* thing I should have been concerned with.

My folly then astounds me, even now. Traipsing around junkyards was fun in college; it's downright dumb as a Junior. (Coincidentally, my efforts at thriftiness backfired: we paid more than we would have for new-car payments...not even counting mental anguish.)

This is not contrary to the preceding lecture on spendthriftiness: you should spend your very hard-earned money very, very carefully, but you should *willingly* exchange your money for stress- and time-saving new professional essentials.

Do what you can to clean up your act *before* you start practice. You must be almost obsessive in focusing on your work. Soon enough, you'll appreciate the value of your time. Remember the story of Jack, work, and no play?

Well...you get a waiver.

MOVING TO NEW PARTS

A minor point: If you do move to a new city, you'll need to arrange a hundred minor details. You can rely on the firm for *some* of this, but be careful. Don't list Seniors as credit references (an apartment rental, for instance), even if you've dealt more with them than with others. It's annoying for Seniors to receive calls from unknown creditors, only to be asked about a new Junior.

Instead, rely on the *office manager;* it's her job. Before you do so, however, extend her her professional courtesy due: let her know that you'd like to ask for a certain reference, or favor, or whatnot—and ask permission. Or ask how you might accomplish whatever it is you need. Most will be quite helpful, in part because of your *potential* standing, and in part because of their courteous ways. Reciprocate.

Double-check these *before* your move. Call the office manager, and ask for help with these details before you're diverted with bar review studies. Don't pester, but don't be shy, either.

ACTING THE PART

You're a professional now. Act like it.

Be *quiet.* Law offices are rarely designed with acoustics in mind. (Not only volume, but direction and pitch are concerns too; you'd be surprised how some sounds travel. I remember a fellow law student who, though nice enough, had this booming, gravelly voice that could be heard from the next building. Yes, it wasn't really his fault, but, still, it took superhuman control to not throttle the guy.)

Giggling, loud talking, slamming doors, and the like are not only discourteous, from a Junior they're flatly unacceptable. Cursing is, unsurprisingly, a no-no...except among fellow Junior foul-mouths.

On the humor front, don't be too sarcastic (if that's your preferred defense mechanism). It is easily misinterpreted, especially among the literal-minded majority. If it's less than obviously funny, it'll be more than likely irksome. And, if it's at all sexual, political, or religious, you're just asking for trouble. You needn't give up your ready wit. Just wait until you've been invited into their inner sanctum—and know their particular bents—before forging ahead with your stand-up routine. This isn't devious; it's wise social skill.

On the tele-front, excessive private (or long-distance) phone calls *will* be noticed, one way or another.

If you use a speakerphone...*turn it down*. If you expect a long (or loud) conversation, close your door. Speak softly and carry whatever legal stick you need. If your office has old phones (with the then-new but crappy feature), don't use the speakerphone. It sounds as if you're calling from a toilet. Even with newer systems, which are better, ask if the other person minds. If there's even the slightest hesitation in response, pick up the phone.

Voicemail is your friend, but don't overdo it.

Now to the latest ego-feature, call waiting. But first, a disclaimer: I *hate* call-waiting. It's rude, pretentious, annoying, and unnecessary. (In a real emergency, there's always an "Operator Interrupt".) Be circumspect before putting someone on hold. It's less rude—and more professional (and less frazzling)—to call someone back...with your *undivided* attention.

Common sense stuff, when we take the time to think about it.

Now for something shallow: Don't wander around empty-handed. Even if you're just taking a walk to stretch, take along a file.

While we're at it, don't walk around too much. It's disconcerting to your floormates, and, once someone starts to pay attention, it might become one of those silly, yet injurious, little peeves. Go to your room.

SMELLING THE PART

Personal hygiene...brush up on it. Don't be an olfactory nuisance.

MORE HYGIENE

Brush and floss after lunch. If you have halitosis—it's hard to tell by yourself, and embarrassing to ask, but if you notice an odd, pasty taste and coworkers backing away—check with a doctor. Also, brush often and keep a bottle of water handy; they lessen the effect.

SOCIALIZING THE PART

Most firms organize social events to capture, or create, *esprit de corps*. Even if you're running low on *esprit*, go.

If they go to the trouble of preparing an event, you can darn well get off your butt and attend. Social events are a relatively innocuous part of the job...but a part nonetheless. Even Seniors who otherwise wouldn't care will note your absence. To paraphrase Horton, a snub is a snub, no matter how small.

Remember too that a technical proficiency is only part of the law practice equation. Social skill—especially as you climb—is an increasing part of every Senior's job. At the lower end of the social-skill spectrum, there's never any time when a major *faux pas* won't reflect on you, badly. There's no need to go to the opposite extreme of bland hollowness (nor should you), but when near anyone remotely connected with the firm, act as though you are always being observed, because you are.

Oh. Keep the overt brown-nosing to a minimum. They get enough at the office, and, ironically, they'll probably respect you more if you simply enjoy yourself. (But do realize that law practice is a *business,* and serious undercurrents of professional posturing cut beneath your path. This is especially true if *any* outsiders are involved. If it's with a current or potential client, be on your *best* behavior. Otherwise, be on your best behavior anyway, as a signal of your earnest appreciation of this most important part of lawyering. If that's asking too much, feel free to goof off...while planning your next career.)

ALCOHOL

Moderation.

OTHER VICES

Don't. Otherwise, careful.

BEING THE GOOD SPORT

If you're in any normal office, there are pranksters lurking about. As long as it's not spiteful or in abusively bad taste, *play along.*

And, though you shouldn't go overboard in the reciprocal game of jokestering one-upsmanship, *learn how to take a joke.* Not only will it make your stay more enjoyable, it will reduce the likelihood of your being on the receiving end.

DRESSING THE PART

Hermits and tenured intellectuals excepted, image matters. Clothing matters not only as a social commitment, but also in attitude. You feel and act differently when you're well-dressed, which is reflected in deference and respect. We not only *do* judge books by their covers, we create sub-industries whose sole task is to burnish them for sale.

I have to admit here to a little disingenuousness: I chose a firm in Hawaii in part because of its relaxed atmosphere and dress code. When necessary, I can meet or beat anyone in the Wall Street look. Yet I sometimes let my disdain for fashion, especially in my Junior years, interfere with common sense. Do as I say, not as I do.

Your dress should be targeted at, or slightly above, the image of your Senior...and a well-tailored cut above the Junior norm. But not *too* much higher. And *not* fashionable. Unless you work in sports or entertainment law, think conservatively about office clothing.[87] You don't want to look slick. You want instead to look, well, *professional*.

Years ago, John Malloy examined business clothing more as science than as fashion. His then-revolutionary books are worth reading.

For men: Don't let women choose your business clothing. Women usually prefer fashionable men's clothing. You don't want *fashionable* business clothing. You need *business* business clothing. There is a difference. Take the time and make the personal commitment to learn about professional attire, and suit yourself. Yet save the GQ look for Saturday nights.

For women: Your advantage is that you've probably thought more about clothing in any season than your male counterpart has in his entire life. The downside is that this is not necessarily an advantage, because you've been concerned primarily with looking good, socially. You don't want to look good, *socially*. You need to look good, professionally.[88]

Your choices: Conservative. Conservative. And Conservative. Dark blue and charcoal wool suits. *Very* subtle patterns. (If you can see 'em, they ain't subtle.) Shirts must be pressed (or ironed); it *does* make a difference. For guys, bright white shirts or *subtle* varieties thereof.[89] Keep the ties tasteful—skip the Disney® collection during your Junior years. Women can be a little more adventurous with accessories, but the result should be strikingly professional.

Now, now...this is the model. Deviate at your conscious will. But first consider that now's not the time to take fashion liberties; wait until you're a rainmaking Senior before blazing your fashion trail.

---

87 Well, maybe you should dress conservatively *especially* if you're in sports or entertainment law.

   ...Wouldn't want to be confused with the talent, would ya?

   (I have it on good southern California authority, though, that this footnote and accompanying text are for amusement only; entertainment lawyers—all dozen of them—get to make quite the fashion statements.)

88 And you *absolutely* do not want to look good, sexually.

89 Contrary to what everyone seems to think, straight (not button-down) collars are more formal, and are thus preferable. They're also easier to handle.

There's a new fashion movement afoot: Casual Fridays. I'm skeptical. For one thing, dressing down is actually more work: you'll need to spend *more* time coordinating an office-appropriate casual look.

For another, it's easy for this to degenerate into dress-down *every* day. (Indeed, that's what happened in Hawaii: "Aloha Fridays" were the day to wear aloha shirts. It became apparent pretty quickly that aloha shirts were vastly more practical, and now dress shirts, jackets, and ties are very much the exception for everyday office wear.) This isn't wrong, especially in tropical climates, but it does heighten the need to be careful to choose dress-down clothes *well*. Even in Hawaii, it's obvious which attorneys dress sharply and which do not. Care to guess the correlation between dress and success?

You don't dress for yourself. You don't even dress for your Seniors. You dress for your *clients*. It is they who pay your salary. Unless they all wear cut-offs—*Gee...what're the odds?*—what you wear at the office reflects on everyone in that office, all the time. I dislike sounding so fuddy-duddy about this, but the approach of Casual Sloppy is simply *wrong*.

Think you work too hard, and others should ease up? Guess again. Most workers work hard, and many must face the public, with a professional image, *all the time*. They cannot hide in a *personal* office. And few make even a substantial fraction of your salary.

Think you're expressing your individuality? You weren't so "individual" when you wanted the job. Think formal dress is uncomfortable? It is, if you're dressing poorly. Think clients should love you for your brains? No. They *assume* you've got brains. They love you for your *professionalism*, which is closely tied with how you present yourself.

Think it's all unfair? *Yup,* it *is* unfair that you expect someone else to pay you an astoundingly high salary (just ask anyone on the street) and tolerate whatever *you* decide.

You're not the King. You're his servant.

Franklyn Kimball, of Kimball Legal Consulting in Chicago, put it this way: "As you get dressed, ask yourself whether the CEO of the firm's most substantial client would approve of—not *tolerate,* but *approve of*—the way you dress."

As a corollary to my admonitions elsewhere to "Spot the Issue, and Solve It", certain things should *never* be an issue in a professional setting. Clothing, and other matters personal, are among such things. "Correct behavior" isn't applauded. It's *expected*. Don't let this become an issue with *you*.

Think you're giving up a little of your soul?

Well—*News Flash!*—you are. Your idealistic dreams in law school have been sold to pay the price of reality: Student loans. Big houses. Fast cars. New spouses. If you think you're so fantastic that no Senior ought to even breathe a note of derision whatever your Holiness decides to wear...think again.

Still think it's trivial? Can you guess why the military requires uniforms?

If you're truly a fashion rebel...get outta' Dodge. Or, more accurately, get *into* Dodge. Small-town firms tend to be considerably more relaxed, and, for many, more enjoyable.

Fortunately for everyone, business dress changes at a glacial pace compared with its casual cousin. More to the point, clothing is every bit as class-oriented as we like to disbelieve. The higher the fashion— real, not *haute couture*—the less it changes. Remember Cary Grant? Perhaps a *bit* dated, but he'd still pass in today's poshest gatherings.

(In large part this is because he knew how to *carry* himself, which, one more time, is tied with attire.)

You should think of business clothing as a cost of doing business. Dressing the part costs money. Women ought to get stipends for the exorbitant cost of women's fine business clothing, plus all the expected accessories. Write your Senators. (Be careful which ones, though.) For men, if you're spending less than a thousand dollars a year, you are probably underdressed. If you're spending much more than that, however, you're spending foolishly.

Some insist on buying new suits every few months. That's absurd. Better to build a well-tailored, timeless wardrobe. After the first few suits, the combinations of styles rapidly approaches a diminishing-returns excess. Do you really need more than a dozen?

Whatever you're chromosomal affiliation, pay attention to clothing. And—as long as you don't go overboard—don't worry about this expense too much. Besides, you can always save that expensive suit for your inaugural address. (*Gosh*, this is an upbeat book!)

One way of going about it: First, read. Second, make an appointment (when you know you'll be in a particularly good mood) to meet with the top tailor in a nice suit shop. Third, *be* in a good mood. Fourth, have a light snack, rather than a full meal. Fifth, take a long shower. Sixth, dress to the nines in your best business clothing. Seventh, introduce yourself, admit that you're just starting out, but ask to be outfitted *and trained* in the best of businesswear. Eighth, don't be embarrassed. No one is born with a cummerbund.[90] Finally, relax. Most times, they'll be impressed by your interest, and will earnestly help you. If not, leave.

Oh. Treat yourself to a nice dinner afterwards. Shopping for business clothes is serious business, and, if you're doing it right, tiring. Don't forget to wrap that little gift you buy for your SO.

Others offer different advice. Follow your own disposition, but don't let a negative one harm you, here.

---

90 Then again I haven't been at many deliveries of billion heirs. Perhaps this is one of those well-kept secrets of the monstrously wealthy. (I'd hate to be the one on the house staff chosen to clean icky little cummerbunds, though.)

If you're truly strapped by student loans, donations to your twenty favorite charities, or wild imprudence, you *can* dress well for less. It just takes even more attention. One of my nicest (and best-fitting) suits was bought second-hand for less than many designer shirts cost. One of my favorite shirts (a designer needle in the Goodwill haystack) cost twenty-five cents. The satisfaction of dressing well for a *lot* less than others spend is itself a reward.

If you're still in school, this is a good time to start learning about professional clothing. You don't have to spend a fortune, but you can spend some time. (Sticking with conservative colors and styles will go a long way to "enhance" off-the-rack clothing.)

Finally, look around. Junior see, Junior do...a little better.

DRESSING THE PART—JUST IN CASE

You're a scout. Be prepared.[91] For those inevitable mishaps, keep an extra dress shirt (pressed), jacket, and tie, as well as an extra pair of pants (pressed) and shoes (shined), in your office.

DRESSING ALLY

In an episode of *Ally McBeal,* a judge took exception to Ally's exceptionally short skirt. Ally, naturally, was offended at the imperious and obviously sexist view from on high. Interestingly, the subtext seemed to defend *her* position: it was her right to dress as she wished, it had no bearing on her qualities as an attorney, and if anyone was offended, that was their problem, not hers.

Wrong.

Now, I like looking at Ally's thighs as much as (...or lecherously more than) the next guy—which is precisely the problem. A judge, a juror, an opponent, *anyone* in the courtroom...ought to focus on an advocate's arguments, not legs.[92] This is especially fitting given that women's admittance to the bar followed a decades-long insistence on the irrelevance of gender. Were *I* the judge, I would have given her *less* warning before throwing her in jail.

Thou shalt not dress inappropriately. It is immature. It is unnecessary. It is *unprofessional.*

For those who're thinking: *"Geez,* lighten up, buddy—you must not get out enough at night. [True enough.] Our clothing is an *expression* of ourselves. We have a *right* to express ourselves. We have a right to *our* body piercings. You old fogeys just don't get it."

---

91 ...and help little old ladies to cross the street, if you get the chance.

92 Would you feel the same if *Billy* wore cut-offs—even expensively tailored ones? This would never happen, of course, because no male would ever expect to get away with it. (Nor would any but the most seditious want to try.)

No...*you* don't get it.

Youthful exuberance is fine, but it relies on a stable norm against which to rebel. Lose that norm, and *we* lose much more. (What would happen if all of our parents were as anarchistic as you claim to be?)[93]

Know *when* to rebel, and when to accept. And don't be too quick to reject—most norms are *good*—but don't accept a norm blindly. Accept it instead with *insight* to the deeper values being accepted.[94]

Representing your clients is your job. Your appearance—within relatively broad parameters—is part of that job. For the twenty-third time, *this should not be an issue.*

For many, this section raises a straw woman: few lawyers would dare to dress as does she. But for those few who might, the lesson applies with full, undiplomatic force. And the lesson applies to more than skirts:

Dress well, dress neatly, and dress conservatively. If you want to wear a toga (or less) to your weekend soirées...fine. But in the office, as in the courtroom, *Schoolmarm* McBeal is the better model.

SHAVING THE PART

Facial hair. Generally, no...unless you have a slender face *and* it's a liberal firm (i.e., Seniors *and* clients have beards/moustaches).

I had a moustache upon entering the Air Force (a dash of daring-do, or so I thought). The Air Force specifies, in greater detail than you might think possible, the trim specifications for proper facial hair. No matter. Our Flight Leader brusquely announced to the handful of neo-hippie renegades that shaving would commence, post-haste. A few commenced, instead, to argue. *Wrong.* That was neither the arena nor time for individualism. (And even if it were: Knowing that *some* higher-ups wouldn't like it, and that *your* survival is at *their* discretion—which is the better course?)

---

93 Pardon my amusement at the, well...*conventions* of cyclical "rebellion". Each generation—each counterculture—is *insistent* upon its own dress *code.* (If you think not, try a season as a fashion buyer.) The only difference is that whatever the "suits" (parents) wear is bad, and whatever is acceptably defiant—hairstyles, inseams, tatoos, piercings, whatever—is good. Even more amusingly, what is rebellious for one generation becomes stodgy for the next. Thus each generation looks unintendedly to its grandparents for models of rebellion. Fashion cannot be concerned with progress, only with vacillation.

94 For those enamored of "postmodern" philosophy, the unlearned discard of convention: (1) isn't *quite* what they were getting at; (2) is cannibalizing; (3) is a path to annihilation; and (4) if it *is* what they were quite getting at doesn't rise to the level of moronic. As with most revolutions, later and lesser dissidents take a useful insurgency too far—for their own ends—ignoring forces and realities of deeper import.

ARCHIVING THE PART

Keep a camera—digital, disposable, or Polaroid®—in your trunk.

'Never know when it'll come in handy.

ADDRESSING THE PART

Correspondence. If your name is sexually ambiguous (or is downright misleading), either let your correspondee know, or don't be offended by an inappropriate title.

No...that's still not quite fair: you should warn your reader. Sure, this hardly ranks as a high sin, but it's embarrassing to respond in a letter if *you're* not sure whether *Mr.* or *Ms.* is appropriate.[95]

It might look a little funny to add a *Ms.* (in parentheses) before the typewritten "Chris Johnson" below your signature in your first letter to (Mr.) Sue Jones, but it'll be one of those little things that smoothes the legal way between you and Sue.

ESQ.

Many lawyers insist on adding *Esq.* to their names.[96] If your firm's letterhead has your name on it, this is overkill.

If your reader is confused whether or not you're a lawyer, then you're not writing good letters.

It *is* important for your reader to know that you're an attorney, but this status should be conveyed by the letterhead and by your message. To call attention to yourself detracts from what you're trying to accomplish; if intimidation is the intent, it will be seen as—and is—a sign of weakness instead.

Well, perhaps that's a bit much. Still, most lawyers don't even think about this appellation, which always struck me as pompous. In any event, wait until *after* you've passed the bar before affixing this appendage.

---

95 We could, of course, follow the Federation and call *everyone* "Mister".

96 *See* Pinheads, *ante*. Curiously, *Esq.* (short for "Esquire") is *not* exclusive to lawyers. It referred, many moons ago, to *squires*...candidates for knighthood who acted as attendants and shield-bearers for knights. *Esquire* was also the title applied to a knight's eldest son, or later to the younger males in a noble house, whose title passed only to the eldest son. In more modern times, it refers in England to a member of the gentry ranking just below a knight. It has, relatively recently, come to refer to lawyers, both male and female.

One non-lawyer gentleman found himself in court to defend his use of the suffix, and—*Lo and Behold!*—the court discovered to its shock that lawyers have no franchise on the letters. Thus, Ted's impertinence in his and Bill's excellent adventure was simply bodacious, dudes.

Just so you don't get too snotty about it.

Oh, yeah. If you do use *Esq.*, you don't need *Mr.* or *Ms.*

You probably should address *other* attorneys as "Esq." in writing, though. Flattery, though maligned, is one of those helpful social lubricants that smoothes the flow of personal interaction. Even better…it's free, and doesn't leave too bad a taste in your mouth.

DR.

As long as we're on titles, you will almost never hear a lawyer refer to himself as *Doctor*. Just for fun—and lest you assume this is correct—you *are,* by degree and scholarship, a "Doctor".

The Juris Doctor degree follows the completion of rigorous (as if we need to be reminded) post-graduate studies, just as are Ph.D.s, M.D.s, D.O.s, D.D.S.s, D.V.M.s, and so on.

Historically, physicians did *not* have a lock on the title. Indeed, the origin of the word *doctor* relates to teaching (and, more broadly, to scholarship), not to healing.[97] Jealous of the honorary respect shown to university scholars, 18th-century medical schools (particularly Edinburgh, in Scotland) began addressing their graduates as *Doctors,* since, by that time, medical students had (usually) also earned bachelor's degrees, and were thus, the schools argued, entitled to the title that scholars enjoyed.

Guilds lustful of credibility assume the title by fiat, which is generally successful after a few decades of snickering. And, following one of our more petty instincts, the correlation between insecurity and the compulsion to aggrandize with decorations creates constant pressure for the expansion of the ranks of "doctors"…beginning with those jealous 18th-century physicians.

(Trouble is, a title of honor loses its elitist cachet when too many are allowed into the clique.[98])

---

97 Early physicians were learned professors who almost never administered their prescriptions, which would have been beneath their dignity. Also, the early state of medicine was considerably more lax than the clear split now between physicians…and everyone else, including dentists and apothecaries (pharmicists), who originally performed similar medical services. This split has carried forward with continued disdain *among* medical professions: Doctors of Medicine, Doctors of Osteopathy, Doctors of Veterinary Medicine (whose study is every bit as rigorous as "regular" doctors, though diagnosis is somewhat more complicated), Doctors of Chiropractic, and so on. Interestingly (and even more parenthetically), in England many surgeons prefer *not* to be referred to as "Doctor", which they regard as fitting only for lesser medical souls). Only non-doctors think of doctors generically. But all are unanimous in admiration for that spicy granddaddy: Dr Pepper.

98 And, if you'll pardon yet another tangential phonetic rant, *clique* is preferably pronounced "cleek", not "click". As much trouble as the French sometimes are, it *was* their word. (Still is.)

In concert with such lust comes an upping of the credential ante. Legal training, along with others, has expanded over the centuries from a loose apprenticeship—*Psst! Got five bucks for the bar fee?*—to a structured, mandatory, postgraduate gauntlet.[99]

An essential requirement of "real" doctoral scholarship is *original* research of some import: The expansion of knowledge. Although this is stretched by many a Ph.D. candidate today, it is the rare physician who expands medicine (and the not-quite-so-rare-but-still-exceptional lawyer who expands law). Yet, by a perverse twist of time, most now assume that only *medical* doctors are the "real" ones.

This somewhat silly section might even tie into the future status of the law, which, by constant attacks and a beleaguered corps, seems ripe for a flanking maneuver. (Gotta' hand it to physicians, though; they withstood the snickering *early*. It'd be deafening, now.) Still, it'll be interesting to see if titles elevate after the ol' *LL.B.*s die off.

'Til then, *Mr.* or *Ms.'ll* do ya'.

HABITATING THE PART

You will spend considerably more than half of your waking hours with your Junior butt in a moderately comfortable chair in a moderately pleasant office. Fix it up.[100]

This goes to more than narcissism. As you enter your berth each morning and moor yourself with your legal umbilical cord, take a look around. Corny or not, there *is* a connection. Not necessarily a pure cause-and-effect one, but a real one nonetheless. Entering a sparse office each morning reinforces no psychological bond between you and your office, firm, and even profession. Dressing your office to suit your (tasteful) taste changes your outlook over your place in *your* office, firm ... and even profession. Really.

There's no need to keep a decorator on retainer, but do pay some attention. (Taste is an elusive entrée. The store-bought variety rarely pleases others' palates. Better to prepare your own.) Keep it conservative. Professionally framed diplomas in tasteful, not tacky, trimming. (Put a crowbar to your wallet for non-glare glass.) Nice prints, nicely framed. Elegant artwork, if that's your thing.

Less is more. (If you have more than a few, it ain't elegant.[101])

---

99 The United States is unique in its postgraduate law programs; others learn law as undergraduates. Although a bachelor's degree has been required for most of this century, only recently did U.S. schools change the title of the degree from *Bachelor of Laws* to *Juris Doctor* (or *Doctor of Jurisprudence*).

100 The *office,* not your chair or butt, silly. *But cf.* §Exercising Your Parts, *infra*.

101 ... or you're in the wrong line of work. Besides, if advertising (and design) theory helps, unadorned space is as important as the focus of attention.

Avoid the fringes; shock (or *schlock*) art goes unappreciated by an alarming (and discerning) majority. Handsome architectural or mechanical prints for you testosterone-laden chaps.[102] Historical maps are always in style. Later, a standing globe adds a nice touch, if you have the space in your corner (or oval) office.

Classical music or light jazz, softly played, adds refined ambience. (Save Beethoven's Fifth and Tchaikovsky's 1812th for late, late nights, though, when the adrenaline'll come in handy.[103])

Sophistication is appreciated, within reason. (If you've gotta' call attention to it, it ain't sophisticated.)

Keep the school memorabilia to a minimum, and make your office a place that others—particularly Senior others—compliment, even if only subconsciously... and that *you* enjoy.

CLOCKING THE PART

Ever see that old movie, *How To Succeed In Business Without Really Trying*, in which the protagonist pretends to have slaved at the office overnight by dumping old cigarettes over his desk, mussing his hair, and so on?

The good news: you don't have to do that.

The bad news: you really *do* have to work hard. And, if you're smart, you'll *act* like you're working hard, too. Don't be obvious—or obnoxious—but do arrive before your Seniors... and leave later.

Not that you will have much choice with your workload, but this is another of those little, expected reinforcements to justify your place in the scheme of things.

WEIGHING THE PART

If you're overweight, lose it. Regardless of emerging medical evidence, the perception of nearly all to those who are fat goes beyond reasoned dislike. Deeper psychologies are involved. In many, a visceral pity, disgust, and even hatred is raised, like a feared skeleton from one's own darkened closet of mirrors.

Fair or not, society proclaims a near-irrebuttable presumption that fatness is perfectly correlated with laziness, weakness, and a profound lack of intelligence. If you wish to make an issue of it, there are (at least) two ways to think about it: organizationally and personally.

---

102 Now was that sexist prepositional phrase really called for?

103 Don't forget Bach's *Toccata* for Halloween. If, by the way, you don't *like* classical music, well, that's too bad. You're missing one of life's great aural pleasures.

Every group—professional, social, even countercultural—demands an almost theological obedience to its dogma. A member who disobeys is subtly, then more firmly, reminded of the Rules. If uncooperative, he is punished, and, eventually, becomes a heretic to be excommunicated. Weight is not quite so extreme, but it's not *too* far off the mark. Contemporary fashion, both in response to and as a catalyst for societal views, mandates slenderness as the model for success.

Whether you accept it or not, you *will* be judged accordingly. Think about your own perceptions. When you see an obese person, you unlikely assume, all other characteristics of said subject being neutral, that he or she is a neuropharmacologist genius on loan from Oxford. More likely, you assume that he or she is a slob, which is reinforced, as a practical matter, by the unavailability of well-tailored clothing in larger sizes (and by our perception that an amply filled waistline cannot be complimentary). Granted, you might not guess the occupation of every covert neuropharmacologist, but the example is extreme in degree, not principle.

Fat is an easy adjective. Being so probably won't mean your job, if you already have one. It will, however, preclude you from most high-paying ones. And it will affect you, whether by being the butt of jokes, by increasing the hesitance of Seniors to let you roam with clients, or by shortening the fuse that all Juniors face... and likely all three. It shouldn't be necessary to write, but all are antithetical to being regarded as a professional, and, consequently, are a sidetrack on the Junior trail towards partnership. Fair or not, it ranks right down there with bad breath, sweaty palms, and uncleaned vomitus on your eyeglasses from excesses at the firm party the night before.

Regardless how dainty the bite, a fleshy face masticating is seen to be piggish. No matter how restrained the off-hours, nor how energetic the exercise, triple-bacon-cheeseburgers are reserved for ectomorphic athletes. Order accordingly.

Finally, added weight does tax one's physical resources. This only reinforces society's stereotypes. At the risk of sounding like an aerobicized, iron-pumping jock—stereotypes, anyone?—physical fitness *will* do you a world of good.

Enough. A personal note: I've been both fat and svelte in my life. Svelte is better. Unfortunately for me and many others, weight and stress are positively correlated. Both are linked to that odd fellow, genetics. Do what you can.

DINING THE PART

Be on your good-to-best behavior during group outings... even lunches with senior Juniors. (Be cautious, unless you know that *every* person within eye- *and* earshot is a decent sort.) If you really need to let loose—which you *will,* regularly—choose your company carefully.

EXERCISING YOUR PARTS

Practicing law is stressful. In itself, stress is neither good nor bad. In moderation, it attunes your senses for battle. In excess, it overloads them. In short bursts, it brings your abilities to their zenith. Over time, if unbroken by rest, it eats away at those same abilities, leaving only a debilitated shell.

Mother nature wisely enabled us with the tool of stress to handle confrontation with those nastier elements in life. But you must know when to fight and when to recharge. Rest serves an important role. Not only is it pleasant, it *increases* your capabilities when you *do* work. If you are constantly fighting the demons of legal opposition, without a break, you're risking more than you think. Something's gotta' give. It won't be the job.

Stress—intense, unrelenting—feeds into attorneys' short tempers, and thus, indirectly, clients' and society's negative stereotypes of us. This, in turn, heightens the alienation many lawyers feel. At the office or in court, use stress *positively*. Don't fight your nervousness, or tell yourself it's a sign of immaturity. Take advantage of that somewhat nauseating rush of adrenaline...and *do your job*. But set your sights in the right direction. In a legal battle—particularly for an inexperienced combatant—stress is a necessary ally. In a longer battle between stress and you, though, stress wins.[104]

One way to eat some of your cake and have it too: Exercise. Choose something less than torturous, force yourself to stick with it, and you will improve your level of tolerable stress. You will also feel better, physically and mentally. (...And your butt will look cuter, which is, after all, a meaning of life.)

A personal note: I've been both lethargic and lively. Lively is better, if sometimes bothersome. (Someone once said that athletics is life with the volume turned way up. True...but silence is nice, too.)

Whether hyperactivity is genetic or learned, avoid the edges...and steer well clear of couch potatohood.

LEAVING FOR PARTS UNKNOWN

In the wise words of those searching Pythoners: *Run away!*

Take advantage of a Junior ability to go incommunicado. Although it might be difficult to take all of your vacation time: *use it*. You *need* to unwind. As long as you take care to let everyone know what's going on—and document all of *your* goings-on—you'll be able to take off without fear of endless phone calls from the office. As you'll later come to appreciate, this is a luxury few Seniors can afford.

As a Junior, you're not yet quite *that* valuable.

---

104   ...which reminds me of the quip: A heart attack is Nature's way of telling you to *slow down*.

Do leave *some* forwarding information, though. And call in a few times to make sure all's right with the world and firm (...especially if you've left something simmering).

Use your vacation time wisely. Try not to take it all at once. A two- or three-week absence is more than uncomfortably disruptive to your officemates...and it'll skew your billable hours tally. Also, the law of decreasing marginal utility prohibits maximum enjoyment of all that extra time in the middle.[105]

It's better to take two or three one-week vacations (scheduled at regular intervals *after* your annual review). That way, you'll enjoy nine-day frenzies of *non-law* exhaustion. And, if you can, take some three- or four-day weekends. Don't get too comfortable, though; you'll start to question life.

Also, try not to bother your Seniors when *they're* on vacation. Instead, ask another Senior, if you can. If not (unlikely), narrow your question...and make the disruption as short and sweet as possible.

APPRECIATING NEW PARTS

For those who move to a new land: For your near-term sanity and long-term survival...lighten up.

Don't compare your new home with your old one. Don't pine, in homesickness, for your homestead. Enjoy, instead, the benefits your new locale offers, and be big enough to overlook its shortcomings. Every place has unique benefits (...and drawbacks), and every other place is *not* your hometown. Don't expect it to be.

A positive attitude will repay you manyfold and—funny thing— you'll miss your *new* home when you revisit the old.

ASSIMILATING INTO THE PART

And now for a discussion about minorities, and women, in the law. A disclaimer: I decided to practice law in Hawaii in part because of its multicultural environment, and in part because I liked and admired the firm, which, incidentally, had one *haole* name on its marquee.[106] (And, in *direct* violation of the laws of probability, every partner was genuinely nice.) I liked that nearly half of the partners were women. It didn't bother me in the slightest that we male haoles were out- numbered. Thus, my experience might not be completely telling to the

---

105 Okay, so it's not a *real* law. (But don't say that to an economist.)

106 *Haole*, colloquially pronounced "how-lee", commonly refers to Caucasians, which brings to mind yet another wisecrack, in light of a debate in Hawaii about the racial appropriateness of the word: *Haole* is derogatory only when preceded by an expletive.

minority/female legal experience generally. Still, this section will cut both ways. It'll either annoy you...or, more optimistically, make you think beyond the stark views so easily proffered by either side.

Some criticize the law for its exclusion of various outsiders. Stop. Law practice is an equal-opportunity oppressor. It's hard for (and *on*) *everyone*. (This reminds me of a skit on *Saturday Night Live,* in which the tremendously talented Eddie Murphy plays a black guy who goes "undercover" as a white guy...and is shocked to learn that, when around only whites, everything is free. The sad thing is that there's more than a grain of truth—not to the gifts, but to the suspicion that white folks get a free ride. It just ain't so. And it especially ain't so for *poorer* whites.) Don't succumb to the conceit that everyone else is cruising through life. This has only gotten worse: It used to be that neighbors tried to keep up with the Joneses. Now we're all resentful that we can't keep up with the Gateses. It's a losing game, folks.

Similarly, women feel especially harassed. Although this might, in fact, be true, it's equally likely a harassment that's shared among men too. Indeed, most men *expect* a *higher* level of (work-related) harassment, and are in turn expected to "take it like a man".

Woe unto the male who cannot.

Finally, even the genuinely upper-crust have no picnic. Few have a guaranteed slot. (And those who do might not have the *right* one). And even if it is the right one, it's still a long journey. What's important is not what you take in with you, but what you take out...and what you make of yourself, in the process.

Along the journey, many false trails—and thickets of thorny underbrush—are encountered. Perhaps the most hurtful involve race. Everyone is racist, and sexist. Some are just a little; others, a lot. Some is based in kernels of difference. Much is not.

If someone attacks your work or your actions, that's painful, but at least you can fight back, or defend yourself, on a less-than-completely personal level. Anyone who is attacked for who he or she *is,* however, cannot fight back so easily. When the attacks come steadily and stealthily, Vietnam-style, the result is fury...usually directed inward in the forms of self-doubt, depression, and self-destructive adaptation, Vietnam-style.

It is unjust that some are forced to deal with such a barrage of *ad hominem*—no, ad *categorium*—attacks. If this speaks to you, my apologies, as a fellow human, and my sympathies, as a fellow. No one—especially no *new* one—should be forced to withstand an unprovoked, incessant onslaught of venomous indignities. Sadly, such mistreatment—which would, almost reasonably, lead some to assault riflery—is the rule, not the exception. Read the writings of Lawrence Graham, if you're curious...or doubtful. (If, by the way, *you* are guilty of a more-than-modest *-ism,* from whatever angle, knock it off. It's not too far removed from pulling wings off butterflies...or from Adolf.)

Were it that easy, though. One reason this is such a treacherous area is the riddle of intercorrelation, in which several factors, including *but not limited to* racism or sexism, are involved in a predicament.[107] The mixed-motives dilemma. It is difficult—too difficult for most—to separate the legitimate from the wrongfully hateful.

Yet—if this rings a bell—that is part of your job as a lawyer.

Well, that's a neat observation...but what should *you* do if confronted with a hostile environment? First, confirm that the environment is, objectively, hostile. Don't be too sensitive; not all slights are intended...or worthy of federal action. And it's quite possible you're being slighted as a *Junior,* not as...*whatever.*

If you *are* in hostile territory, consider whether you'd be better off fighting or leaving. Be reasonable. In most cases, the latter is preferable; you cannot change others' thoughtless idiocy, and, even if you could, you shouldn't be burdened by the task. Plus, once you're out in the real world, you'll be better able to find better firms, where such gratuitous slurs are unknown, or at least rarer.

As the one who better sees, you'll have to thicken your skin. This might seem unreasonably harsh to those whose skins have already grown densely calloused by piercing insults past, but the fastest way to disarm an opponent is to take away the joy of victory; the more you can be pushed, the more likely will be the pushing. Yes, it's unfair, but another of our human traits is a dislike of those who can't take a joke...no matter how bad the taste of the jokester.

Here's yet another perspective: Regardless of race, creed (does anyone still use this word?), gender, national origin, weirdness, or however else you care to classify yourself, you can also classify the world in two ways: Personal and Professional. What little personal time you still have is your own, and if anyone interferes (...relatives excepted), then you are within your rights (...if not comportment) to tell them to buzz off.

On ever-voracious professional time, however, they own you. Thirteenth Amendment notwithstanding, your butt—of whatever hue or curvature—belongs to them. You're working on *their* time. In the Bad Ol' Days, if you weren't the right color, or if you were an innie rather than outie, you would never have gotten past the gilded reception area. That doesn't make it right; it does make it more understandable. Even more radically, there's a further—valid—perspective: Get that chip off your shoulder. There *is* a responsibility to assimilate into a public persona acceptable to others: legal, social, and other.

This should apply to *all*...not just to the ever-fluctuating plethora of minorities.

---

107 If you've studied calculus, you'll recognize the potential fallacy of co-dependent variables. As always, pun intended.

It is not a matter of pitting the old assumptions of cultural absolutism (which, taken to its logical extreme, creates Nazi Germanies) against the newer idiocy of cultural relativism (which, taken to its logical extreme, *justifies* Nazi Germany). Societies operate—or not—based on the solidarity each member feels for himself within society... and among others. Sins of the sword are perpetuated not out of the *existence* of cliques, but instead by their too-often rigidly exclusive, non-accommodating (and, worse, xenophobic and xenoviolent) nature.

Law and its servants are in a peculiar position in this still-raging debate. We are the gatekeepers of freedom (not idle words, as events have repeatedly proved), and adherents to our own cliquish ways. That, too, is changing. But, as a Junior, yours is not to be on the front lines. It's not a matter of destroying your identity; just put it aside until you survive and gain the abilities to make a difference, if that's your passion.

Take a look again at one of the passages in the Preface: you must adapt to meet your environment as it meets you. Take a look also at the heading to this section. (Unlike contracts law, there's no hiding behind a "Headings" disclaimer.) If you want the goodies that law can provide, then *you* must assimilate into the part, not vice versa.

Sure, society should expand to accommodate all, but the burden is on you, as Junior, to adapt...not the other way around.

Finally, at the risk of politically indecent contrariness, consider that the situation isn't quite so black and white...pardon the almost shamefully unavoidable pun. The disadvantage for most middle-class minorities—which includes nearly all who go on to law school—is no longer universally stark, and is now possibly inverse.[108] If anything, most will bend over backwards to prove their good faith.[109]

---

[108] A 1992 study reported in the *National Law Journal* found that salaries of minority law graduates *outpaced* the salaries of non-minority graduates. Specifically, the median salaries for minorities entering academia were 11.1% higher; for industry, 5% higher; for government, 4.5% higher; for public interest, 10.6% higher, and for private practice, a whopping 17.8% higher. In only one category, clerkships, did parity exist. *Median Salaries,* NAT'L L. J., May 30, 1994 (Special Supplement) (citing the National Association for Law Placement Employment Report and Salary Survey, Diversity in the Legal Community: The Search for Opportunity by Women and Minority Law Graduates, Class of 1992).

[109] If they ask *you* to bend over, however, then you've been presented with a dilemma in which I'm out of my league. However, if you feel after serious contemplation that you face real discrimination or harassment, your better option is, unjustly, the same: *leave.* While you still have the chance. Don't wait until it blows up and you're pounding the pavement. It might not be fair, but *you're* the one hurting, and you may be left with little option but to strike back legally. And as we usually counsel our clients, that's rarely the better option. Unless you can afford—and handle—the title of gadfly, think serious-

MORE SEX

If you happen to be homosexual, advertise that fact with caution. Even sympathetic moderates who, intellectually, are eager to approve will feel uncomfortable when sex is a more-than-subconscious subject. Actually, sex is *always* a more-than-subconscious subject, but, when curve balls are thrown, even the best hitters can miss. And a different sexual outlook *does* qualify as a curve ball.[110]

If you're adamant about your sexuality, you should take a long, hard look at potential employers. You'd fit in in few.

While you're at it you might also take a long, hard look at *yourself*. An in-your-face attitude is offensive, regardless of where *your* face is coming from. Take another look at that sentence just a few lines up: "If you're adamant about your sexuality...."

Notice that I did not write *homo*sexuality. What is unacceptable from a heterosexual should be equally objectionable from a *homo-, bi-, a-,* or *anti-*sexual.

You should be neither ashamed nor proud of *what* you are.[111]

But...discretion *is* a better part of valor. There is a difference between asserting what is fair (...assuming we could agree on that amorphous concept)...and demanding more. Regrettably, those denied are forced to demand more—and demand stridently—in the hopes of getting what is fair.[112]

The trick is knowing when to stop (...which is especially difficult when revenge becomes institutionalized).

The best course for most homosexual folk: keep it to yourself, at least until you've figured out what you need—and what others expect. Take a look around. If you'd feel uncomfortable if the Seniors, or some of them, knew that you're gay, you should think seriously about finding a more accommodating place. Although this can be hard for law school activists, think twice when leaving the nest of academia.

Don't ask, don't tell.

By the way, I happen to be prejudiced *for* homosexuals. I think they tend to be better people, if only because their uniqueness has forced them to confront questions of humanity sooner than most.

Don't be so hard on others, though. Usually, it's a matter of growing accustomed to the different.

Don't chastise: we're *all* under the spell of conformity.

Hey, it's your species, too.

---

ly before taking your case to higher authorities. Sadly, the choice is sometimes between what is right...and what is practical.

110 An editor noted that it was a good thing *this* ball wasn't plural. *Touché.*

111 ...which maxim should apply to all.

112 Worse, fairness is a rather slippery creature; it keeps moving on us.

YOU ARE WOMAN. WHAT'S THAT ROAR?

Geez... still *more* sex.

For my credibility (and personal safety), I must preface the following discussion: I am a feminist. I am also, however, a male who likes females... a *lot.* I like them professionally, and I like them personally. I like them socially, and I like them *socially.*

I like them, Sam I am.[113]

I do not, however, feel bound by the assumptions of either side in the supposed battle of the sexes. Yet the influx of women into traditionally male roles *has* strained our social fabric. 'Twas so much easier when a haircut told you everything you needed to know. (I didn't write *fairer;* I wrote *easier.*) To deny this helps no one.

An important, if difficult, point: Women often handle power badly. Sure, men sometimes handle power equally badly, but usually for different reasons, and, most unfairly, it's not as objectionable. This extra baggage gives women little room to maneuver. Many thus feel compelled to out-asshole the worst male around. For whatever reason, the result is no less unpleasant for those who are forced to work with—or worse, for—femmes from Hell.

Women can be worse than men when in positions of power for the same reasons that junior Seniors are often worse than senior Seniors. Add to this a stress—all too frequently substantiated by thoughtless (or mean-spirited) others—that they're *not* men, and thus somehow must compensate. Sadly, "others" all too often includes other *women.* You ladies have it all over us gentlemen when it comes to internecine warfare.

If *you're* confronted with a hellish femme, try to work your way into another Senior's graces. If that's not possible, or if you *like* her or her line of work, adjust to meet her style. Few are prepared for this, and you might find yourself in a solid relationship if you can persevere where others fade (particularly if her harshness is a front, which is not at all unlikely).

If *you* are a hellish person, you will only cause yourself trouble.

Especially as a Junior, you should not be abrasive. And, even later, it isn't necessary. Really. (A friend—a female attorney—once told me that the worst thing an opponent could do was to be *nice,* which made it all the harder for her to be strict.)

Meanness should be a badge of honor for no one.

Should you be *assertive?* Sure. Indeed, you *must* be assertive as a lawyer...any lawyer. But playing the bitch will cause as many antagonisms as it'll solve (if it solves any). And, if you carry these grudges with you, you'll only be—and make others—miserable.

---

113 Lest my S.O. get the wrong idea, the Marine's motto is mine as well: *Semper fidelis.*

This has little to do, by the way, with the differences between how men and women think. Whether a result of different biochemical wiring, or of very different socialization, men and women *do* tend to think differently. With all due respect, you should think like a man. That's the way the law works, and that's the way our society is organized. And, as someone who's tried—with *very* mixed success—to be the sensitive guy, it's generally a more effective way to handle most of life's hardness. Unfortunately, in law as in life, hardness is the rule, not the exception.[114]

This should *not* imply that "thinking like a man" means acting like an asshole. Rather, it means accepting the world as a fairly cold, impersonal place—especially when money's on the line.[115]

We might, someday, more appreciate women and their way. Until then, keep in mind the ever-vexing dilemma between reality and ideality...and your role, in the former, as Junior.

Yes, the crap that is forced on women Juniors—in addition to the crap that is forced on *all* Juniors—isn't fair, but that doesn't excuse you; everyone gets a cross to bear.

The answer?

Look at those Seniors you admire—of whatever chromosomal affiliation—and *emulate*. (You'll find that the best bosses are demanding yet generous and caring.[116]) What makes some people better and others worse—as Juniors, Seniors, lovers, captains of industry or nations, or anything else—has little to do with genitalia. This is not a *sex* thing; it's a *quality* thing. Excellence is not a gender.

A good lawyer is knowledgeable, careful, swift, and polite.

A good Junior is intelligent, eager, careful, swift, and polite.

---

114 I was thinking of adding a joke about hard laws being good to find, but that may run dangerously close to crossing a ruinous line. *Aw, hell*...where'd that line go?

115 But...a warm nest is not mutually exclusive. Part of the problem is that men and women operate in parallel worlds that only accidentally resemble the other, each with divergent rules, expectations, and (in-)sensitivities. What is expected of (and among) women is often unthinkable, socially, for men...and vice versa.

This doesn't make it right...or wrong. It does make it difficult to even enter the fray without losing one's sense of gender grounding. The point? A little circumspection before you—whoever you are—race about.

116 I was about to write "paternalistic", but thought I should limit my offense quotient at least a bit. On second thought, though, there *is* a difference: *ma*-ternalistic doesn't quite cover it, because the *demanding* part is stereotypically lacking. On third thought, note that "generous and caring" fits our image of women more than it does of men. Yet even a casual study of great (and aggressive) leaders shows this more "feminine" side. Thus, a renewed endorsement of the original premise: both genders have something positive to contribute to good leading, and either is incomplete without the other.

By the way, I happen to be prejudiced *for* women.

I think they tend to be better people, if only because their generally unfavorable position in life has forced them to confront questions of humanity sooner than the unfair sex. But don't be quite so hard on others. Usually, it's a matter of growing accustomed to the different. Don't chastise: we're all under the spell of conformity.

Hey, it's your species, too.

NURTURING THE NEXT GENERATION

Now for the real trouble. (For me, not you.)

Of the Senior women I have known (or known of), few have been good mentors. No, that's not quite right. I'm trying to recall someone who makes that statement true, but I can't.

Of the Senior women I have known, or known of, *none* have been good mentors. ...Why?

Well, although the reasons are understandable, the result for you is no less forbidding. Women face additional pressures of which most men are utterly unaware. Worse, the gender and power dynamics operate differently for women than for men, with a profound impact at the office. This difference is seen not only between women and men, but also among women.

The source of these different dynamics? Allow me to play amateur industrial psychologist: Junior males are no threat to senior ones; only *lateral* fights are necessary. (If there's too great a difference in seniority, the junior male loses...and he knows it. Thus, no contest.) In general, a junior male has no real hope to supplant a senior one. This is the law of the jungle, carbon-based or concrete.

The junior male's hope is to generate a paternalistic bond with the Alpha male (or, at least, with *a* senior male). Why? The lieutenant gains access to things of great value (status and sex) through the boss's reflected power. (The higher the boss, the greater the value.) The boss, conversely, is not threatened by a junior sycophant. Quite the opposite: he *needs* such subordinates to win against *other* senior males, and to maintain his perceived power base. He minds not at all tossing his scraps (social and sexual) to subordinates; as long as he gets first dibs, there's no loss to him—only gain. Males have thus worked out an honest, if cynical, relationship within the male ranks.

Women, on the other hand, are moved by a different dynamic. Senior women *are* threatened by junior ones. They're certainly threatened, sexually, even if the junior female has no intent (or even knowledge) of her bewitching attraction. A woman fights to *maintain* what is hers *within her group of females*.

Worse, women are no longer fighting only for access to powerful males (through which they gained things of value—protection and property); they're now fighting for power, itself.

Senior males face no comparable pressure: they need only fight, occasionally, other *senior* males to maintain what is theirs.

Senior females must fight nearly *everyone*. (Under the civilized rules of the *gentle* male this really isn't true, but it doesn't matter: Women *feel* the compulsion, nonetheless.)

When *you* work for a female Senior (even if you're a male), understand this pressure that women face, uniquely. There's not much you can do about it, but do try to avoid unnecessary battles. You will lose.

FELINE FIGHTING

As a corollary to this problem, women face an especially difficult time *among* women. Pulp fables of the *Lifetime Channel* to the contrary, in the workplace women generally don't get along.

I have known of *few* genuinely positive female-to-female work relationships.

(Again, I think I'm being generous. Perhaps I just don't get out enough, but I suspect my experience is universal. I raise this question in classes I teach, and am greeted regularly with vigorous agreement among women students—especially *older* women students.)

The effect in practice is unfortunate, and unlikely to abate.

Most men get along with Senior men. Most women get along with Senior men. (Sometimes too well.) Most men work fine with, and for, Senior women. It's that last pairing possibility—women and women— that causes the most calamity.

For men, avoid even the *appearance* of challenging a woman's professional competence. (The same is true of a Senior man, of course, but again you'll only create an enemy with a man. With a woman, you might lose valuable *personal* property.)

For women, avoid, as much as you can, even the appearance of challenging a woman's *authority*.

This includes appearing to be too much the ladder-climber. (True for men, too.) I'm dangerously exceeding my sphere of experience, here, so I'll end with just the cautionary note throughout: *be careful.*

PLAYING WITH FIRE

If you happen to be a woman, and you're thinking, in the back of your mind, that you'll get special treatment from a woman (or man) boss... *think again.*

If you happen to be a *man,* and you're thinking, in the back of your mind, that you'll get special treatment from a woman (or man) boss... *think again.*

Senior/Junior relationships are fitful enough without adding yet another extract to the brew. *Using* gender—positively or negatively— is a *very* sharp, double-edged sword. Think again.

PLAYING WITH CLIENTS

A Senior, who was a Junior herself not too many moons ago, once told me of a (male) client who refused to accept advice from—*Gasp!*—a woman (her), despite her obvious expertise. Fortunately, most clients are now light years ahead of that clod.

If you're presented with a similar problem, which will be unlikely as a Junior, go to your Senior for instruction and support. (If you get neither, it's time for you to find a more accommodating place to work.)

PLAYING WITH OTHERS

Sadly, women *will* likely face some variety of sexism, as many of you faced in law school and before. I'm not sure what I can write to help. You have a fine, unfair line to walk. In most situations, you should be nonchalantly, but firmly, above it. Sometimes, however, you'll need to draw upon a reserve of courage you shouldn't be forced to use—to challenge your tormentors.

Go to sympathetic Seniors (the higher up the better), and ask for help. (Most) Seniors aren't callous; this stuff (now) offends them, too. And they're not foolish. As Baker & McKenzie found to its dismay, harassment costs *serious* money.

Beware the quandary faced by all potential losers in law, however: those who sit in judgment must do so on the words of others. Thus, a battle of unprovable verities. Though you're at the disadvantage, you can reasonably expect some support. If not (and perhaps either way), it's time for you to move on.

CRO-MAGNON MAN

If, by the way, *you* happen to be a sexist, racist pig...shame on you. First, you're not that good. Second, you'll find that there are lots of people out there (of all stripes) who *are*. Third, you obviously have no understanding of statistical theory. Finally, it's not fair that you give pigs a bad name.

What'll it take to destroy your provincial and petty (and pestilent) preconceptions? Examples?

Beth Kirby, my flight instructor (...way back when) is an *awesome* pilot. She has an uncanny sixth sense—acute situational awareness—when she flies, and she can *fly* like nobody's business. (She's also dis-armingly *cool*...without even trying.) I'll match her aeronautical skills against yours...*anytime*.

If you're *still* a sexist, racist butthead, and can't think of a *legal* example of a non-*you* who'd kick your behind, intellectually, but who suffered by prior-*you*s, unjustly, read about Ruth Bader's Junior year. I'll match her legal skills, then, against yours, now...*anytime*.

HOMO ERECTUS

A reviewer (who happens to be female) wrote a comment beside my declaration, a few pages back, that I liked that nearly half of the partners in the firm in which I worked were women.

She wrote:

> *Why?* Was it because you liked an environment where you could look at sexy bodies, or because you genuinely find them intellectually stimulating?

Actually, neither.

At first, I wasn't going to dignify the question with a response. As it was posed in earnest and might not be an uncommon thought, however, it deserves an answer.

In indirect reply to the sexy-bodies part, I'm reminded of another Air Force training experience. I was speeding down a corridor in a dorm that housed both men and women Officer Trainees. (Sex is *verboten* during training. If proved, it's a speedy ticket out.) One woman, who happened to be *very* attractive, was bent over scrubbing her floor for an inspection. Her butt was protruding gallantly into the hallway. I remember thinking how odd. Any other time, I'd've saved that image for serious later mental investigation. Under the circumstances and extreme stress, however, it was just another butt.

In more direct reply, I tend to prefer women because it's easier to drop the male-competitive instinct. True, there are other problems, but life wasn't advertised as simple. Perhaps the reason I have little problem working with—or for—women is that I don't even think about it. I respect others for their experience, intellect, and humanity, not status. (Maybe that's why I'm not still in the Air Force.)

I like looking at women.

To steal a line from Jimmy, I too have lusted in my heart.

Yet that has not much to do with proper office conduct, and it offends me—I'm not easily offended—that many, many people can't get these two things straight. I wouldn't object to an offered defense of "sexist shit" in a swift-kick-in-the-balls suit.

Indeed, I think another swift kick appropriate, with all court (and cobbler) costs taxed to the kickee.

Dammit, guys...stop.

And don't deny the problem: *Someone's* doing the harassing.[117]

---

[117] I'm not referring to the latest "hostile-environment" wrinkle, which arguably goes too far. Rather, hard as it is for *gentle*men to fathom, there really *are* sexual *quid pro quo* predators lurking about.

The truly sad reality is that such predation is, on the whole, rewarded.

Look. Appreciate. Copulate.

But keep it all behind a courteous smile. To do more is to expose yourself to serious trouble, as a Junior...and it's disrepectful as hell, as a person.

Like children who only initially can claim innocence to the evil of hurting animals, you owe an intellectual—and moral—duty to look at the world through the eyes of your victim. Part of the problem, granted, is that those who harass tend to believe that their advances are desired (...whether the target admits it or not), or are just made in good fun (...with the hearty hope to get lucky). Go to Hell.

As far as the intellectually stimulating part, I'm again offended by the implied correlation. Women who are intellectually stimulating are no superior to men who are.

SUPPORT

Find someone—preferably a senior Junior or junior Senior—in whom you can confide questions about what you should be doing, how you should be doing it, and how you should handle difficult situations.

This applies to *all* Juniors; *everyone* needs help at first.

And, for perspective, take a look around. The best test is also the easiest: How do *Senior* women (minorities, gays, etc.) fare? Numbers are less important than the *real* test: Are they *treated* well? If there's even a hesitation in your response, find a better firm...or build one.

MORE PERSPECTIVE ON THE NUMBERS GAME

A woman once advised another woman on a law listserv (adding the unsolicited issue of the "glass ceiling" to an innocent question about a joint MBA/JD): "Don't go for the MBA. Very few women ever make senior executive."

Yes, very few women ever make senior executive.

...But very few *men* ever make senior executive, either.

Pause.

In our conceit, we look at our problems through only our own eyes. Too, we sometimes fail to look at all. *Of course* very few women have made senior executive. (And many of those who have have done so through family ties.) This isn't sexist; it's common sensical. Women entered business schools in great numbers only in the past decade or so. It takes *everyone* at least that long—cyber-folks excepted—before even the most promising candidate is a serious contender for a *senior* position. In larger companies, it's a beauty contest (of a very different sort) *and* a lottery...*in addition*.

This assumes, as well, any of a variety of other serious managerial issues that few are willing to discuss, dispassionately.

Perhaps the overcorrected lens of our present sensibilities isn't the best one through which to view this issue. A thousand generations of behavior, both learned and lineal, cannot be so easily liberated.

Perspective.

All together now:

Lighten up. If you look too hard for something, you'll too easily find it.

— 8 —

Dancing with Lawyers

Whatever you might think you'll get away with in the law, you won't avoid dealing with other lawyers.

THE SLOW DANCE

When assigned a project, you will often be matched with a Junior counterpart from the other, evil side. This is a fairly nice arrangement, as you both can stumble about without too much fuss.

Just as often, however, you'll find yourself up against a seasoned opponent. Through such trials by fire, you'll learn much…and you'll learn it quickly. For your client and for yourself, be on your toes, and don't allow yourself to get schnookered.

Once, when I was *very* junior, I had to fill in for a litigator who was ill. It was a silly little hearing for a (second) default judgment on a commercial dispute that had festered for *much* too long. In court, I was approached by another attorney, who announced abruptly that his client was ready to settle. I shoulda' smelled a rat.

A down payment was generously offered. *My oh my*. The case had become Kafkaesque in its absurdity. Not having the slightest idea what to do, I excused myself and called the office for instructions.

"Fine," said my Senior, "Get a check."

I returned to find opposing counsel disappearing…but not before saying, over his shoulder, *"Oh,* go ahead and enter my appearance, and we'll take care of it. *Bye."*

Uh oh. What should I do? The docket was passing quickly, and our case was almost up. *Our* client was paying for this. What should I *do?* I wasn't sure whether it was appropriate to…*what?* Just appear and let the other side hang? (*Could* I?) Or be the nice guy, and tell the judge all was right with the world and our clients?

Being the nice guy, I called his office later to ask about the promised payment. The, er…gentleman wouldn't even return my calls.

Suspendatur per collum.

If you find yourself in a similar situation, which you likely will in some way or another, find the strength to say "…I don't *think* so."

Never again. OK, I'm calming down. For everything you do: document, document, document. When in doubt, *write it down*. Document your work. Document your phone calls. Document your conversations. (Anal retention is a solid asset, here.) Create a paper trail for yourself and for those to follow. It will improve your lawyering, and it will cover your tail.

A quick memo to the file, at a minimum.

Nothing's worse than staring at a piece of paper...and not having a clue as to why you did it that way. (This happens more often than we might care to admit.)

When in doubt, *explain it.*

You will rarely be faulted for being *too* deliberate. When you make changes to a draft, send a redlined copy, with comments in a cover letter. Eventually, you'll not need to make quite so many changes, because you'll get it right sooner. Until then, assume that the other side has forgotten every word of your last conversation, and needs a fresh reminder of why you did what you did. Also, (Senior) others who weren't privy to your discussions will pass judgment—or not—on your work. Let them in on your reasoning.

(Don't be condescending, but do recap: "It's my understanding that your client's primary concern was *x*. Our client has addressed/is unable to address...." "To confirm our understanding, I have incorporated the following: (1)...; (2)...; etcetera." And so on.)

Respond.

Don't let a letter, fax, or voicemail lie fallow. It's amazing (and appalling) how often lawyers simply ignore correspondence (a word that implies reciprocity). That's a sign of sloth, and it's not a good way to conduct your practice. Respond *promptly* to incoming messages, even if it's to say "I am unable to respond to this right now, but I haven't forgotten about you. I'll get back to you as soon as I can."

And then, darnit, get back to 'em.

When in doubt, *consult.* Don't hide unpleasant news from Seniors. (Or, later, from clients.) Let them know what's going on, so that they can direct your next move. This is no professional intrusion; it's wise lawyering. And it's your job.

THE TANGO

This is the slow dance...after a few years' lessons. By then, your projects will have become a little more demanding, and so will you.

When your client's position requires that you hold fast...*hold fast.* Better attorneys learn to use their creative talents to maneuver out of *I-Wanna'-Win-You-Gotta'-Lose* predicaments. True, sometimes there's no escape. More often than not, though, there is. And, even when not, *how* you handle a hard-line position is almost as important as the position. Generally, let 'em know, but don't rub it in. They're not stupid. They can grasp a firm stance, and respond accordingly. Add unneeded baggage, and you might just force them, psychologically or really, to reciprocate in kind.

Play it *cool* with other lawyers. Don't let it get personal. This is just one aspect of *professionalism,* and it will reward you tenfold once you get the hang of it. Honest.

THE TWO-STEP

Sorry, this section is for Texas practitioners only. Unfortunately, our market research indicates that this group lacks sufficient after-truck disposable income to warrant its own section.

THE *LAMBADA*

A friend once wrote:

> Thane, my man, no offense, but you have not the makings of a trial lawyer. You have no instinct for the jugular. You gotta' go for the bastard's throat. Only if he puts up a good defense, or manages to get *his* teeth close to *your* throat, do you become reasonable. Otherwise, it's kill, kill, kill.

In unfairness to the writer of this passage, I'm splitting his words to make two points.

You will encounter gunslingers in your career. You must learn how to sling back. If your opponent is playing hardball, either because his client wants him to or because that's his M.O., then, by all means, reciprocate. *No*...more than that. You *must* reciprocate. To do less is to do harm to your client.

You need to fight—*Fight!*—for your clients. That's the way our system, for good and bad, is organized.

But that's different from being professional. You can be assertive, without being rude. You can be effective, without being conniving. You can be successful, without being Machiavellian. You can be *good,* without selling your soul.

An essential reality—and criticism—of advocacy is the importance in our judicial dispensary of the advocate. Your client *relies* on you. If *you* suck, *he* loses. You might feel not-so-bright, but it's *his* case. And it's a hard pill for him to swallow that the outcome relies as often on your skill as it does on Lady Justice.

One client's Rambo litigator is another's zealous representative. This will always be a dilemma in law practice. Yet zealous does not equal discourteous...or dirty. What's important is that you not be a hardass with other attorneys just because you *like* being a hardass (...or, perhaps worse, because you're on a crusade).

Rather, know *when* to be tough. It is more to your client's interest if you have the *capacity* for attack-dog lawyering, but know *when* to release the beast.

Older lawyers are better at this, either because they're running low on piss-and-vinegar, or because they've mastered the difference between the flanking maneuver and its heavier (...and less friendly), frontal-assault cousin. Heavy artillery isn't needed for every battle, and, worse, friendly fire isn't a good way to go down.

Lawyers get a bad rap—deservedly so—for being too legalistic. As a corollary to the above admonition to do battle (when appropriate), learn when to use the light touch.

Especially when dealing with non-lawyers in positions of authority over something you want (who almost always can give you what you want...if *they* want), go easy unless you're *forced* to do otherwise.

Remember the human element in the law. People are people, who act according to motives not clear even to themselves. When pushed imprudently, they'll as likely dig in as give in. This is a lesson freely forgotten come wartime; morale is a difficult beast to destroy...and an even more difficult one to master.

For now, accept your marching orders from your Senior: Don't get carried away on your own. Even in a metropolis, you'll bump into the same professional adversaries again and again...and again.

Keep the gratuitous pissing to a minimum; in confined spaces it tends to splatter. (And, yours isn't the only urinary capacity.)

THE LAW

At the same time you're learning to deal with bosses, colleagues, secretaries, staff, salesmen, clients, and opponents, you cannot take your eyes off the ball. You must *dedicate* your early years to learning the actual rules under which lawyers are supposed to operate.

You must learn *The Law*. Some attorneys—*Gasp!*—make it up as they go along. Some attorneys *really don't* know the law. Period. Or perhaps they don't care. Either way, this makes your job both harder and better. Harder because you'll end up fighting about nonsense, and because your clients (...and their money) will be stuck in the middle. Better because, if you *do* care, you'll (eventually) do right by your client, and you'll do very well, by yourself.

First, *learn the law*. Confirm the rule and issue at hand. Then, *stand your ground*. If you can, leave the other side a face-saving out. Better to serve your client than to make a gratuitous point. (You can file for sanctions and a disciplinary hearing, later.) In the meantime, keep your *client's* interests foremost, and don't let the other side get away with what other sides shouldn't get away with.

THE LETTER CONTINUES:

> And I'm going to kill that son-of-a-bitch [another lawyer], figuratively speaking. He really fucked [a mutual friend] over. She and [her infant twin children] wouldn't be in the predicament they're in if he'd just done his fucking job. I will not forgive him for that. And I will not let him walk away. He's gonna pay. Simple as that.

The lawyer who is the object of the writer's ire deserves each ounce of venom. The former had been retained for his (supposed) expertise, which the latter lacked. Yet when the "specialist" screwed up—on a case he *wouldn't have had,* otherwise—it reflected badly on the generalist, who had set the secondary representation in motion. Guilt by association, and highly damaging to the generalist's reputation with his (former) client and (still former) friend.

Finding a good lawyer—like finding a good physician, dentist, or mechanic—is chancy enough under normal circumstances, but being in the middle, as a peer professional, heightens both an awareness that something's wrong...and an anger that it doesn't have to be.

The specialist had committed malpractice; he had *knowingly* placed his new client—and her children, (very) premature twins—in a grave situation; he had, by his representation and by his acceptance of her money, precluded her from seeking other help; he didn't seem to appreciate the non-rainmade gift thrown his way; and, generally, he didn't seem to care.

A DISH BEST SERVED COLD

This brings a sad, sad feature of our humanity to light, made all the sadder by our ubiquitous presumptions of righteousness: We cannot feel others' pain.

Worse, enough of us don't care.

After a great deal of thought, I have come to an unpleasant—but, I think, inescapable—conclusion: Unprovoked violence must be dealt with with greater violence.

We do ourselves a tremendous disservice by disbelieving that we are animals...and are able to rise above our instinctual emotions only irregularly and with great distraction. Worse, the beast tends to rise quickly, and often.

In the law, you should give the benefit of the doubt...the *first* time. You should presume reasoned intentions, and act accordingly.

But, if proved wrong, you must respond in kind, *squared*.

Again, he sums it up better than I:

> It's like the [choose the ethnic cleansing/zealotry flavor of the year]:
> You try to reason with them, you appeal to their humanity, their com-
> passion, and they keep raping, maiming, executing, etc., etc. So you
> finally just blow the assholes away and be done with the problem.
> I tried the Nice Guy approach with that prick, and he didn't even have
> the courtesy to answer any of my several letters to him.
>
> I was not trying to make the point that only those who were Dober-
> mans in a previous life have what it takes to be good trial lawyers. But
> once the fight is on, being able to transform oneself into a Doberman is
> the only way to deal with the problem—and one has no choice.

RECASTING THE LESSON

I once learned fencing, in college. The instructor made much of the various rules of chivalrous engagement, and I did try to stay within the bounds of proper play. During one of our final matches, I played a ruffian, who cared not for the finer points of the game.

I held my own for a point or two, and then began to fall behind. He continued to disregard the rules, and score. In human form, I became angered, and matched him—and more.

I won... and earned a *B* in this minor collegiate battle. Indeed, the instructor was so disappointed at my civic debasement, she lowered my grade for the entire (one-credit) course.

Should I have remained the "good" player—and lost—or should I have allowed my anger to help me win?

This theme is persistent: In life, in poetry, and in movies involving stars and wars. (The urge among screenwriters for the happy ending is relentless, and false.) It's one thing to ponder this for a (relatively) meaningless college course; quite another for a *client.*

When confronted with aggression, you will have the same choice. I would like to recommend that you take the high road, but, in good conscience, I cannot. When confronted with aggression, you must push back—*hard.* And you must let the other side know that there's more where that came from. (This is a *tremendous* benefit with a firm, as the implied "threat" has already been laid.)

And you must be prepared to *back up your promise.* This goes to the much maligned (and equally effective) geopolitical doctrine of "mutually assured destruction"; all hope rests with the *threat,* for beyond that awaits nihilistic, sweeping demise.

But, to the more difficult question: Should you respond *in kind?*

My inclination is to write *"Of course not!"* You *can* be an effective, tough—yet gentle—advocate. And the gutter is a dirty place. I cannot answer this for you. And I wish the temptation weren't so seductive.

Be careful down there. [118]

---

[118] I was bemused, and dismayed, at the beginning of a criminal law course. (The professor had written the text, which in its pro forma explanation of criminal punishment had pooh-poohed the role of retribution.) Retribution is, sadly, among the *strongest* justifications for punishment. (Not in itself, but in recognition of human nature and, more precisely, human response.) The other reasons range from wishful thinking to disingenuous. Deterrence, for example, *cannot* be a rationale for *any* specific punishment; one cannot be punished for the effect on others. It is, instead, an aside benefit, generally.

This aside rant is notable mostly because these two sections run against the feel-good impulse among "civilized" folk. Civilized, that is, until somone's pounding on *your* door.

This section, in fairness, raises solemn questions far beyond the scope of this book. Nonetheless, you cannot allow your client's interests to be harmed by your refusal to accept reality, or respond to it.

DEFENSIVE PRACTICE

In all of your work, you should be aware not only of how your actions will appear...you must be able to *prove it*.

Be aggressive in your maintenance of records, and in creating a paper trail in the first place. Yes, it is a diversion, and yes, it is inefficient. But it is also a reality of practice, and the more you incorporate defensive tactics into your practice, the less hazardous will it be. (Just picture a judge asking whether the other side knew *x,* and your whiny response: "But your Honor, I *told* him over the phone!")

This applies to everyone: to your opponents, to court folk, to your own client. Not that you should be suspicious of motive; simply that you protect your client and yourself.

This applies equally to dealings with courts. One litigator friend was involved in a drawn-out family law case, in which everyone seemed dissatisfied, including the court. The case was going badly, and he was worried about preserving his options for appeal. At one point, he called a Master in the Field, who asked: "Did you get a certified copy of the docket sheet?" *Hmm*...why would he need to do *that?*

Well, anyone in the court with access to the file—or friendly to the opposition—might have altered the docket sheet, or back-dated something that would later be crucial. (Guess what? It *happens.*)[119]

If it *were* to happen and he could *prove* it, that would be embarrassing to the offending party, and more importantly, it would preserve his client's case. It'd be separate grounds for an appeal, if need be. Quite likely, it'd be a fast win. *Without* proof, he (...and his client) would be dead. End of story.

Practice defensively.

PROFESSIONAL RESPONSIBILITY...*ONE MORE TIME*

You *will* be the defendant in a malpractice suit. That oughta' scare, well, something out of you.

Unhappily, it's probably true. Legal malpractice is a growing field, made all the more attractive by the bounty of legal mistakes out there...and by wronged clients' growing impatience.

Yes, *all* professionals commit some malpractice. It's part of the joy of statistics. It's also part of the risk of playing an uncertain game with imperfect players and complicated rules where the objective of the other side is to prevent everything you want. To paraphrase Abe, you can fool some of the risks all of the time, all of the risks some of the time, but never all of the risks all of the time; in a certain percen-

---

119 ...and not necessarily for bad reasons. Sometimes, it's an innocent oversight, or a clerk going the extra mile. Still, it wreaks havoc with fair play, and, if you're on the losing end, it won't seem so fair even if it is.

tage of cases, something's bound to go wrong. It's also front-loaded, which means that Juniors, not surprisingly, are prone to greater trouble. Thus, few Juniors have unsupervised, malpractice-breeding contact with clients, and fewer treat live clients carelessly.

Still, there is a difference between inexperience—which afflicts us all—and malicious indifference, which requires a special breed. Inexperience is tempered with supervision. (This is yet another advantage of working for an established firm, where Junior can draw upon the experience of the best in the business.) Make sure your Seniors know what's going on...particularly if you suspect that you're on thin ice. Though it might cause as much trouble, an honest mistake is easier to answer for...and less *likely,* if truly honest.

If you're guilty of malicious indifference—or uncaring greed—you deserve armpit nests swarming with the fleas of a thousand sickened camels. There's just no excuse for that attitude or behavior.

One of the many reasons we are so disliked as a profession is the relative impunity with which we've had license to screw unto others. And, as anyone who's been on the receiving end knows, it ain't pleasant if it ain't consenting.

Our profession has only belatedly begun to deal with malpractice. Cynically, it's been just enough to keep the pressure off.

The legal profession is, now, where the medical profession was a few decades ago. Still, the pressure's there—and growing—to set a few examples. Don't be one of them.[120]

As clients become less forgiving and the law grows ever more complex, so too do our duties. Although it might be churlish to complain that higher standards will now be applied—*Gee, we'll actually have to follow the rules*—than were applied to our predecessors, that *is* what is happening. The (mis)use of rules designed for honest mistakes to instead cover malevolent behavior is tolerated less and less.

The danger in cheating—which is what bad lawyering is—lies not only in the (im)moral, but also in the human: The first time you cheat you might feel the guilty twinge of a receding conscience. The next time, he recedes further. After a while, it becomes easier to ignore him altogether. Worse, cynicism and hypocrisy give chase, and run dark and deep. Finally, you get to the point where you feel *entitled* to the proceeds, to the power to inflict harm on others who get in your way, to deeply resent any challenge.

---

120 You might even begin to empathize with physicians, who've been under lawyers' watchful scrutiny for a while. It's especially difficult for a professional—who's *used* to being in control—to suddenly find himself at the mercy of hostile plaintiffs in a less-than-pleasant system. As physicians make lousy patients, lawyers make for mischievous defendants. More seriously, physicians are, on the whole, better at their craft than we are at ours. It's been easier to *hide* legal malpractice, but that doesn't excuse us.

For some, it's a reliance on the incompetence of *other* lawyers who don't care. Never-ending battles of mediocrities. For some, it's a matter of (not) getting caught. For you, it should be a matter of relying on the experience—and vigilance—of Seniors to minimize the dangers of your own inexperience...and susceptibility to the seductive powers of the darker side.

I once cheated. Ninth grade. Algebra. I'd blown the test off, and like other JDs (*Juvenile Delinquents*), I looked afar for the answers. I wasn't caught, but what struck me, as a practical matter (the cheatee was no Steinmetz): I would've done better had I figured the test out on my own. Either way, my grade was deserved.

Just to reinforce a little professional pensiveness, note that the lawyer in the passages above—unlike most who do the same—is in a world of hurt because of his choice to cheat the wrong client.

Molesters are the least favored among prison populations. Beware whose interests *you* molest.

Less flippantly, don't take advantage of your clients...even if you know that they'll never know.

Integrity.

ETHICS

The vast majority of Junior projects are mundane to the point of stupor. Rarely will you encounter a serious ethical problem. If you've kept your nose clean, the world will spin about on its axis just fine, birds will sing in the trees, and luxury car dealers will offer their wares with ever such broad smiles. On occasion, though, you might stumble across an ethical landmine.

First, confirm that the situation is truly as serious as you suspect it to be. The world is a scary place to a Junior; higher-order judgment on ethical matters is almost asking too much, too soon.

Yet the law—and the Bar—*do* ask.

OK, now you're sure something's amiss. Know this: you're in trouble. As a Junior, you have professional authority in theory...and little maneuvering room in practice.

Do not pass **GO**. Do not collect $200.

At best, a disciplinary hearing is embarrassing, time-consuming, and expensive. (...Or so I'm told.)

Ominously, the net is expanding. The arrogant rule that applied to the professions—arduous to enter, but *laissez-faire* once in—was unwise, and is increasingly unacceptable. Add to this a nervousness Seniors now feel over the deep-pocket theory applied to *them,* and you've a recipe for professional abandonment...and a personal nightmare.

Plus, the institutional interest in upholding the face of the guild—protecting bad lawyers at the expense of (expendable) clients—isn't interested in you, anymore (...except as an accessory).

You still have your responsibilities, though.

Ask the offending party, as innocently as you can, what's going on. Don't overreact, or threaten.

Do *not* violate your duties, or go outside the firm or to the client. That's a *certain* route to trouble. Instead, inform a Senior.

Note the word *inform*—don't screech Chicken Little's line. Your job is to confirm that your Seniors know what's going on.

Document your actions, with memos to the file *at a minimum*.

Keep copies for yourself. If you're truly worried, then have copies notarized, mail them to yourself, certified, and hold them, unopened.

(The glorious part of lawyering is the realization that just because you're paranoid doesn't mean they're not *really* out to get you.)

Prepare a new résumé. Prepare to leave, preemptively. Chalk the experience up to...experience.

And live to fight another day.

9

Dancing with Clients

All power in the Firm is related *directly* to clients. Don't kid yourself. Whether they're honest about it or not (...though few are shy about acknowledging their billable trophies), Seniors are rewarded for their clients and the money each brings in. Not surprisingly, your exposure to clients is limited during your Junior years. Still, you should prepare yourself for this part of lawyering. For some, it's the best part.

RESPECT

In the past, many lawyers—perhaps the majority, even—started their professional lives solo. They hung out a shingle in a small town, or perhaps a small city (firms were lower on the horizon, then) and set about the arduous task of building a law practice. They learned, after a few years of paying rent on a small office, with only the occasional walk-in at first, the true *value* of a client. Most did other work, including odd jobs, to support their families until they could build their practice and reputation. Today, that scenario is obviously the exception, rather than the rule. Though you won't have the hard-knock reasons to value your clients as did your predecessors, you should value them just as highly, in any case. A law practice—and the clients upon whom such a practice depends—deserve your *profound* appreciation.

Your client is not your toy. Nor is he your possession.

As I write this I know that, cynically, clients *are* notches on lawyers' Mont Blanc pens...and many lawyers treat them as such. We're condescending, officious, querulous, snobbish, boorish, and expensive. These are among only the main reasons people don't like lawyers.

What other response would you expect?

Your client *is* your responsibility. Remember the law of Agency: What you do—and how you act—on behalf of your client *affects* your client. A client is known to others as an extension of his lawyer. You. If you're a jerk, then so is he. Again, don't punish your client with a thoughtless, steamroller approach to the opposition.

Contrary to what some lawyers seem to relish, your client's interests are not best served by unthinking attack-dog tactics. Instead, think about your *client's* interests, and mold *your* approach to fit *his* needs, not vice versa.

You must *care* about your clients. If not personally, then professionally. This requires some level of commitment beyond mere competence. Most clients go to their lawyers in fear of their ignorance, in shame for their problem, and with resentment, however unintended, over the uneven relationship. All too often, this resentment is roundly deserved by lawyers who do not care even to conceal their contempt. (Not that it would help; contempt is a hard beast to tame.)

This is worsened by a fundamental difference between client and attorney: to you, it's just another case. To them, it's likely one of the most important events in their *lives,* if not *the* most important.

You've little to be contemptuous of. Clients are regular folk, living regular lives, and making all the regular mistakes that we'll all make for as long as we're here. Even sophisticated clients sometimes make foolish mistakes. You must guard against the tendency—to which many lawyers succumb—of treating them all like children.

REVERENCE

As a corollary to the clients-are-everything sermon, tread carefully around clients. (This is rarely a problem for Juniors, but you mustn't let down your professional guard, even after you've established a good working relationship.)

You need not, initially, gather your own clients. But—here's the danger—if you do *anything* to endanger a Senior's hold on a client, *well*…there's no happy ending to that story, for you.

Your efforts must support your Seniors' and you must strive not to cause offense. Thus are made the dreams in which all therein live happily ever after.

REVERENCE II

As a corollary to the above corollary, maintain a professional balance around clients. Be respectful always, but subservient never. Some clients treat their attorneys as lowly minions, and will expect you to play the role. Decline, politely but firmly. You are there to serve, but not to kowtow.

It is important that your client respect *you*. This is an issue with some clients, and it raises serious professional issues beyond the scope of this book. (This is of increasing relevance in the increasingly competitive climate firms face vis-à-vis *holding onto* clients.)

First, follow the lead of your Senior. (One odd benefit to difficult clients is that the *Senior* is usually equally frustrated; this is a good chance to build a firm, sympathetic relationship.)

Second, honor your own professional role.

This can be tricky, but you will likely earn *their* greater respect if you stick to your professional guns (in those few cases where the law *clearly* goes against what your client wishes), rather than rolling over. Remind them that you work *for* them—it's your solemn obligation— but that the courts and regulators (and prosecutors) do not.

And it is *they* you both must ultimately please.

REVERENCE III

How about a corollary to a corollary to the first corollary? (...And you thought you'd avoid the third degree.)

If you are *certain* that your client wishes a bad legal strategy, stand your ground. (Again, after serious consultation with a Senior.) But first, you must be *absolutely certain*. This you should not be.

"No" comes too easily to a lawyer's lips. It's a bit harder to figure out how to get to a *different* "Yes".

A client cannot expect you to violate the law—nor should you comply, even by omission—but he *can* expect you to rummage through the many, many rules hidden therein to figure out an alternative that accomplishes the same goal. (This is one advantage of doing at least the occasional plaintiff's work, as it forces you to be more creative.)

The practice of law inculcates an attitude that seeks to *derail,* rather than set right. Young lawyers especially find it easier to see a dozen reasons why a case should be lost, rather than the *one* reason why it should be won.

Re-admit *common sense* into your analysis—let it tell you where justice would lead—and then figure out how to achieve that outcome. Your mantra should be *"Constructive* Advice", not mumbling along as the legalistic naysayer. Figure out the *result* your client wants (sometimes obvious, sometimes not) and think your way through the alternatives. After all, that's what the law is all about. (And that's what will cement a strong relationship with those clients who count.)

RELATING TO CLIENTS

Most lawyers are condescending toward their clients...even if they don't mean to be. Not only have you no right to be condescending, you have an obligation (and will be rewarded) for being considerate.

It's no mystery: People like...*what they like*. Some clients like the soft touch; others like it hard. Some like to be kept informed of every detail; most prefer stealthy results. Some like every facet explored; most want the job done fast and cheap.

Deal with your clients the way each would like to be dealt with. Pay attention...not only to the details of your clients' cases, but also to the details of your *clients*. If they are bored (...or glance nervously at their watches and peek with concerned frowns at their bank statements), stop ranting about odd precedent from another circuit. If they are impassioned, lend them your (expensive) ear. If they are curious, explain the law...carefully. But don't talk down to them.[121]

If they're...*whatever,* model yourself to fit *their* needs, rather than railroading them with yours.

---

[121] If you *really* know the law, you should be able to explain portions of it in less-than-coma-inducing bites. Make it interesting. It *is*.

LISTENING TO CLIENTS

Learn how to listen. *Sure, sure...* you already know how to do *that.* After all, you've got ears, right?

Wrong. Listening is a skill not easily *developed.* Rather than focusing on what others are trying to convey, we unthinkingly filter their words through our own, dissonant translators. And we rarely turn off our internal voices, each begging to be heard.

How many times have we each heard *"You just don't understand!"* or *"You're not listening!"* (...especially from those closest to us)?

Well, often it's *true.*

Few concentrate, intently, on the words that are said, the context in which they're spoken, and the manner in which they're uttered.

Listening—*truly* listening—is hard work.

The majority of your interaction—say, fifty to ninety percent—should be spent listening to, not lecturing past, your clients. The exception is where you and your clients deal with others, in which cases you will (usually) be your clients' knight. When alone, however, you're their counselor.

Act as though you *want* to be there, to *help* them—not as though you're doing *them* the favor. (For the fifty-fifth time, it is *they* who are paying your mortgage...although that shouldn't be the main reason you care.) Show courtesy to *everyone,* regardless of age, gender, or "official" rank.[122] Learning to deal courteously with those from *all* walks of life is a signature of the most successful members of any profession. If you find yourself treating those from lower walks poorly, stop. It *will* trip you, one way or another. (If *you* are treated poorly by someone against whom you have no immediate recourse, how freely are you going to vent your rage when you *do?*) You should not be nice because you *have* to, and not even because it makes your job, and life, easier...but because it makes your job, and life, *better.*

Your clients are more than billable units. Most are individuals—untrained in law—who, when they need legal help, also need more. As their attorney, you're emotionally detached from their problems, which, you can be assured, hit close to home, to them. This is an essential element of lawyering, but it's also cause for distress when you fail to relate to your clients' extra-legal needs. Most are *scared*...just as we *all* are in the dentist's chair. No one likes the feeling of powerlessness in anticipation of over-imagined torture, even if we know it's for our own good. Clients can be halting or misleading (or both), their stories held back by makeshift emotional weirs of hesitancy and embarrassment...or gushing unimpeded through floodgates opened wide by an urgent desire to tell all.

---

122 You wouldn't like the ending of the story of the attorney who was rude to the secretary of the Chairman of the firm's biggest client. (Although, again, that shouldn't be the main reason you care.) *Oh, yeah...* she was his wife.

The Chinese word for *listen* (pronounced "ting") is comprised of the character components representing the eyes, ears, heart, and mind. Use *all* of *your* senses.

聽

Be patient. Be sensitive. Be comforting. Be *interested*.

Find out what they *really* want. Find out what they really *need*. Find out what is negotiable and what is not. Figure out how much hand-holding they will expect.

Don't cut them off. Don't look at *your* watch. Don't answer the telephone. (Your secretary should know that only God gets through when you're with a client; the Pope—and Rehnquist—can wait.[123])

Do *lead* the conversation. When ferreting the facts, ask careful, even purposely uncomprehending but always non-threatening questions (...*à la* Columbo). But don't dominate, and don't worry too much about this, now. It's unlikely you'll be exposed to more than the occasional client, but you can perfect your skills in listening to *Seniors*. (Beware. Some Seniors are among the *worst* listeners: to them, everything's so repetitive—and their hourly rate so rapacious—they sometimes race off hastily in a direction the client might or might not have wanted. Don't imitate.)

At the end of the conversation, make sure that you're both operating from the same manual. Rephrase the other person's statements, to confirm your understanding and task.

Do not focus on the client's mistakes. Most, oddly enough, don't like that. More worrisome, it's easy to slip into an "If only you had done *x*...." routine. That's an *invitation* to an ethical, perjurious quagmire. (What do you do if your client calls back and says *"Ya' know,* maybe I really did remember the facts differently...."?)

Look *forward,* instead. Think of solutions, not recriminations.

Before you become annoyed, or angry, at another's words, confirm the *feeling* behind them. This is especially important if the speaker is from a different culture (or sub-culture) or circumstance. At the same time, consider the effect of jokes...or even off-hand comments.

(For those who've seen Ally McBeal and think the "Smile Therapy" of The Biscuit odd...*it's not a bad idea*. Keep the option of friendliness alive; you'd be surprised at how often a self-effacing comment, with a broad smile, will resuscitate a stalled or even poisoned negotiation. Emotional amnesia can be a powerful negotiating tool.)

In all circumstances, you'll want to maintain an even, courteous, *professional* demeanor.

For every lawyer...try your hand at poker: It's good preparation for this ceaseless demand of our craft. You might also read *Sun Tzu*.

Be *aware* of your approach to the other side: this is crucial, and a ham-fisted advance will almost always serve your client poorly.

---

123 If God does call, mention to your client, afterward, that he shan't be charged for the diversion.

Keep in mind both the other side and your own. Even experienced business clients, who in their own worlds command others without challenge, are uncomfortable in their role as the needful, ignorant client. Even if not irritable, they'll be annoyed at the distraction of it all.

(They will quite likely treat law, and you, as a "black box"—a fixed cost to be assumed away. The downside is that their expensive box had better *work*.)

As an aside, most business folk *love* to discuss their trade.

Don't cut them off. You can learn much by listening, and they will appreciate your interest. Too, this industrial knowledge will make you a better attorney, for them and for others to follow.

In every case, pay attention. The client/attorney relationship is just that: a *relationship*. Like any other, it requires effort—serious, *personal* effort—to start, to keep... and to weather the storms.

Through it all, you must *care*.

THE UNGRATEFUL CLIENT

Once upon a time, a lawyer met his client at the airport, just as she was about to board for her first-class seat. This lawyer had called her, several times, to remind her to drop by the office to sign the papers she had requested. (Oddly enough, as these things go, these were very much to *her* favor.)

She never did drop by. It seems she couldn't be, well, *bothered*. On the last try, the exasperated young lawyer learned that she was leaving for an extended trip; if the documents were to be signed, there was only one way to do it. *Funny thing*...the client was not filled with joyous appreciation to see her attorney rushing, with notary in tow, to greet her at the departure gate. Nor was she particularly pleasant. She was, instead, *irked* to be disturbed before her trip.

The moral of this story? In large measure, clients *cause* their attorneys to *become* gruff, obnoxious, even uncaring. You should, first, attempt to rise above such emotion. Anticipate the *consequences* of the natural human response of treating clients badly. Try to moderate your feelings. For those clients who are "unworthy", do your job, remain courteous, collect your fee, cover your posterior, and focus your emotional energies on those clients who *are* worthy.

THINKING LIKE A CLIENT

Few clients know how law is practiced. They don't know what goes on when you're sweating in the library under a research deadline. They don't understand why lawyers don't have immediate answers to nebulous questions, or why case law is such a pain in the brain. (Most *assume* that you *already* know the law—*all* of it.)

They generally don't even accept that things *are* so nebulous...particularly with *their* just cause.

They *do* know that they have a legal problem, which they expect you to solve...quickly and cheaply. They also suspect that their legal bill will shock even their jaded, wildly high estimates. When the bill does arrive, that sense of shock is replaced by irritation, anger, and, sometimes, a phone call (...or, worse, a letter).

This is aggravated by poor—and all too common—client handling. Much discontent can be avoided by wise client massage. This is neither grand deception nor cruel manipulation; it is wise business grace.

Don't promise what you can't deliver. Deliver what you *do* promise. Don't give clients unrealistic or simplistic expectations. Keep them informed. Pollyanna aside, integrity counts: You should not only *be* honest, you should *show* honest. And the truest test of integrity: being honest even when no one else would know.

Make sure your clients understand that *they* are supposed to call the shots; you "merely" provide alternatives and advice. *Merely* is in quotes because you should be forever in awe of the trust placed in your judgment. If you're a lawyer who makes clients' decisions for them, stop. First, it's wrong. Second, it's dangerous. Third, it's unnecessary. Give them the options. Give them your recommendations. Sure, there's room for persuasion, but do try to be the counselor, not the dictator.

Beware the Grey.

Clients don't like to pay for fighting the many monstrous creatures that infest these marshlands of the law. They smell a rip-off.

Wouldn't you?

Finally, when you hear those words of infamy, *"...but it's a matter of principle!"*, remind your client, gently, that *wars* have been fought over less. Much less. And, unless your client has a treasury bursting with monetary troops, retreat—or compromise—in the face of an enemy with its own troops and principles is often the better, if less noble, course.[124]

REPORTING TO CLIENTS

Don't be secretive, either by design or laziness. Clients don't know the legal maneuvering that's going on, which is frustrating for them. Just think back to the last time you took your car in for that strange thumping noise...and empathize.

---

124 Ominously, yet another quirk of human nature is that such a client will often *assume* that you should fight for his principle *at your expense*...and he'll be just as incensed upon receiving your voluminous invoices, which are sure to follow to correct the original injustice. Beware.

Keep the relationship clear: *Who is your client?* Sound easy?

Well, not when the client is a company. Or a couple. Or a child. (Including childish adults.) Figure this out... and *keep it straight*.

Find out also how much autonomy you have. Are you supposed to report directly to the client? Are you supposed to take up issues directly with the client? This is usually obvious, but sometimes not. More on this in just a bit.

Find out how much reporting is expected. If you're not sure, err on the side of *over*-reporting. Send them copies of all substantive documents or pleadings. This justifies as well as informs. (It's also best to send drafts of proposed major letters, pleadings, or documents for the client's approval.) If it involves a restatement of facts or recitals, send them a draft *well before* the deadline. They're busy, too. They might not be able to return that affidavit or verify that exhibit the day before it's due, and they won't appreciate your presumptuousness.

Find out what forms your client prefers, and use them. Most won't know or care... as long as they accomplish whatever is needed.

Make sure they do.

Don't assume that clients know what's going on... or understand the importance of legal maneuvers. Toot your own horn, at least just a little: If you win a summary judgment, let the client know—in *his* terms—what that means. If you're in-house, phrase your successes in terms of money saved.

In whatever terms you use, *include your client in the praise*.

Don't be overly aggressive in marketing yourself, and don't hog the glory: You will be working with—and receiving business from—your clients and your peers and even your staff. (A quick aside: Keep a list of your victories for a pre-annual-review memo to your Seniors.)

WRITING FOR CLIENTS

Your clients will often need to respond to business associates (or adversaries) to protect a contract or other right. Just as often, it's useful to first respond at your *client's* hand, not yours. But *you* should draft the letter. This raises a few problems, and an opportunity.

One problem: Clients write in a different voice, with different motives. It's thus obvious whether the letter was written by the client or by you. Because your legal voice *is* so different, you must be careful not to be too legalistic: *Receiving* a letter from an attorney—any attorney—is an invitation to immediate difficulties.

The important point is to set the *facts* straight (...keeping in mind the legal posture), not to threaten specific legal consequences. Rely on the client for a natural tone and accurate details, and make sure that those facts are indeed in place.

An opportunity: if your client is in your conference room, dictate the letter, *then and there*.

Clients *love* this.

First, they see a legal mind—"their" legal mind—in action. (This is helpful when your *bill* is received.) Second, it lends a warm, cared-for feeling...kinda' like milk and cookies after a scrape, a Band-Aid, and a maternal kiss. Third, you can confer with your client on the facts, quickly and accurately. Finally, it makes it much more likely that the letter will be written, correctly. (Many clients will let it slide, by inattention or indifference. Sometimes that's fine, and oftentimes not.)

Ask your secretary to type a draft, while you chat with the client, who can then have it redone on his letterhead (...with a copy to you).

CONFIDENCE

Make sure also that your contact with the outside world adds to—and does not subtract from—your representation.

Do not voice your doubts to outsiders, or to clients. It's easy to do this, and you must edit yourself in both your speech and writing.

A *senior* Junior once had to respond to a bizarre proposal for a new municipal venture that might have obligated the client to a multi-million dollar boondoggle. The corporate promoter was both insistent and most unhappy about the involvement of a lawyer. (*"Hey,* we do these kind of deals all the time, all by ourselves.") The client [an elected official] *wanted* to do the deal, and was in no mood to hear the myriad risks (and probabilities) associated with the details. The senior Junior had less than 24 hours to respond—the *third* red flag—and wrote:

"I don't know anything about *x,* but...."

How much credibility do you suppose that particular attorney had, with either the client or the promoter? How much easier was it for the promoter to tell the client, "Well, if he doesn't even *know* what he's talking about, then why should you listen to him at all?" (Which was *exactly* what was said...*and done.*) The result? The residents of this particular community were indeed obligated to a multi-million dollar deal; whether it becomes a boondoggle is not yet known.

The important point is that the attorney was not able to adequately represent the clients'—the *citizens',* not the official's—interests.

Don't you ever write "I don't know anything about *x,* but...."

If it's true, then you'd better *learn* about *x* before advising on it. More importantly, you *don't need to be* an expert on *x.* Yes, it's helpful to know what you're talking about, but the law is the law, and legal principles are going to apply fairly uniformly—especially when basic issues of liability, etcetera, are concerned. The law has a dual nature: It is both a substantive discipline, with rules and procedures, and it is a "transparent" structural overlay, constantly seeking the input of all other disciplines for both factual and public policy determinations. Your job is to master the substance, and the structure, and apply that knowledge to whatever facts apply to your client.

When confronted with such a dilemma, respond instead:

```
"Before making a final legal determination on
issues a, b, and c ... it is first necessary to
explore the following [engineering, accounting,
technical, whatever] issues: ...."
```

If you're on a 24-hour deadline, and you (or your client) aren't already an expert in the field, the answer is: *Decline.* Yes, it is useful to be able to jump on the now-or-never deal. But the now-or-never deals *worth accepting* are very few, and very far, between. And they're only worth accepting if your client is *ready* to accept them. Smart clients already know this. The world will still revolve, tomorrow. (And, if it doesn't, a missed deal will be the least of your client's worries.)

TIME

Don't respond immediately in a heated situation, if you have the time. Better to take that extra day, to edit it right.

THE MOTH

Juniors face a steady transition from rear-guard support flunkie to front-line commander. You will start off as the invisible assistant to your Senior. You'll prepare picture-perfect drafts, write those shining memos and letters, and run around to check whatever pesky details need to be checked. In the beginning, this work will be done for your *Senior's* signature. Eventually, you'll be introduced to the client, who will then see paperwork with *your* signature on it. This is an important shift...for everyone. Take it seriously. Finally, the case will become "yours", and you will check in with your Senior only for updates and strategic questions.

Unless the client is a big one, your Senior is only too happy to give the case to you. Senior still gets the credit (read: $$$), but will have only supervisory and schmoozing responsibilities. This ties in, as well, to the wider path leading to partnership: from the moment of your interview, you are being evaluated for your ability to interact with clients. At first, you needn't catch your own: You will be fed. You must, however, not only become self-sustaining with what's given you, you must also show promise to catch your own...*and* catch enough, eventually, to feed the next generation of hungry Juniors.

Look. Listen. Learn. Then be prepared to take over on silent signal from your Senior. (The smaller the client, the sooner this'll happen.) Try to keep this relay progression smooth. Don't rush it, but don't linger either. Ideally, it should happen without missing a beat.

If the client notices, you've missed a beat.

YOUR FIRST CONFERENCE

If you're at all awake, you'll be terrified in your first first-chair conference with a client. You will have spent some time as junior gofer in previous conferences, though, and will ordinarily have dealt with that client before.

When in doubt, do what most do: overprepare.

Excessive hours are a lesser sin than embarrassing the firm. Not that you should spend a zillion hours: Just prepare until you're comfortable with the facts of the case, and core of the law. (This might be non-billable time, by the way. Ask.) The clearer a picture you have of your client's situation, the better a job you'll be able to do.

You *do* need to start thinking like a Senior, though. Law carries a high fixed cost: Arguing over a $10,000 issue is not one-thousandth as hard as a $10,000,000 dollar one. Many times, it's *worse*.

The problem is inherent in the law, and many clients find themselves stuck in a losing battle against prudence. Don't exacerbate the problem. Develop a sense of proportion. For now, rely on the discretion of your Senior, with an eye towards developing your own discretionary talents.

Know your clients' cases. And appreciate your Seniors' concerns. They'd prefer to avoid the embarrassment, expense, and inefficiency of a malpractice suit brought about by throwing a Junior into a tempest completely beyond his ability.

Keep in mind, though, that it'll feel as if you've been thrown to the lions...despite the absence of growls.

When with clients, remember that, to them, *you* are the firm. (Even when you're doing work for other clients, to them you're *still* the firm.) Also, they expect you to know what they've told *others* about their case. You don't like repeating yourself to bureau clerks, do you? (...And you don't pay clerks by the six-minute meter.)

Don't be cowed by extravagant opposing counsel. More often than not, it's an immature attempt to conceal *their* feelings of inadequacy. (...Small consolation as you face Attorney Rambo ranting abusively about something.) If you've done your homework, then preparedness will be your shield—which will only strengthen with experience.

This is a subset of situational awareness, which, in military terms, refers to an acute cognition of, and command over, one's immediate surroundings. Perspicacity. Experienced commanders have it. Pilots have it. Race car drivers have it. If they lose it, even temporarily, then they—and others—die.

Once, when scuba diving, I was told by the Divemaster to stay near the boat; it was not to be a drift dive. I cheerfully agreed, and dived down to frolic to and fro among the coral, fish, and stray shark or three. As the needle in my air gauge fell into the time-to-surface range, I looked up for the comforting, familiar shape of the dive boat.

Hmmm… nowhere. Curious, I surfaced and found, to my surprise, that my dive buddies and I had drifted far from the boat. I stayed on the surface above the others—who were still happily wiggling about below—so that we could be found. What struck me is that I hadn't even *realized* that our group was being swept away by the current. Each maneuver through the coral seemed like a random path in the same area…not a constant drift from safety. I was not aware of my surroundings—no small sin—or location relative to the boat. Had other circumstances been different, the dive might have been deadly.

The stakes aren't (usually) so high. For most Seniors, situational awareness is easy; they've been around the Courthouse block more than a few times, and are familiar with its contours.

You have not, and have to ask directions to the information booth. This, too, shall pass.

When it comes to your job, don't stick your head in the sand. If you think something's not quite right, get your bearings and *check it out.* Then, if you're sure you're on solid legal ground, *stand* your ground.

Better to ask a "dumb" question, in relative privacy, than to fake it and end up making a dumb *move,* in public.

The worst that can happen is that you'll be made to look foolish. So what? You have a *duty* to your client. That's more important. Besides, ninety-two point seven times out of a hundred, the other side's bluffing—or staking ground—and'll back off.

Try it. You might like it.

If you truly don't, and lust after the fetal protection of the library instead, then you're in the wrong field. Skip ahead to the last chapter. There's lots out there for you.

You have yet another tightrope to walk: While you can't give up, you cannot ignore your internal warning signs, either. If, upon serious reflection, you really *do* think you're in over your head, let your Senior know. Don't be embarrassed to the point that you say nothing, and thereby harm your client's interest…and expose yourself to even greater grief. Also, avoid painting yourself into a rhetorical corner.

You should think not only tactically, but also strategically, about the ever-important exit. This can be real, as with a condition in a contract, or it can be emotional, as in not letting *your* emotions dictate a premature conclusion.

Social anthropologists use a tool known as the Hoffstede Power-Distance Index, which measures the power relationship between two people, as perceived by the weaker. If you, the Junior, are afraid to speak up where you legitimately think something's wrong, mistakes are more than just likely, they're darn 'near *inevitable.*

Seniors cannot know everything that goes on in a transaction or case, and they wrongly delude themselves into believing that you know what you're doing. Irritating as it might be, it's better to raise the question than to keep silent against your own better judgment.

Let's not be so indirect. Aircraft accidents are bad, right? Well, it's interesting that two regions of the world are positively correlated with a higher incidence of faulty procedure-related accidents: Latin America and Asia. Also notable is that members of these cultures tend to score high on the Index. Translated to the flight deck, an Asian or Latin American copilot is obedient (and equally effective, under normal circumstances), but less likely than his American or European counterpart to tell the Captain that they're about to fly into a mountain.[125]

Don't let your ego write checks your competence can't cash.

"SUGGESTIONS"

Now for the hard part. Seniors are comfortable with *their* knowledge. It's difficult for them to relate to *your* nervousness in carrying out their suggestions. If they ask that you demand x payment towards settlement, or y days as an ultimatum, you *must* follow their lead— even if you're embarrassed, in your insecurity, by your position.

Give your Senior some credit. First, you likely do not know the whole story: Juniors rarely know more than a tiny sliver of the facts. Second, you're probably being used as a pawn in the negotiating game (*their* negotiating game). This is, as we all come to appreciate, one of a lawyer's greatest values to his client; the addition of an agent will almost always improve the bargaining position of the principal. Third, you should take advantage of a cooler head to moderate your tendency to overreact...positively *or* negatively. Finally, it's your *job*. You *will* be uncomfortable. If you're remotely normal, you'll be *frantic* the first few times in the hot seat. Hang in there.

---

125 This is not culturally exclusive: The Dutch captain of the KLM 747 was the *star* of his airline. His copilot was not. Their flight had been delayed, and the captain decided to refuel. (This blocked another aircraft, a Pan Am 747, for an hour.) Flight-time limits and marginal weather made both crews anxious to leave. With only one runway, each plane had to taxi its length before turning around for takeoff. The KLM captain turned his craft, and began to run his engines up for takeoff. His young copilot warned him, in an *audibly* distressed voice, that the path was not yet clear. The Pan Am *crept* along in severe, patchy fog. After a few minutes, in his growing impatience, the KLM captain *again* began the takeoff run, without confirming that the Pan Am aircraft was clear. The copilot dared not challenge his captain a second time.

Five hundred eighty-three souls were lost that day in the Canary Islands.

Another tragedy, showing a reciprocal tendency to ignore "inferior" commands, involved a skilled Mexican crew, which had inadvertently altered the autopilot into a shallow dive, at night. Just before hitting the ground in their perfectly flying machine, an automatic ground-collision warning, in the voice of a woman, warned them to *"Pull Up! Pull Up!"* The last thing recorded was *"Shut up, Gringa."*

NERVES

Conceal your nervousness. *Your* client is looking to *you*. For answers. For alternatives. For professionalism.

I once saw, as a potential juror, a jury selection conducted by an inexperienced plaintiff's attorney and a *very* experienced and polished defense attorney. It's unlikely this difference played a *deciding* role to the jury—most will go far to overlook such disability—but, still, the other potential jurors looked as embarrassed for the plaintiff's attorney as was I.

She commented—*several times*—about her complete lack of trial experience. It would have been *much* better for her (...assuming she had no option to turn the case down) to have kept her doubts to herself and gotten on with the case. Even though she felt (correctly) that everyone could see her inexperience—and her grand fraud would thus be exposed—we just wanted the facts, ma'am.

Sure, everybody loves an underdog, and nervousness can be used by a skillful litigator to connect with the jurors (who are nervous too), but her distress was palpable. Worse, her poor client, who was nervous enough at the outset, became downright *frightened* as the jury selection wore on...with the trial yet to follow.

There's not much her lawyer could have done to *not* be nervous (...other than trying smaller cases first), but her comments were bad lawyering, and truly unnecessary.

Even if you know that you know less than you should, your client assumes that you know all a lawyer should, and more. Somewhere between *arrogance* and *deer-in-the-headlights* lies a safer and more satisfying middle path.

One way to conceal nervousness is to *slow down*.

Allow yourself time for composure. Circumspect slowness will be perceived as deliberation (good), not stupidity (bad).

I once took my brother, Brus, flying. (He then flew C-130s in the Air Force, and I had learned how to fly in college. He was qualified in jets and multi-engine turboprops, but not in the bug-smasher variety of aircraft.) I was then in law school, destitute, and hadn't flown for a year or so. I arranged to take a required biennial flight review with a flight instructor before taking Brus on a sight-seeing and gravity-defying cruise over central Texas. Brus thought I was crazy for attempting to take a flight exam without taking refresher lessons first. During the flight exam, in an attempt to cover my rusty command of flight procedures, I slowed down. Everything I did, I did with exaggerated deliberation. After the flight, I was *complimented* by the flight examiner on my smoothness and skill. I joked about this with Brus, who went on to scare the crap out of me with his jet-imitation maneuvers...in our rather non-jet Cessna.

This personal analogy gets better. What if there'd been an emergency, and my skills hadn't been up to snuff?

Good question.

I would not have endangered myself or others with a true lack of proficiency, which is relative to the task. Had I needed to fly over unfamiliar territory or in marginal weather, I would, indeed, have taken refresher flights, taken along an experienced pilot (were an instructor-pilot not present), or made other arrangements.

Your Senior will (probably) not put you in a position completely outside your competence. (It will only *feel* that way.) On the other hand, the process of learning requires that you advance to increasingly difficult projects, which necessarily requires that you—yet more aviation jargon—"ride the envelope" of your competence.

Occasionally, you *will* get a project beyond your reasonable capability. Yes, it's unfair. Attorneys, who darned well ought to know better, are sometimes the worst violators of the objective rule dictating what you *should* know. When put in this precarious situation, punt. Do what you can, rely on the experience of others, and ask for help as often as you can get away with.

If you get into a situation where you realistically feel you're out of your league, to the detriment of your client, calm down, politely ask for a recess if the situation warrants it, and contact your Senior. Relate the situation, and ask for advice. Let your Senior help you get your bearings.

If the responsible Senior is unavailable, ask someone else (preferably someone who practices in the same area) for help. If everyone in the office has deserted to the annual picnic to which you weren't invited, then punt some more. Rather than citing law you don't know (which you probably won't), tell them you'll check on that particular point and get back to them…fast. And then, dammit, get back to them…*fast*. Unless it's a basic question of law that you really *should* know, clients generally won't mind, and *will* be impressed, if you get back to them, quickly, with an answer.

I once got a call from the president of a corporate client. He needed the answer to a banking law question in a new case. *Frau Comandant* and her *Oberleutnant* were unavailable; I was it. I had no idea what the answer was, and I told him I would read the file to which he was referring and get back to him. I found the file, skimmed it, and asked another Senior for the answer. Answer in mind, I called back. He was *amazed* that I returned his call twenty minutes later.

Your clients should be similarly amazed…but not for long.

They should come to *expect* exceptional assistance from you. Simple stuff like returning their calls in minutes or hours—not days (or, worse, not at *all*)—and keeping them in the loop are what will cement a positive bond between you and your clients.

Note the possessive pronoun preceding "clients". You must quickly learn to think and act as if each project given to you is a direct link to a client, to whom you are *personally* responsible. You might not have immediate contact with clients, but soon enough you'll be dealing directly with lots of 'em.

The more they become *your* clients, the better will be your position, later, among your *fellow* Seniors.

PRIDE GOETH...

Beware however a natural, false confidence. After you've survived a few scrapes, you might succumb to a natural feeling of invincibility.

Careful. Fate has a way of defeating the invincible.

CEREMONY

We are a species to which ceremony is important. Your clients pay a lot of money for you. Yet they usually only see the tip of the work iceberg. Make it sparkle.

It might seem silly to you, but it does make a difference to them. Just imagine a stately, ritualistic Victorian closing—leather binders binding, quill pen scripting, wax seal cooling, and blue ribbons flowing—and understand the impression such (supposedly non-essential) extras make. Less shallowly, it *is* important to impress upon the participants just how serious this stuff is.

Before you can impress, though, you must learn the dance that accompanies transactions. If you're responsible for a closing, you must learn the steps to avoid delay...and embarrassment. Your secretary will know far more than you about such office protocol. Pay attention. Take a moment to make sure you know which documents (and exhibits) to prepare, in what order and quantity. Your secretary should tab the signature lines; it smoothes the process and looks professional. Think through the event: doing too much in front of your client makes them nervous. The smoother the event, the happier the client.

If there's a hiccup in the process, you've not done your job well.

When I was 17, Brus and I bought a duplex (in serious disrepair) for renovation, because, *well*...we were such fun guys. At the closing, after both sides had signed the documents, the attorney slowly rose, walked around to our side of his desk, assumed a deliberate stance, and signed the documents and deed with such a flourish as to scare little children in the street below.

Very impressive. He had taken a course in calligraphy, and his signature *was* beautiful (...especially next to our amateurish scribbles). A bit much, perhaps. But, connection or not, we paid his bill without complaint or controversy.

SCRIPTING

Some attorneys' letters include signatures that look as if scrawled in haste and puerile defiance by a second-grader (...held back, twice, for poor penmanship).

Your letters will be on display for all to read, for all time. You *will* be judged by the quality of *every* component you produce. Your signature must never look childish. It should never be quasi-block written.

If it's ugly, improve it.

If it's just okay, improve it anyway.

And for *all* signatures...don't rush it. Savor the calligraphic experience—a sign of closure. In an unstudied flurry, are you really saving that much time?

MONEY

Once upon a time, there was an attorney.

This attorney was told to meet with a new client, who had been referred by a friend of a Senior. Before starting the case, the attorney faced an annoying housekeeping chore: In an embarrassed rush, the attorney asked for the retainer.

The client, with a broad smile, told the attorney, innocent to the ways of the profession, that the retainer was "not necessary" in this case, and the bill would be "taken care of" in due course. The attorney, flustered and wishing not to make an issue of it, went ahead with the case. Nor was the Senior consulted—to double-check the "special understanding"—before starting the work.

Needless to write, the bill was not "taken care of"—in due course or otherwise. Also needless to write, this attorney learned in a most poignant and persuasive way the importance of pleasing the gods of firm accounting.

The end.

DANCING WITH DISSATISFIED CLIENTS

Despite your best efforts, a client will lose. A case. A contract. A child.

The client might react well, or he might react badly. You're a close target for anger...and a convenient scapegoat upon which the firm may affix responsibility, justifiably or not. It goes with the territory. If you have done your best, try not to lose sleep over it. The situation will pass, or it won't.

Either way, there's not much you can do about it. Your Seniors will probably support you in the long run, even if they must temporarily abandon you to save the firm's ever-more-important face.

If a client calls in a huff, be professional. Try to find out what the problem is, and promise to check it out.

Don't get defensive. Do *not* shout back, no matter how bad it gets. End the conversation as courteously as your can, and check with your Senior, who might take over. If not, it is *your* responsibility to make amends, promptly.

The more professional your demeanor, the less likely any gaffes will be an issue—and the easier will be your handling of them.

Also, it's easier to go from a super-professional model to a friendly one than vice versa.

You *will* make gaffes. If they're serious enough to be noticed, they are usually best handled with a prompt and sincere apology. Rarely will lasting damage be done. Perhaps most importantly, these experiences will remind you how much nicer it is to do the job right the first time around.

WHO'S ON FIRST?

Don't appear too friendly to opposing counsel in front of your clients. You have a fine line to walk, here. Your clients pay you to represent their interest in an unfamiliar, often hostile system. If clients see you as overly buddy-buddy with the enemy, they might—legitimately— conclude that, rather than being an honest forum for disputes, it is, instead, a clubby, greedy contrivance... at *their* expense.

Explain to clients who are unfamiliar with lawyers that you're courteous to opposing counsel in part for their benefit. Be courteous to *everyone*, but, in combat, keep it professional.

THE HORIZON

Yet another part of being professional is keeping your distance—both emotional and subjective—from your clients. This is not disrespectful, nor is it dishonorable. It's a necessary component of law practice; if you cannot be objective about your client's situation, you won't be much help. A lawyer, by definition, provides legal advice unencumbered by a direct, personal interest in the matter.

When clients come to you with their problems, look beyond (...and sometimes behind) what they are saying. Keep a healthy distance. Clients are like everyone else: they have feelings, which are hurt by being wronged (...or *wrong*). Whether subconsciously or otherwise, clients mislead.

Without threatening their honor, carefully challenge their version of the facts. This will both help you in your representation of them... and avoid embarrassing (and *very* damaging) blunders, which follow ignorant lawyers like imprinted geese.

Be disinterested. Not *un*interested...*dis*interested.[126]

MAINTAINING THE DIGNITY

As if I don't already sound like a broken record: You must be *exceedingly* careful how you phrase your thoughts. To your clients, to your opponents, to outsiders...to *anyone.*

Once upon a time, an attorney was up against a family law mess: a hostile judge, a greedy attorney *ad litem,* a scheming and perjurious opponent, fraudulent documents, and, well...not much was textbook about the case. Worse, the opposing witness was upstanding—a nurse with a confident, convincing manner—while his young client displayed a less-than-honorable past. The battle was for a child, the *natural* child of the client. The nurse had attempted to steal the child from its mother with a forged affidavit of termination.

A lucky star under which the mother sat shone as a foundation, in another state, which employed her grandmother. The foundation had agreed to pay for a portion of the case. As it dragged on, seemingly endlessly, the attorney felt it necessary to explain the case oddities to the client's grandmother (who was also paying for the representation) and the foundation. As the legal bill mounted precipitously, the attorney was increasingly embarrassed for the entire profession: Why was this case becoming such a bottomless pit of their money?

Here's a draft of a few paragraphs to them:

> The woman who is trying to take x away is the most polished liar I have ever seen in a courtroom. She is older than Ms. X, a professional nurse with a good work history, and is on sound financial footing, unlike Ms. X. She is also far more articulate and sophisticated than Ms. X—which is one reason why she tried to victimize Ms. X. (The other reason, I believe, is that she calculated that Ms. X would not be able to find the wherewithal for a court battle.)

> The judge is largely deferring to the court-appointed attorney, at this point. Further, she has insisted on delving into areas that are legally irrelevant. She is doing so because she his bending over backwards to get all the facts, no matter what the controlling law. She is trying to do the right thing; but in doing so, she is doing the wrong thing—in part because it's driving Ms. X's fees and costs up so far.

---

126 Sorry, I just can't help myself: *disinterested* and *uninterested* have too interesting a history. *Uninterested* originally meant *impartial.* Its meaning fell into disuse during the 1700's, however (...along with the original meaning of *disinterested*, which then meant *not interested*). Their meanings have thus flipped: *disinterested* now means *impartial,* while *uninterested* now means *not interested.* Being the contemporary guy, the meanings intended here are the modern ones.

Here's the revised version:

The woman who is attempting to take x away is exceptionally convincing in court. She is older than Ms. X, she is a professional nurse with a good work history, and she is on sound financial footing. She is also far more articulate and sophisticated than Ms. X, at least in a court setting.

The judge—despite controlling law on this point—is understandably insistent on securing the "best interests" of the child (which does, indeed, fall within the court's power and duty in most family law cases). I believe the judge is trying to be painfully fair, but the result, unfortunately, is a difficult process for Ms. X, and an expensive one as well.

Your support of Ms. X in her case is both admirable and greatly appreciated. Perhaps one reason this case has arisen is that Ms. Y calculated that Ms. X would not be able to fund the substantial burden of a court battle. With your continued support, I am confident that we can eventually secure for Ms. X recognition of the legal right to keep her own natural child, x.

DANCING WITH WITNESSES

You'll likely deal with non-interested witnesses (and a few interested ones), especially if you're in litigation. You should take care in dealing with, and even in approaching, these individuals.

As a rule, *lighten up*.

If you start a conversation using words like "affidavit" and "legal proceeding" and "subpoena"—what would you expect? The natural reaction is to clam up tighter than a, *uh*...clam.

Begin instead with a gentler touch. The weather, a favored sports team, their blue-ribbon, silver-coated pooch...whatever.

Keep it *aw shucks* friendly, and enjoy the fruits of friendship.

Be respectful, both in manner and of their time. (If it's a bad time, return at *their* convenience.) Moreover, you needn't be sneaky. (If you *do*, it's likely a job for a private investigator, not you.) Tell them up front who you are and why you're there, but keep the paper and pens hidden, at first. If they *do* clam up, don't bulldoze ahead. That'll only make it worse. Instead, change the subject, in your ever-friendly way, to something innocuous. *Then* lead them back to the subject, gingerly. Don't rush it. Polite persistence pays. More often than not, a few minutes of non-threatening conversation, followed by a non-threatening discussion, will produce vastly more than a coerced, uni-directional interrogation. They're witnesses, not suspects.

After you both have discussed the matter a while, mention that a writing is a good idea: *"Well,* I suppose a short summary of what you've just told me would be helpful." If there's resistance, you might mention that it's for *his* benefit as well: "Sure, you're *welcome* to take a look at the summary—I'd *like* that, in fact—and if there's *anything* wrong, you just tell me, and I'll fix it, to *your* satisfaction. That way, no one will be able to twist your words, later. *Deal?*"

When you draft the statement—written in the first person—do so informally: in language the witness both understands and would normally use. Nothing fancy: almost as if the witness were *speaking* it. Start with ministerial data: when, where, and at whose request the statement is made (...so opposing counsel cannot later claim deceit). When finished, ask the witness to go over the statement *carefully*. *Don't rush it.* Don't let *them* rush it. Make any corrections, and make sure it's genuinely satisfactory. (Writing a statement will often draw out additional facts that might be missed otherwise.) At the very end, ask for a signature. (Don't even *mention* this, earlier.) If they refuse, defuse it by saying "Fine, no problem."–but ask again if the statement is accurate. (Even without a signature it *is* usable, if more troublesome, in court.) Ask them to initial any changes, to inoculate against a claim of forgery. (Ask for correction initials, even if it's *not* signed. Most folks assume, incorrectly, that initials "don't count".)

If it becomes, or is likely to become, difficult, consider a private investigator, who, unlike you, *can* testify in court to a witness's statements and actions. (Assuming, of course, first-hand knowledge.)

If the witness "remembers nothing"—try to get a statement to that effect. (*Hold* it for the cross-x upon a newly "discovered" memory. *Ah*...the joys of impeachment.) If you absolutely cannot get a written statement, write one anyway, as a memo to yourself, with special attention to the details of the meeting. (Place, exact time, etcetera.)

CONFIDENTIALITY

Start thinking in terms of confidentiality. You're no longer valued for your fount of gossip. This is important not only as a matter of good taste and social manners, it's the *law*. Take it seriously.

If knowledge is power, the ability to *withhold* knowledge is controlled mastery.[127] In law, emphasize the *controlled* part. Be *careful* discussing cases with others, even *within* the firm: Lawyers...usually no problem. Secretaries...getting muddier. Mail room clerks...nope.

Do *not* discuss cases outside the firm. Unless you're discussing the case with an expert specifically brought in on that case, you are *not* at liberty to discuss *confidential* information. (...And the definition of "confidential" is quite broad.) This is serious stuff, taken seriously by those with power over *you*. Act accordingly.

---

127 Do not react with immediate disdain: Power is neither bad nor good. It simply *is*. Well, no...not simply. It *is* both necessary and inevitable. The test of goodness lies in its use, or relative lack of abuse.

Confidentiality and confidence are related. If a Senior learns that you've been blabbering about a client to an unauthorized person, you'll be up for a dressing-down, at least. If your Senior sees instead a mature new lawyer who knows how to keep his mouth shut when his mouth should not be open, then you're on your way.

Confidentiality. Confidence. When your work for clients gives them confidence in you, then you're on your way.

Which leads right into a discussion of rainmaking.

THE RAIN DANCE

It's probably a little early to get your wetsuit on, but you *can* get into the proper frame of mind.[128]

Rainmaking—getting new clients, or getting new and better business from existing clients—is the *raison d'être* of the law firm game. He who brings in the most (paying) clients, wins. Even among egalitarian, ex-hippie, down-to-earth partners...money matters. The game is just too serious for it to be any other way. And in most firms, the game is dead serious.

This should not imply that you must schmooze your way through one soirée after another (...although that's sometimes what it takes). It *does* mean that you seriously consider the allocation of your time, and reserve time to make sure that: (1) your present clients love you (which ought to be your Standard Operating Procedure, anyway); and (2) potential new clients learn of you, consider you, and hire you.

Don't assume that bar association goings-on are a sidetrack. Quite the opposite: they are central, and they are encouraged by firms. This aspect of practice is, *inter alia,* an investment in your career.

Keep track of those you know and meet. This includes your college and law school buddies. Start and maintain a filing system. (If you're doing it right, by the time you hit Senior status you should be well on your way to several overstuffed files, or their electronic equivalent.) Don't be obtrusive, but do take the effort: maintain contact with your contacts. You needn't become a glad-handler or serial joiner, if that's not you, but neither should you become a hermit in your legal cave.

Another, related way to start is with your business cards. It might seem like playing the pretend grown-up (...and, in a way, it is). Even so, your business cards will be among your best friends in the world of practice. Distribute them freely. (As a Junior, they are free.) Don't be pushy, or hand your cards out when socially inappropriate (...when in groups, for instance); it'll backfire.

Do hand your card out unobtrusively, one-on-one, with a genuine smile. (Not for a *quid pro quo* or as a tacky sales job, but as a gesture that you truly enjoyed meeting them, and think highly enough of

---

128 Sometimes it's a tight fit, I know.

them to observe the fading rules of social etiquette, and wish for them to have a record of your meeting—for reference as an acquaintance or perhaps for a future friendship.)

When someone gives *you* a business card, take the time, after the meeting, to jot on its reverse a few relevant details: (1) the date and place where you met; (2) personal information, such as interests and spouse/children's names; (3) business particulars; and (4) other information that might be helpful to remember.

You should then periodically add this information to an electronic assistant, either portable or desktop.

Who knows? You might just (eventually) catch yourself a client. Bringing in even a small client—approved by a Senior—is a *big* prize. (In some firms, you might be *expected* to start bringing in clients soon. Very soon.) Later you'll become more selective, and won't worry about setting such a wide net. Still, it's nice to get calls from prospective clients, even if you end up referring them elsewhere (...which you likely *will*). It's also important to develop the interpersonal skills that are essential to Senior practice.

You cannot solicit business. Yet firms survive only by keeping their clients happy, and by attracting new business and new clients. "Rainmaking" is a form of marketing less crass than the commercial variety. In a sense, it's a subtle form of solicitation. (With a strong professional emphasis on the *subtle*.)

For some, such hands-on rainmaking is beyond their personality limits. Fear not: there are other ways. One of the Seniors for whom I worked had this affliction. She couldn't (or wouldn't) schmooze to save her life. Yet she is one of the most successful attorneys in Honolulu, she is well-respected, and she is a genuinely good person.

She attracts clients through her reputation, which is earned by being extremely good at her work. It helped that Seniors senior to her had protected her earlier from much of this process, and allowed for her development, over time, of a top-notch reputation. This is crucial in any career, and will go a long way toward making up for introspective tendencies. To repeat, this is among the greatest benefits of practicing in a firm, which goes unappreciated by many therein: If you survive, you will be *given* your practice.

No small gift, this. Seniors give you your first clients. All you have to do is...*take care of them*. If you can do that, you will gradually, eventually become the lead attorney for those clients. Usually, Senior has moved on to bigger and better fish, and is more than happy to give the smaller fry to you to clean.[129]

---

[129] A reviewer noted the Freudian metaphor in the context of a discussion of lawyers' maltreatment of their clients: clients as fish to catch, kill, clean, and eat. His point is reinforced by a common phrase for the distribution of profits to partners in proportion to rainmaking: "Eat what you kill."

Competence with one client leads to contacts with other potential clients. If you're *serious* on the Partnership track (or corporate counsel track, or judgeship track, or everything-else track), you must plan for your eventual rainmaking tasks.[130] For now, your job is (relatively) easy: *Take care of your clients.* Do good work. Go the extra mile.

Appear to be super-sharp, and actually *be* super-sharp.

Notable, however, is the reality that most successful attorneys are both very good and very "political". They combine the interrelated elements of excellence: technical, managerial, and marketing. This is a critical difference, which applies as well to firms that meander, and those that become (and stay) legal powerhouses. (Not, mind you, that a legal powerhouse is necessarily the place to be. Indeed, it is often a less-pleasant cousin to the friendly, satisfied variety of firm more content with its moderate size and clients.) Decide for yourself what you want, but know, going in, the score.

Finally, bide your time. What's the rush? The bounty will be yours soon enough.

RAINMAKING: THE SECRET

Well, that sounds awful' purdy. But how, exactly, should *you* go about getting new clients?

First, that's a misconception. Most law work is *retained* not from new clients, but from *old* ones. You're at an obvious disadvantage, there. (Not only with clients from your own firm, but also clients with any *other* firm. "Stealing" clients—from other, established firms—is no easy feat.) Don't waste your time.

Second, some lawyers assume they have to "get" clients. This is another misconception, and a bad approach. The *best* attorneys don't "get" clients. *Firms* consider it beneath their dignity to "get" clients. (Well, officially.) They'd rather the *clients* get *them.* (They then graciously reciprocate, and accept the firm's end of the representation.) Granted, this is a genteel, almost quaint notion in the post-*Bates* age of personal-injury ads. Importantly, the firms (and attorneys) with money *and* power operate the quaint way: they position themselves, and let the clients make the "first" move. (Of course, *positioning* is the trick, here.) How, then, to get the client to move first?

Two quick answers: one cynical, the other more pleasant.

If you're in it for the money, then that's where you should go. Make yourself known in the right circles...*outside the legal one.* (*Lawyers* don't make the best prospects.) This, of course, requires a universe of other qualities, which are likely in inverse proportion to

---

130 Yes, even on these other tracks you must make rain: In a corporate position, your "clients" are the general counsel and senior officers; in a judgeship, it's either the governor (and the senators), or the voters.

your initial standing. (In English: the more you need it, the less likely you'll have it.) You must—as a start—be presentable, likeable, and sociable. This requires as serious a commitment as the one to the law.

The second (and I think better) option is: avoid the trap in the first place. Rather than stalking potential clients (...the worthiest of whom already have long-term ties with established Seniors, thank you very much), go instead where your heart takes you.

Enjoy yourself. Seriously.

If, for example, you like sailing, then go sailing. Don't lie in wait to snare someone; they can *sense* that. Have *fun,* instead. They'll sense that, too. And they'll likely like you, more.

And, when the need arises, guess whom they'll ask, first?

One attorney had an excellent hobby: classic cars. He met with new friends, discussing a mutual love: old, classy cars. He did not trawl for new clients; they came to him. Not as a nervous client, but as a friend (or at least, acquaintance) with a mutual *non-law* passion. He was very successful, and he let that success come to him. And he didn't force it. And he enjoyed himself.

Now, let's not *all* grab a paper for the next classic auto show dates. Find something *you* truly enjoy. Find something you *truly* enjoy. (If it's solitaire, you might rethink a partnership goal.) The important point is to have a life, both professional and personal. Yes, there will be conflicts between the two, but don't let either dominate the other, permanently.

Also, become involved in your local community. At a minimum— especially if you're new to the area—read the local business paper, religiously. This will give you a better idea of the local goings-on, and will form a base of knowledge in your later dealings with clients. Choose local events and organizations that interest you, and the rest will follow.

As long as I've mentioned religion, however obliquely, you should participate in "personal" organizations—religious, political, or philosophical. These provide not only a venue for meaning and friendships, they give you the opportunity to impress (don't overdo it) and, most importantly, to perfect your public speaking and socializing skills.

(Don't lock yourself into only a narrow group or interest, however, and don't assume that only "high-class" venues offer opportunity. Sometimes the opposite is true...yet that shouldn't be the immediate goal, anyway.)

For the sixty-ninth time, these "soft" skills apply across disciplines and are *crucial* to success after the initial, technical phase of learning subsides into a more difficult one. Ever more true, *making* partner is easy compared to *staying* partner.

For now, keep your eyes on the ball: take care of your *existing* clients. Insist on excellence—*demand* it from yourself—without overdoing it, and the rest will follow.

RAINMAKING FOR OUTCASTS

If you happen to belong to a group that, by whatever characteristic, has been at the fringe of power—legal or otherwise—you might have special difficulties attracting clients.

High-powered (or even medium-powered) law is a clubby business, which, not surprisingly, rewards those who are already part of the socio-eco-racial-gender-religious-power-genetic-politico Club.

This is not malevolent. It simply *is*.

It is not a conspiracy, but is, rather, an elemental group-orientation that we each favor. As Marge Simpson put it, while whisking Lisa from the company of a (black) jazz saxophonist who had befriended the young midnight-runaway, "It's nothing personal. I'm just afraid of the unfamiliar."

The answer, if you are (or feel) excluded, is to do what anyone given a lemon should do: Make lemonade. Where others see limitations, you should look for unseen opportunities. If you have no contact with potential clients in your city's upper-crust club (to which *very* few, of any stripe, have access)...*do something else.* Anything. There are lots of possibilities, once you free yourself from the constraint of thinking like everyone else. (In which case they win, don't they?)

Sure, you might well have to work twice as hard to get half as far. Yes, it's unfair. It's also the history of this and every nation...and the law of inertia, applied to first-generation-nobodies all. Yes, it's unfair.

Get over it.

Perhaps most counterrevolutionarily, it is only within the context of our modern, Western, legal precepts that the *notion* of inclusion is possible. (If you think not, a challenge: Look to *any* society that does not fit those three qualifiers.) Something to ponder as you rage against The Man.

The vast majority of attorneys (and neighbors) are *eager* to accept. Let them.

Scout around for firms in which you'll have greater opportunity to shine. Rely on the contacts you're given by association with your firm. Use whatever other contacts you have...or make.

Yet your first, best shot remains: *Take care of your clients.*

10

SECRETARIES, STAFF,
AND OTHER
FUNNY CREATURES

The Attorney-Secretary relationship deserves special attention, as dealing with The Secretary can present perilous pitfalls for the unwary Junior. As often as not, the problem is of *your* making.

Most likely, you'll be given the *very* part-time assistance of a busy Senior's extremely busy secretary. Rather than take umbrage, accept this as a necessary and beneficial arrangement: you don't yet warrant your own assistant. More importantly, you should take advantage of this talented resource. Experienced assistants are a blessing not to be taken lightly. It is they who will make the difference between a mistake (*your* mistake) being corrected, or not, before it goes to a Senior, or—God forbid—outside.

Always, always, *always* take care of (meaning, for now, *be nice to*) them, and they will take care of you. Not only can they save your posterior on those occasions when it needs to be saved, they can greatly reduce stress (*your* stress)...or not. The choice is yours.

Don't be snotty. Unless you've waited tables, dug ditches, or shoveled manure in your life (I've done each), you are in no moral position to sneer.[131]

You should be friendly, courteous, and respectful, but not too familiar. The friendly, courteous, and respectful part should follow based on (un)common good manners. It should also be in recognition of their true contribution to your work and to the firm.

The last part is a warning: Attorneys and Staff exist in separate, if intersecting, worlds. Mistaking friendliness with deeper friendship can easily strain the place of both attorney and staffperson in their respective worlds. Moreover, some Seniors (including senior *staff*) are Pinheads, and take the Social Order thing quite seriously. To them, fraternizing is the worst sort of social crime. Too, sexual harassment laws are increasingly intrusive, for much good and some bad, into the workplace. (Oddly, Social Orderers seem to have had the most trouble adjusting to this little legal trend. *Hmmm....*) Given that most Staff are women, and especially given that Seniors are now increasingly mixed, it is prudent to maintain strictly professional, if pleasant, relations in the office.

---

131 If you *have* lived life in the trenches, you'll be either graciously understanding...or insufferable (in which case you've learned the wrong lesson).

In a related vein for men, forests have been cleared in discussing office romance (and mere liaisons). Sure, you can appreciate the view, but don't be a clod. If you can't contain visions of sex with secretaries, receptionists, and office furniture, take another look at that rapidly burgeoning field of sexual harassment law. In any office, it's better to keep your privates private for at least your probationary period.

(Besides, if you have *that* much spare energy, perhaps you should be in politics, not practice.)

THE OFFICE ROPES

Back to more innocuous stuff: Take advantage of secretaries' knowledge. Learn from them. Not necessarily legal stuff (...although they might just surprise you), but office details. It is they who know how the scut work is performed. And, coincidentally, part of the learning process as a Junior is to become familiar with the scut work of law.

Keep in mind, however, that a Junior's learning is done with an eye towards a bigger picture than they need worry about. And don't be uncritical of their advice. They usually aren't aware of legal issues, or of Seniors' unspoken expectations of you.

You cannot take substantive direction from staff, without clearing it first with a Senior. It sounds a little tinny even to say, *"Gee,* boss... my secretary told me to do it this way."

TWO-WAY STREETS

You should attend to the needs of your secretary, just as she attends to yours.[132] If she has a personal legal problem, point her in the right direction and, with the consent of a Senior, actively help if you can, or refer, if you cannot. Be careful; you don't want to get trapped in the middle of an emotional mess. In most cases, you'll refer. In nearly all cases, a sympathetic ear is the favored contribution.

(By the way, don't forget to advise her to check the library first, to get some basic information about her problem. That's good advice to everyone, for nearly everything. Most would rather be spoon-fed, true, but...you get *paid* for that.)

If she has a personal *personal* problem, be understanding...but, again, don't get sucked into an emotional morass, out of which there is no gentle escape.

It is unlikely that you will be concerned with wild incompetence. (Seniors rarely have to worry about competent assistance.) If she is a

---

132 Okay, you caught me. "She" *is* more appropriate, though, given the near universal preponderance of women in secretarial jobs. Don't lecture; I didn't say it was *right* (...although few men could do the job as well). Sorry, that parenthetical was alarmingly sexist, but, dammit, it's true.

good assistant (almost certainly), you should forgive, within limits, minor transgressions. If, however, her personal problems seriously interfere with her job, discuss it with your (mutual) Senior.

Careful, though. You should be *exceedingly* circumspect before pressing this issue. (See "Squeaky Wheels" a few pages down.) If you do complain, do not attack or criticize personally: it's quite likely that the *Senior's* loyalty extends (much) farther to *her* than it does to you.

PERSONAL STUFF

This can be a problem. As you climb the ladder, you'll have less and less time (and patience) to take care of the personal clutter that bogs down everyone's life.

Some Seniors expect their secretaries to run personal errands, while others are too embarrassed, or think it too aristocratic, to ask. Some secretaries don't mind, while others are offended.

There's no simple perspective on this. There *is* an economic justification for such a division of labor; it makes sense to pay a secretary to do tasks that free the attorney's time for more "valuable" duties. This can't help but be a loaded discussion, because the word *valuable* can be interpreted economically, or in a different, moral sense. Worse, it's too easy to confuse the moral with the practical.

Secretaries' assistance is *in*valuable, meaning lawyers could not do their legal work, well, without them (and they should be accordingly appreciated...and compensated). But, in strict comparison, their work is more fungible than yours. We Americans, in particular, are uncomfortable with such aristocratic trappings, and resist overt recognition of class. Thus, for us, the dilemma.

You can avoid this trap by, first, not being officious, and, second, confirming that *your* secretary isn't offended. As a Junior, you should not ask for more than *minor* personal favors. (Request only those favors that you'd be happy to return.) And, as with everything else, *pay attention*. Most secretaries are willing to do small stuff, especially for bosses they like, but don't let it go to your head. If your secretary *does* mind, either because she's too busy with Senior's work (...or personal stuff), or because she's offended...*back off*.

Once you've climbed far enough, you'll have the opportunity to find yourself your own *chargé d'affaires,* if that's your style. You should, however, let prospective secretaries know, up front, what you expect.

If it's part of the job and understood by everyone, *ex ante*, then you're on firmer footing than if you expect higher-caste goodies just, well...*because*. Better yet, hire an extra gofer for *everyone*; secretaries' time is too valuable to waste, too.[133]

---

133 In the words of a famous feminist: *Everyone* needs a wife.

ADONIS AT WORK

Firms are fertile grounds for sex. Power (or illusions thereof), money, deference, activity, and courtly coifing—aviewed aplenty—are potent aphrodisiacs all.

For you boys, it is possible—even probable—that a secretary will become infatuated with you. The magnetism in office life is just too conducive to attraction.

For you girls, it is possible that you will become infatuated with a Senior (...or fellow associate).

Before you rush off (again) to the Sexism Patrol, understand that, most unfairly, the sexual tensions that inhere to office life inhere almost universally to the benefit of men. True, at the office *everyone's* at their best—there's no mussed hair, dragon breath, or improper scratching,[134] as at home—but our genetic code rewards physical and social attractants we are (now) loath to concede.

For everyone, take it easy. You will have neither the time nor the emotional *je ne sais quoi* to successfully handle a romantic (or merely physical) *tête-à-tête*.[135]

As the citizens of Hellas would remind us, the fate of Aphrodite's obsessive attention was not simple.

GIFTS

You should be generous (but not too personal) when Secretary's Day rolls along. (If you *do* rely on your secretary for personal favors, you should be especially generous when it's time to reciprocate.)

For mixed company, a nice lunch is okay...*if others go too*.

A thoughtful gift is always in good taste. Yes, you've just come from studenthood and poverty, but you now make many multiples of her salary, and spending some lunch money on a well-thought-out token of your appreciation will be, well...*appreciated*.

On the other hand, don't be extravagant. First it's inappropriate. Second, it breeds contempt, rather than appreciation; as an odd part of our psychological profile, we more easily appreciate the reachable rather than the extraordinary. Third, it too easily stirs resentment in others...including especially other *secretaries*. Finally, it might make your *Senior* look miserly in comparison.

Juniors who make Seniors look bad are not long for the firm.

---

134 An editor suggested *inappropriate and prolonged,* instead. Nice touch.

135 Some of you, however, *are* fully prepared to take advantage of the sexual possibilities. Sorrowfully, this ability is highly correlated with an utter lack of concern for the feelings of the other, which brings to mind yet another of my many laments in life: The wrong guys get laid.

POWER GAMES

Various games are being played, simultaneously, as you merrily skip to and fro. Some staff play what minor cards they have...against you. Whether as vicarious revenge against Seniors who lorded over them, or out of resentment, or just *because*...beware.

This is a rare situation where you should *not* pay (too much) attention. Try to stay on *everyone's* good side. It won't be possible, true, but it *is* preferable to gratuitous choice of sides (especially if *your* side is not the victorious one).

Take advantage of your quasi-invisible status as a not-yet-important one, and stay above (below?) the fray.

SQUEAKY WHEELS

Pity your secretary, who's racing to keep up with your Senior's work. She then sees your eager face, anxiously piling something on her desk. More work.

Most will strive valiantly to please two bosses. Just understand that you're a *very* distant Number Two behind Senior Number One.

If you're consistently put in a bind because of the demands on your secretary, discuss it with your office manager or Senior.

Let *them* fix it. Do not blame; ask for additional help. (Indeed, you should approach the problem *from,* not against, your secretary's position: ask for help for *her* benefit as well.)

The squeaky Junior gets the oil (and, again, greater respect if it's a legitimate squeak). More importantly, you won't be forgiven for late or sloppy work because you've lost your assistant.

If you're still left high and dry, then complain again. They will get someone for you. If it's the ineffective assistance of a secretary who's swamped by *another* Senior's work, complain again. Not officiously, but seriously: You have *work* to do. And—though you might not yet realize it—you *do* need secretarial assistance.

Don't be a pushover. Don't just hope that it'll get better.

Let them hire a temp. The economics of this problem are odd, but the solution is an easy one for you. Without secretarial help, your productivity dives from the tank top into the toilet bowl, unless you know what a computer is. (But, even then, you should not spend your time, and your client's money, fidgeting with the details of preparing signature blocks, captions, and so on.)

Without help, *you're* the one who is harmed, directly. But—here's the funny part—the additional cost of a temp isn't even *noticed* by the firm, but the benefit is given directly to you.

Problem solved. *Next.*

PRO FORMA CRITIQUES

Once a year, you might get a slip of paper on which you are supposed to "evaluate" the performance of your "subordinate"—a secretary. *Don't you do it.* This common managerial tool, regularly misapplied in commerce, is downright silly in a law firm context.

It is *dangerous* for *you*. Just as your Annual Review is important to you, so too are these Performance Reviews vital to your secretary.

Do *not* criticize, or even attempt to offer a "helpful" critique.

In the monochromatic world of personnel administration, there is no such thing. Fill in the blanks, instead, with pro forma pleasantries. Any serious comments, *if* appropriate, should be conveyed, *orally,* via other channels. It's doubtful your written comments will be taken seriously, but they are embarrassing and have been known to reduce, or even negate, a merit raise. (*Then* go ask her for that special favor.)

Let more Senior warriors fight these battles, and deflect wounds that might be fatal to you.

YOUR AGENT

Take advantage of your secretary and other office staff. They have the knowledge, skills, and, most likely, *enthusiasm* to help you get the job done. Let them.

Give them drafts (...well before *your* deadline) to type and polish. Ask them to confirm office or minor details. Ask them to call bureaus. Ask them to pull files. Take advantage of their expertise.

Take advantage also of their *existence*: Don't give out your direct office line number. The receptionist and your secretary are *valuable* intermediaries for you, just as you will be for your clients. Even after you're on a first-name basis with other professionals, let *your* professional assistants screen your calls. (Also, it's more comfortable for the *caller* to be passed through a receptionist; it gives them time to collect their thoughts and sound professional.)

Take advantage.

DICTAPHONES®—PART I

It's ironic that in this age of technology, a younger generation has gotten away from the time-saving tools of the office Dark Ages.

Some Seniors are (still) nincompoops when it comes to the winning ways of Windows, Mini-DVD, and their newest cousins, H- 'n XTML. Most are wizards, however, with Dr. Dictaphone.

Set aside your mouse for a minute, and pick up that little black box issued to you on your first day. *Use it.*

It will increase your productivity (and *quality*), and make your job go faster (and more pleasantly).

Start with letters. When you're about to draft one: *speak*, don't write. It'll take a little getting used to, but it'll be worth it. You'll soon learn, and will graduate to meatier stuff. Tasks like restatements of fact, deposition summaries, and recitals will fly off your desk.

Sure, the *total* time required to process documents can be greater (at first), but *your* time, as the law-wielding attorney, will be lesser. That is the underpinning of economic development the planet over.

Do what you do best. (Dictation software is improving, and might someday supplement or even supplant this dictacentric office routine, but we're not quite there yet.)

Not least, your Seniors will feel a happy glow of parental pride at your fledgling Dictattempts.

DICTAPHONES®—PART II

When you use your Dictaphone, follow (unwritten) dictation etiquette that will speed the process and ease your secretary's burden.

Speak clearly, into the microphone, and don't speak with music or other noise in the background. Spell out odd or frequently misspelled names or terms. Sound out punctuation:

> ...comma...[blah, blah, blah]...open paren, open quote, *ex why zee* corp, period, close quote, close paren...[blah, blah, blah]...period.
>
> New paragraph. Mister Zema's...*zee eee em ay 'zzz*...duties as an officer of the corporation are appropriate only...[blah, blah, blah]... period. The board's actions were thus ultra vires...ultra *vee aye arre eee ess*...comma...unless...[blah, blah, blah]...period.

After you develop a dictation rapport with your secretary, you'll be so blindingly efficient they might have to set up a JUNIOR X'ING warning sign near your door.

(Careful...Juniors are worth double points in season.)

WHILE WE'RE ON RAPPORT...

You must become increasingly efficient in your work; anything that hinders your efficiency hinders you.

You must give your secretary work. If you try to do too much of your own work because you think it's too much trouble—or you're too embarrassed—to get your secretary to do it for you, you will soon hit a productivity ceiling.

There is a skill to working with a secretary. As long as you are not officious (which, again, you should *never* be), you can (and should) let them know what you expect. *Communicate.* Explain your quirks. Point out your abbreviations, shortcuts, and whatnot.

Develop a mutual *modus operandi*. Work as a team. *Be nice.*

If she is curious, take a moment to explain why you want something done the way you do. (You might realize just how petty your peeves are, though.) Explain why legal language sometimes has to be so detailed...and *always* has to be precise. (She'll likely be *way* ahead of you on this score.) Your idiosyncrasies will make more sense to her, and she'll have less of an urge to resent or rebel.

Make her feel that what she does is important too, because it *is*.

Oh. Take note if *anyone* is discourteous or disrespectful to clients, clerks, or passers-by. Again, this shouldn't be a problem. (Indeed, it would be astonishing.) But, just as clients and the firm are known to others by *your* behavior—note thee well—so too are *you* known by the behavior of all in your office.

SECRETARY AS HOUNDDOG

Don't force your secretary to chase after you. It's not fair to her, it's irritating to others, and it won't reflect well on you. (You wouldn't want to be near the mental expletives roiling in the mind of a rushed Senior who's told you're nowhere to be found.)

When you leave the office, *tell your secretary*. Yes, it's somewhat like grade school. So be it. In law, you're on call. Get used to it.

Oh. Don't leave the office too much. Seniors don't like it when their Juniors are unavailable.

GOING HOME AGAIN

You can't. If you happen to be a former secretary, think carefully before accepting a position as an associate attorney with the same firm. It's a compliment, true, but you'll be saddled with the added, difficult job of breaking the perceptions of your former office mates.

The trouble is: you'll still be a subordinate...but of a very different kind. As a former secretary, you'll feel a strong kinship to—and have a lot more in common with—other secretaries. This is admirable, but dangerous. You cannot start your legal career acting like a secretary. If you *do,* others will easily treat you as one.

This isn't (entirely) a moral issue: secretaries and attorneys play different roles. Confusing the two will not only cause you to forget your lines, it'll confuse the other actors, disrupt the play, upset the director, and anger the producers.

DOCUMENTS

Take old ones and reuse them. "I will save time" is your mantra.

If your firm has a form file (which it almost certainly does), check with your Senior and *use the forms*.

Documents will fly out of your office once you get the hang of it. That makes for happy clients, and happier Seniors.

Efficiency is not your first concern, however: *proficiency* is.

Figure out first what to do and how to do it. *Then* you can figure out how to do it better and faster.

If the form file is old (which it might well be), ask your Senior to double-check the form, update the file, and *use it*. If your firm doesn't have a form file (unlikely), ask your secretary to start one. (Start one for yourself, anyway.) Ask your Seniors, look to form books, save old forms, note what others have done (for litigators, the Courthouse is a good place for examples [136]), ask your secretary to create blank forms, and so on—all to improve your work product and *save time*.

DOCUMENTS—THE SEQUEL

When in doubt, *make a copy*.

Naw ... make one anyway.

DOCUMENTS—REVENGE OF THE RAT

Even if not in doubt, *file it*. Now's not the time to disavow your latent pack-rat tendencies. No one will yell at you for sending too much to the fileroom ... and it might just save your posterior, later. (True, it might just *sink* you, later, but the odds—and law—favor records.)

DOCUMENTS—THE BATTLE FOR PERFICERE IV

Be circumspect before criticizing (or changing radically) *others'* documents. A *personal* investment is created with each document, and, no matter how bad something might be (within reason), treading on authorship toes is worse.

Usually, it's best to suggest (or require) those changes necessary to achieve your clients' legal goals and protect their legal interests...and forget the poetry. Once the project is finished, *then* you can await an opportunity to start a *new* project with *your* dazzling form.

DOCUMENTS—THE FINAL CHAPTER

Never insert a hand-written correction to a final document. Have another copy printed. Now's not the time for you to save our forests.

---

136 Don't waste time searching for a serendipitous find, but if you've heard of a case that sounds like a good model, ask your secretary to ask a staff person to get a copy. (And don't overlook the numerous examples under your nose.)

DATING AL CARBON

When you create a document, *put a date on it*.[137] And...include the *year*. Later, after the case has been long forgotten, the year (and date) might be the most important part. An undated document is like an uncollectible judgment: an expensive, worthless piece of paper.

I'm not sure whether you should date Al.

THE OFFICE MANAGER

Office managers range in talent and personality from super-beings to drips. Yeah, that's true of everyone else too, but administrators tend to more immediately affect the details of life. Most are good at their jobs, and will take them, and be taken, seriously. Many are former secretaries, which provides a good career ladder for talented staffers (...and a clue as to their grasp of the firm's goings-on).

Although no one will explain it to you, their contact with you will be limited. (You're happy to see them every other Friday, though.) They will almost *never* become involved in a legal matter (except in connection with billing); they're there to maintain the administration of the office.

They're also there to keep the office productive. If your chair is killing your back, ask for a new one. You'd be surprised at the goodies you can get...if you can justify the purchase.

Just as they won't interfere in your work, though, you should *not* become entangled in administration. Do not delegate (or meddle in) administrative tasks, except in emergencies or in *very* minor matters, without first checking with the office manager. (Rely on your secretary: let *her* take care of it.) Silly as it might seem to you, fiefdoms coexist within the firm, and just because you ignore—or disrespect—them doesn't excuse you. Don't trample on others' toes, just as you wouldn't want Seniors to trample on yours.

Don't be too much the technophile. (Oddly, most new technologies are *not* an improvement, at first. It takes a generation or so of refinement before productivity—the object of the game—kicks in. Smart Seniors and firm managers know this.)

Even if you *can* step in to save the firm time or money, stop first to think *very* carefully whether you *should*. Being the logistical hero can cause more problems for you than it solves for the firm.[138]

---

137 Not just any date, silly...*that* day's date.

138 If you'd like to introduce a new-fangled technology to a non-technologically minded Senior, *and* it presents a substantial improvement, *and* its disadvantages are acceptable...then approach your Senior from the perspective of a problem-solver, not a technology-lover. Mention the [time-saving, client-friendly, etc.] advantages. Then...*relax*. Let it sell itself.

Finally, take note: To the office manager, you are (*much*) closer to the staff than you are to the Seniors. The office manager is there to take care of *their* firm. You just happen to be part of the job.

CAUSE FOR PAUSE

Much of law office life is designed to puff egos. *The staff know better.* They're being polite out of professional courtesy. Don't misinterpret their civility for blind subservience.

Perhaps more tellingly, the office manager, veteran secretaries, and senior staff know what the *real* status line-up is in the office.

You're in training for your (potential) position as a real lawyer... *but you ain't there yet.* Just take a look at the bib (with that cute little gavel monogram) around your neck before you say anything snotty.

CONFIDENTIALITY

One more time...

Do not talk about your officemates to (non-spousal) outsiders.

Do not further, or—Heaven Forbid—*start* rumors about Seniors, senior Juniors, other Juniors, Paralegals, Managers, Receptionists, Clerks, Senators, other Stray Politicians, or Anyone...with the Staff. This is a no-no, and not very smart.

Confidence. Confidential.

Get it?

OTHER FUNNY CREATURES

Larger offices have various administrative staff astir.

These inhabitants can be helpful...if you let them.

They can make trouble for you...if you force them.

Be nice.

VEERING OFFTRACK

It happens. More often than most lawyers, who are too stuck in their own little worlds, know or admit.

There are nearly as many reasons for lawyers leaving as there are lawyers who have left. One reason is a fatalistic psychology that develops in many Junior/Senior relationships, worsened by even minor, but persistent, mishaps. Another reason is a "Sorry, kid. Nothing personal, but we've gotta' kill ya'…" predicament so familiar to Bond fans. And when Junior agents—*now issued Decoder Rings!*—believe (*succumb to,* really) their own characteristically immoderate egos, the disillusionment can be particularly severe. Where familiarity breeds more than moderate contempt, look abroad for your White Knight.

But don't expect a foreign power to be benign. Before racing off, take an *honest* look at what you face either staying or leaving.

Appreciate too the momentum of employment: Were you on the outside looking in—and they had a whiff of whatever problems (real or imagined) you've suffered—they'd give you the time of day only to remind you that the interview was over. Once you're *inside*, though, your advantage is that getting rid of you takes a decision, which isn't usually made (unless they've caught a bizarrely contagious downsizing bug) until they've run through at least some minimal attempts at rehabilitation. Take advantage of this advantage. (Take a look, too, at what you will face after the initial, and ephemeral, euphoria of freedom: more than a career hangs on your job.)

Many Juniors face such problems. Many *Seniors* have faced them, too. Spot the issue, and solve it.

Dare I say it again? You're not loved because you're a genius.

You're valued for your time and competence. Hell, even those few professors worthy of the description aren't *really* valued for their genius, except for the prestige it (sometimes) brings. Come to think of it, genius, or even super-competence, scares regular folk. If you're in the former category, dealing with the latter, *tone it down*.

Tone it down, anyway. If not out of modesty, then out of an awareness that law is fairly brimming with smart, smart people just itching to show off. Worse, those closer to the average tend to achieve status, and thus power, in part *because of* their more moderate endowment.

(You've heard the old saw: "The '*A*'s teach, and the '*B*'s work for the '*C*'s." There is a good degree of truth there, even in the law.)

---

139 To the future bankruptcy attorney: You might wish to reorganize the sequence of chapters to avoid dissolutionary results.

Moreover, with due tribute to the novelist Trevanian, defeats tend to come *not* at the hand of the *more* talented, who might legitimately surpass you. Rather, they come through the jealousies of the *lesser,* who cannot, except by treachery.

Tone it down. Intelligence is threatening...particularly to everyone lower on the curve. Understand it. Don't fight it. Get on with it.

Every profession has a fairly limited bandwidth of characteristics for its successful populace. Sorry to keep bringing another profession in on this, but...most pilots are smart, but not *too* smart. (They might start wondering why instruments work the way they do, rather than just using the information to fly the plane.) Attorneys have wider limits than most, ranging from below-average to stellar.

Figure out where *you* are on the line-up, but avoid operating—for at least your first year or so—on the edges.

WHAT CAN GO WRONG?

A few possibilities are presented: Dislike of work. Dislike of a Senior. Dislike of law practice.

Dislike for a particular variety of work is (relatively) easy to solve: change your practice. The sooner the better, because the greater the investment the firm makes in you—planned or not—in any field, the more difficult and unlikely will be a smooth transition to a different practice area.

If the work is too closely connected with the firm, then follow the same advice, but on a grander scale. As elsewhere, a little planning can go a long way. If the new field is in a different firm or area, start networking, to use a greatly overused buzzword. (Bar associations and law school yearbooks can come in handy, here.) Get the word out that you're interested, and, with luck, they'll come looking for you.

Even if not, you'll still be ahead of the game if you can make the switch on your terms. As one of my brothers is fond of repeating, the best job is the one you have while looking for another.

Dislike of a Senior. This is a bit more difficult, depending upon the firm. Most realize that, sometimes, some pairs just don't click. (It's often related to a clash of styles...and guess who loses?) The best way to handle this is to maneuver your way—quickly—into work for *other* Seniors. When you become busy for others, a disliked Senior will fade from your viewscreen, as if unintended.

Usually all goes smoothly: this occurs to *most* Juniors, in the normal course of practice. (Misfortune can come, later, if a Senior decides to make trouble when you're up for partnership, or even *after* you've made partner. If you have an inkling that yours is the type of firm where such gratuitous backstabbing takes place, you should move before you're locked in. "Golden handcuffs"—those ever more generous perks—start chafing after you've discovered them.)

Keep in mind, however, that nearly everyone has difficulties with (at least) one boss. (If it's *every* boss: For a more appropriate solution take a look in the mirror.) Also, in the irreverent words of only partial organizational satire, remember the Three Ws. Learn: *What to kiss, Whose to kiss,* and *When to kiss it.*

Dislike of law practice.

Many, many attorneys wake up after years of practice, and realize that the dreams of their youth will remain unlived. Many, many attorneys wake up after years of practice, and realize that they dislike who (...or *what*) they've become.

Sure, this is true of most lines of work, but law seems particularly susceptible to disillusionment. Part of this is the type of person who is attracted to law, and part is the reality of law practice. If *you* find a Sugar Daddy (...or Mommy) to take you away from reality, congratulations. Advance to Park Place. If no one owns it, you may buy it.

For everyone else: Adapt, migrate, or die.

FIRMNESS THROUGH ANOREXIA

You might be affected by yet another reality of modern law practice.

Law firms are subject to unusual economics. They've been insulated from the howling winds of competition, yet now find themselves dangerously exposed to the elements...without the managerial outfitting that has seen other industries through. And, in a lemming-like rush to shave costs encrusted from lush times, many find the idiotic ritual of downsizing a refreshing, but illusory, tonic.

It is idiotic because it ignores common sense. The recent practice of downsizing for the arithmetic thrill of it was as foolish as most other management fads. Businesses soon discover that "right-sizing" is not the panacea advertised; it creates as many problems as it supposedly solves.

It was refreshing, only in passing.

It is illusory because it ignores the unique nature of law practice as the nearly perfect labor-intensive industry...and because it is an attempt to maintain "artificially" high partner draws. Previously, law thought itself immune from the vagaries of commerce. It now enters the fray with unjustified relish. For lawyers, the irony is doubly pungent, because the supply of legal services is relatively fixed in each local market, especially in the short-run. Shedding "excess" Billable Units (you) has little—or *adverse*—immediate effect on the economics of individual law markets, but does immediately *reduce* the financial ability of firms to cover overhead and other fixed costs.

Not that the opposite—the unthinking expansion of the 1980s—is any less undesirable. (Yes, it's a foolish way to run a railroad. But it's *their* railroad. And it's not nearly as easy as I make it out to be, here.)

One key to long-term success for any organization is the optimal use of resources, not a mad dash to avoid the results of the previous mad dash. (As one of my business professors disbelieved years ago in defense of a vacuous risk-management matrix, managers are and must be responsible for *all* things internal, for it is they and they alone who have the authority to direct change.)

Perhaps worst of all is the cynic's observation that scorched-earth labor policies (and their reciprocal cousin, spendthrifty Good Times) are a mere recognition of on-going sloth. Well-managed organizations should, ideally, never be in a position where cutting—or losing—*any* staff results in a benefit.

If *you* get caught up in this mess (not too unlikely, at some point), watch your Junior behind, develop a strong niche practice, crank up your billing machine, keep your eyes open for other possibilities, and, *oh yeah*...watch your Junior behind.

GOING AWOL

Working for others is a two-way street. If *you* lose confidence in *them,* leave. If your heart's not in it, either change your heart...or leave. If law practice is not for you, use your legal education to advantage in another field.

Law *is* unique: It is procedural, yet grounded in Rules. It provides practical knowledge—and dynamic skills—that can be applied across a wide spectrum. Art teaches awareness. Science teaches analysis. Medicine teaches diagnostics. The military teaches accomplishment. Business teaches possibility. The law teaches consequences.

I used to think that the saying about "thinking like a lawyer" was just that: just a saying. (A conceited saying, at that.) I thought it should have been: "thinking like an intelligent person". Yet there *is* a difference. I'm not sure it goes as far as Professor Kingfield's arrogant proclamation that law school would turn your brain from mush to lawyer, but a legal education does provide an advantage over others, who rarely separate reason from detritus.

We spend our days thinking ahead, which is striking for those who do not. (Or are too busy *producing*.) A sharp non-lawyer friend once remarked, after watching another lawyer and me edit her (non-law) document, that we both continually searched for, and recommended changes to, her terms based on possible meanings that often were not intended...and that would never have occurred to her to change had they not been pointed out. An eye-opener for her, and for me.

Lawyers are trained to identify and disregard irrelevancies, which is quite an achievement in a world filled with them. True, we sometimes take it too far, but it is a valuable skill, nonetheless. Your legal education is a powerful tool that will open doors in hallways other than the one marked *Law Firms*: public service, politics, commerce, teaching, and, *oh yeah*...writing. All are within your grasp.

LOOKING AFAR

If you're not cut out for a hyper-aggressive practice path, you might consider a position abroad. Many foreign governments and businesses are looking for bright minds just like yours. With the right outlook, expatriate life is the best of all worlds. (With the *wrong* outlook, however, it will be a living Hell...of your own making.)

The position can make a stateside office pale in comparison. You'll work on weighty issues—at a higher level of responsibility—that you wouldn't dream of touching in the U.S. until after you've clocked a good decade of seniority. (I spent some time during my first year in Micronesia as counsel to delegates in their constitutional convention. *Wow.* It's not every day one gets to play with a constitution.)

You'll enjoy (...and endure) experiences that others only imagine. You'll meet (and be instant companions with) people you'd never otherwise know. Not only from diverse places, but also with little regard to rank or occupation. And you'll work in a cordial, positive atmosphere.[140] This worldly, cloistered life is a pleasant change from the provincial, cloistered life lived by most professionals, whose circle of friends narrows, as if by natural selection, to the point of numbing professional isolation.

Best of all, expatriate life is *cool*. It's one of the best-kept secrets of professional career planning. Even if you're a major gimp at home, abroad you're an exotic specimen. Big fish, little ponds, and such. (As an added bonus, most other places aren't so burdened by the negative images of lawyers so readily bandied about in America.)

Don't use language as an excuse. Americans are annoyingly and almost uniquely monolingual. English *will* suffice in most places, but you really *should* learn another language.[141] (Indeed, if you're still in school: minor in a second language. Even if it adds an extra semester, it will be among the best investments you ever make.) Facility in a second—or tenth—language instantly makes you golden. Unless you graduated by the skin of your teeth from (and with generous family contributions to) Fred's School of Cosmetology and Law ("...with one *convenient* location at the lower level of the Maple-Oaks Mall!"),[142] "prestige" credentials mean a whole lot less when the position calls for a law degree and bilingual abilities possessed by few. (You'll be surprised, though, at the top-notch renegades you do meet.)

---

140 Well, I write with experience from laid-back Micronesia, which makes Hawaii look downright uptight, in comparison; other locales are, no doubt, more formal. Still, I think the premise holds generally.

141 Maybe that's too indirect: *Everyone* should know (at least) two languages (...one of which should be English). If you do, you need not worry about the lower needs of your own hierarchy.

142 Free lawsuit with complete makeover!*   *Some restrictions apply.

Finally, for those who wish to mute the criticism that the U.S. has too many lawyers, you can do your part to help.

LOOKING AFAR—THE VOYAGE HOME

Know, however, that once you jump off the Express Train to Partnership...you probably won't ever get back on, because, *well,* it's going pretty fast. And Conductors don't like excess bagga...*er*...passenger movement. And you might just realize that the train's destination is far, far from where you want to be.

LEGAL RECRUITERS

If the market (...and you) are hot, you'll start getting calls from your neighborly headhunter after you've been out a few years. Careful.

Beware leaving the Devil you know for one you don't.

Recruiters can be a valued resource. It is nice to let someone else help with your (personal) sales job, but understand their motivation. Their client is not you: it's the hiring firm. Keep that in mind.

Keep in mind also that your leverage diminishes drastically once you've signed. Ask around about the prospective firm; now that you've some familiarity with practice, you have no excuse of ignorance.

Just as you should in school, do your homework.

IN-HOUSE

Another well-kept law career secret is the life of the in-house counsel. Working directly for a company—big, medium, or entrepreneurial— can be the legal equivalent of mountain-climbing: you will be on the leading edge, guiding others through the legal thickets and up the face of sheer business cliffs from the word GO...unlike your law firm counterpart, who usually only sees a problem *after* it's muddied.

You'll be involved in broader, more interesting discussions. You'll not need to worry about rainmaking, or collecting from clients unwilling to pay (or from those quite willing to raise the collections ante with a malpractice suit). You'll actually have (most) weekends off.

For their part, companies are waking up both to the economies that go with sharp in-house departments, and to the sharpness that goes with sharp in-house departments. In the future, it'll be a matter of competitive advantage to have entrepreneurial-minded legal counsel coursing throughout the corporate body.

A warning: In the past, in-house lawyering was a *very* weak career sibling; everyone assumed that once off the firm path, a legal career was dead. (Many in-house lawyers were senior associates denied partnership; thus the snobbish condescension.) This is becoming less true, and, besides, once you've enjoyed indoor plumbing, you'll not likely want to go back outside.

GOING SOLO

If you're going solo—either by choice or less voluntarily—then you are *really* going to get a look at the world from your Seniors' eyes.

Law practice—in addition to being a profession—is a *business*. Businesses fail. Businesses meander. They can reward, and they can enslave. They succeed through grimly hard work, intelligent leadership, and perseverance. They fail for many reasons.

Good sources *are* available to ward off common mistakes in setting up a law practice. (Again, you might check the publisher's web site, which includes recommended law practice books.)

A few basics:

Be honorable, and be good (figuratively and literally).

Use care in selecting clients. Reject bad clients and marginal cases as often as you can afford. Even if you're desperate, pay attention to the others' advice (and your own intuition) and learn how to say no.

Take no more cases than you can handle, with all your heart. *No.* Take *half* as many cases as you can reasonably handle, and do each, *perfectly*. Perfect means...*perfect*. Physicians are expected to perform medical procedure after medical procedure, perfectly, every time. When they don't, injured patients *sue*. Most attorneys, by comparison, wouldn't be allowed to cut a turkey. Yet your legal procedures—*ring a bell?*—are as important to your clients as your doctor's *medical* procedures are to *you*. Act like it.

Excellence requires *excellence,* not the overused, indolent meaning of mediocre-plus. (Not necessarily an A$^+$, but certainly a B$^+$ or better—a *true* B$^+$ or better.) You'll be *miles* ahead of your overworked counterparts. You'll enjoy better results, with less (...or just better) stress. You'll please your clients: a few happy clients are rather better than many disgruntled ones. And you won't starve. Plus, you'll build a reputation that'll precede you, to the benefit of your clients and paycheck, alike. (Building a good reputation takes tremendous effort; a bad one takes considerably less.)

When you run across clients who don't pay (or who don't cooperate, or who lie)...*drop 'em*. It'll be difficult (both emotionally and fiscally), but the risk and hassle of a malpractice suit, which often follows a fee-collection suit, *aren't worth it*...from every angle. (Credit cards can obviate both cash flow and collection problems, but beware the caveats, including a client's considerable powers to dispute a charge.)

Some lawyers are forced into solo practice. Yet law practice is too tangled for most to practice alone. Find a compatible compatriot for moral (...and real) support. At a minimum, a good office-sharing arrangement provides some economies, and it'll give you a personal and legal sounding board. It's important to your professional abilities, and to your emotional well-being. Don't mingle finances, but do keep an eye open to a future partnership.

If you're not an administrator, become one. Or hire (...or marry) someone who is; you'll need it.

And hang in there. It is scary, but it'll all work out okay.[143]

A DANGEROUS MISSION, HANS

A few guides dance around the deeper question of whether recent law grads *should* set up shop on their own.

Practicing law on one's own is a lonely, *arduous* existence for even an experienced attorney. For a new one, it borders on the insane.

Why?

The first reason is practical: it takes *years,* and sustained effort, to become a good attorney. Without the regular guidance of experienced (and self-interested) Seniors, the burden is overwhelming.

The second reason relates to how solos are treated. The reaction of *many* Seniors upon meeting a solo practitioner? A frown. Perhaps an ever-so-condescending shrug, and a nearly immediate dismissal of the solo's competence. Sadly, such presumption—while impolite—is all too often warranted. It takes skill, experience, and assistance to practice law *well*. It's difficult enough to arrange (and maintain) all three in a firm; it takes a singular dedication without.

An understandable and all-too-common reality is the inclination to just get by—or give up. We thus witness a recurring condition, with a solid percentage of solos, already behind the power curve, deciding (or accepting) a lesser fate.

I'll not beat around the bush: I *urge* you not to attempt a solo practice upon graduation. It will make your first year in law school seem a pleasant picnic by comparison. I do not mean to be condescending, but you *will* be incompetent—regardless of your (presumably strong) dedication. You will likely harm your first clients, who look to you for, at a minimum, legal expertise. Finally, to paraphrase Mr. Dangerfield's lament: you will get *little* respect from "fellow" professionals.

If you *are* forced to go solo immediately (or soon) after law school, plan to spend hundreds of hours in (and thousands of dollars on) CLE programs. (You will likely qualify for discounts, for most.) These are a professional necessity, along with other non-billable activities, and they'll put you on a more firm standing among your peers.

You should also volunteer for a variety of community activities, both law and non-law. These will give you exposure, experience...and they'll give you something to do.

Lest you think this section too harsh: A *dedicated* solo practitioner will become a *better* practitioner than most law firm Seniors—because your own trail will have been so rough. But it *will* be rough.

---

143 For the film version of this book, I recommend a fade to Brahms' Lullaby.

WHAT IF YOU SUCK?

Whoa!

I felt a pull in the cosmic thread of the Universe. (Perhaps it was all those defense shields rising at once.)

Now, now. Some of you, to put not too fine a point on it, won't be good lawyers.

Well, that point's a little dull. A very few of you lack the ability (or temperament) to think (and act) like good lawyers. A larger proportion won't make good law *practitioners,* which is what most think of when they think of lawyers. (Indeed, most probably think only of *trial* lawyers as "real" lawyers.[144])

A variety of factors contribute to suckdom. Paradoxically, intelligence is the least important to your immediate success, and is, at its peak, *inversely* correlated. Far more important are the squishy variables of motivation, motivation, and, coming in third, motivation.

Attitude and talent bring up a close fourth and more distant fifth, respectively. (Yes, luck and connections are there, but it's a cop-out to look to them: You're lucky and connected, or you're not. Either way, you'll still need the first five.)

And now for a word about incompetence: it's *ubiquitous.* In fairness to all who have ever been incompetent (which includes everyone, at first), it's inevitable.

It is impossible to know everything, when you start. It is impossible to get everything right, when you start. (If, by the way, you can't *see* your own incompetence, then you truly are.) What's objectionable is not inexperience, but *voluntary* incompetence.

If you are lazy, or just don't care…go play somewhere else. You'll mess up the playground, you'll cause others to cry, and the game will not end prettily for you.

True, you'll meet klutzes who, maddeningly, seem to get along just fine in life. Still, you can bet with some assurance that the halo that protects them will shine not as brightly for *you.*

More importantly, the picture is bigger: You might be destined for other glories. Save yourself and make the ultimate contribution to your clients…get motivated or get out.

---

144 Come to think of it, a Senior once said something to the same effect:

"You're not a *real* lawyer until you've appeared in court."

As a paper-pushing transactional Junior, I was taken aback…and silent. One reviewer—a former judge—was offended at this, and thought the Senior incorrect, and out of line. Perhaps so, but the prejudice is pervasive.

Another, a litigator-reviewer, commented: "And transactional lawyers probably think you are not a true lawyer until you've [you fill in the blank—I have no idea what you folks do]."

BURNING BRIDGES

Even if you do plan—or are asked—to leave, *be nice to your Seniors.*

Aside from (un)common decency and professionalism, there is a cynical reason for this: Unless you're joining a monastery in Tibet, your Seniors' evaluations will follow you for good or ill.[145]

Once you are working elsewhere, that shouting match with the managing partner won't matter nearly so much.

Until then, smile.

---

145 ... and I'm not entirely sure about even Tibet.

— 11½ (Bonus Chapter) —

On Being a Lawyer...

Welcome to one of the most disliked professions around. Perhaps it's *the* most disliked profession. Politicians (many of whom—*Surprise!*—are lawyers) slither in at second because, jaded as voters often are, they can—occasionally—throw the bums out. Not so once someone's ensnared in Lady Justice's cold arms.

It should not be surprising. We divorce ourselves from our clients; we need not believe as they do. Thus, we're suspicious. Inscrutable. Devious. We expect juries to find the truth (but not exasperation), even when we—*explicitly*—withhold part of the picture from their view. From *their* view—a reasonable one—more often than not we are part of the problem.

THE OLD LAWYER

Law has changed. Many *senior* Seniors look nostalgically, once upon a time, when law was an honorable and professional gentle society. It is no more (...if, indeed, it ever truly was).

For good and bad, money has changed our neighborhood...and we can't go home again. A few firms try. They attempt to duplicate the rarefied airs of 𝔜𝔢 𝔒𝔩𝔡𝔢 𝔍𝔫𝔫𝔰 𝔬𝔣 ℭ𝔬𝔲𝔯𝔱, but the pressures on law practice today, even for the Old Guard, are intense...and unyielding.

(These pressures have found their way into corporate and government practice as well; there is no institutional immunity from the pressure cooker of modern law.)

One catalyst for the change from an elitist profession to a profession/business, then on to a business/profession...then finally to an industry/profession...was the entrance of, and demand by, *non*-élites. Long before the hated billable hour,[146] law was a profession peopled by the élite, and conspicuously a product of that stratum (log-cabined practitioners excepted). This was not without its abuses, but, as long as you were on the inside, it was a cozy place.

Outside, however, cold, cold, cold.

If you were white and male and fittingly upper-class or *very* ambitious, the law was cozy, indeed. Before you deign to judge, either condemningly or wistfully, remember who you now are: an attorney. You will reap the benefits of the new legal industry/profession, just as you are resented, feared, and sometimes openly despised by those who,

---

146 Which was, originally, an effort to *control* legal costs.

a generation ago, would more likely have beamed in admiration. Sure, lawyering has always had its detractors—many soundly supported by evidence—but generations past looked upon a pleasing backdrop against which lawyers were an integral part of an honorable fabric of society. Much of that respectful backdrop, which reflected well on us, has tattered...and what is left is badly faded.

Well, maybe not. Maybe it's just been replaced by a chromacolor screen blaring bites of the latest personal injury ads (between retrospectives on the Simpson ordeal). Sadly, law is ever more like politics: Even those who like their own lawyers dislike the profession.

It's part of the "But he's *my* SOB!" mentality.

Also behind the headlines lies a lust for partner draws that are, by historic standards, astronomical.[147] No, it's worse than that: a few decades of playing with the economics of sweatshop law have whetted the appetites of Seniors, who now *expect* all those dazzling perks and, by exhaustive hardships past, feel them to be their due. With the laboring pyramid of eager new partners and hungry young associates rising taller and less sustainable by each passing billable hour, and by a market grown weary of feeding this ravenous legal beast, economic reality was bound to strike.

So, for everyone, a financial Catch-22: Seniors, no doubt, regret their bidding wars for new associates. The salary ante for presentable associates has been upped...with only marginal benefits among same-stratum firms; now, they *all* pay too much (...leaving the majority of "lesser" law graduates to scramble for survival).

Still, there it is. As a lemming-modeled profession and in fear of losing "star" graduates to other firms, they can't (easily) take it back. And, as humans, we want the best of both worlds: we like the goodies that come with law-as-an-industry, but aren't so sure about economies of scale and other competitive realities that come with the cold, hard world of commerce. Thus, a strenuous attempt to straddle the worldly fence, to hide behind the former (and imagined) glories of the profession, while glancing lustily at all that money flowing about. Further, as non-élites, we're more concerned with generating income as an end unto itself, rather than as an expected means to a comfortable, honorable life. The problems arise when income-as-an-end confronts law-as-a-duty.

Law has changed, perhaps even more dramatically than the society it permeates. We've become more open, honest, diverse, competitive, critical, divisive, and, on the whole, better. This change has come so quickly, and yet subtly, that most have forgotten the gentlemen's

---

147 In 1994, a law partner made 7.5 times the median income, compared with "just" 2.7 times the median in 1951. (Among top firms, the disparity is greater.) Not to be outdone, the average CEO reportedly makes 419 times the wage of the average factory worker, compared with 42 times as much in 1980.

club that is our heritage. And we've even more quickly tossed aside the possibility that *social* precedent might not always be bad.

In our haste, we've crushed much that was good.

Whatever our modern assumptions, this heritage continues to rule our modern ways, like the dead hand of a spitefully resistant but inalterably mortal decedent. *Plus ça change, plus c'est la même chose.* The more a thing changes, the more it's the same thing. Bosses are still "partners", and you're still the lowly "associate", which likely was intended as a continual reminder of the youngster's standing...and august responsibility. The (relatively) gentle apprenticeship of years past has, sadly, fallen into disuse, and meager attempts in law school, although helpful, serve to give you only a small reference to the grand game you're about to play. Stakes are higher, clients more demanding, relationships more fleeting.

Whatever that history, it *is* history. We are among the landed gentry no longer. We are instead amidst a flurry of Rambo-litigators, lean and hungry practitioners, and a logarithmically more complicated and inhospitable legal and social environment.

Whatever the reasons, you will now be paid, worked, and ignored to an extent that might have seemed unprofessional a generation ago. Yet, when you're most crestfallen over some stumble, remember this: Seniors, on the whole, weren't as good as you are. *What?!* Blasphemy! It's true, though. Take a look at a Pre-Law Handbook from 1970 or so. For most schools, law admissions were then *much* looser...and subsequent competition in class rather lighter. (Applicants to even the top law schools rarely faced worse than 3:1 odds—many closer to 2:1— stats more common among regional or even local schools, today.)

True, we shouldn't confuse quantity with quality, but if the figures were half as favorable today, we'd nearly all wear monogrammed turtlenecks and take on nicknames modeled after car-care products.

One outgrowth of maturing institutions is rising standards, which means that those already inside might not have made it had newer, higher standards been applied to *them*. What this means is not that Seniors are slugs. Rather, it means that, because the competition is so much fiercer today, comparing the "average" Junior of yesteryear, who faced a simpler legal environment, with the "average" Junior of today is misleading, at best. (Or insulting, at face.[148])

---

148 Lest you get smug, *you* probably aren't as good as your more recent predecessors. This "Lost Generation" that came of legal age in the early-1990s suffered the worst of two worlds: The most savagely competitive law school application jungle—nearly *twice* as fierce as in recent years—and a *brutal* retrenchment in the law job market upon graduation, leaving many in this talented group to fight not only for professional survival, but also against the beast of bankruptcy. Think I overstate? I know of graduates from some of the *top* law schools who were downsized in mass firings, who went *years* without work...or who were never able to find work in the law, at all.

On the other hand, even the best Juniors, way back when, never received the stratospheric salaries that most of you now hope to get. In short, the transformation of the legal profession into a business has tightened the noose around everyone's work-a-day neck.

THE BAD LAWYER

There're *lots* of bad lawyers out there. True, there're lots of bad *every-ones* out there too, but that's no excuse. *No.* It's more than *no excuse.* It's a contemptible cop-out. Lawyers have duties to their clients and to society...and an unusual measure of power to abuse their station. The two types of bad lawyer: the incompetent fool and the competent cheat. (If you're an *in*competent cheat, *hey,* you've enough trouble without extra bad-mouthing from me.) Both are guilty of the same sin—a lust for unearned riches—if for different reasons. (The former, for laziness; the latter, for anger.)

If lazy, you won't survive. If angry, you won't survive well.

Again, my apologies: One's incompetence as a Junior (is that why it's called *practice?*) isn't bad per se, but it *is* cause for consternation ...and for reliance on the wisdom of more senior others.

And now to the angry, contemptuous—and *contemptible*—lawyer, who does more damage in one case than ten decent lawyers are able to do good in ten cases, each. Nonlawyers aren't aware (and would disbelieve) that lawyers are held to a higher standard of integrity.

Sadly, some *lawyers* also disbelieve. Or, perhaps worse, we think the Rules shouldn't *really* apply to us—a sort of self-granted Divine Immunity. Sure, there've always been bad lawyers...but there weren't quite so many, and they weren't quite so obvious. We see one result of our own cynicism in the severely depressed image of lawyers.

Much as we postmoderns pooh-pooh the notion, there *is* something to the Chivalrous Order of the Officer and Gentleman (which term, in my book, includes women). Perhaps it seems silly, or even naïve, but there *is*—and must be—a higher duty. We are too predictable for it to be any other way; if we don't expect an ideal, we won't approach anything close. (Not that most will live up to that ideal—or that we should ignore the reality that the cape accompanying membership dishonorably protects the bad with the good—but we are a creature of symbolism. Whether a flowing cape will make *you* more honorable is an aside—we have no choice but to hold ourselves to an ideal.)

Regardless, you *are* held to a higher standard. And, most probably, you'll be *held* more closely to this raised standard. Your *client* can lie. That's right. As long as he's not a deponent or on the witness stand, he can fib up a storm...with only his conscience and the threat of shame or retribution as his guide. Not so, *you.* Though the prohibition has been poorly enforced—so far—lawyers may *not* lie.

Look it up, if *you* disbelieve.

THE BROTHERHOOD

As a practical matter, it's not very smart lawyering.

I once was lied to by opposing counsel. Not a major lie, to be sure, but a lie nonetheless. I gave him a few centimeters the first time. He'd get nary a micron thereafter.

And guess where that left his client.

Sure, you'll be able to get away with some things—hell, *many* things—but, even in a large city, you'll be surprised at how often you run into the same adversaries. I cannot be delusive, though: There's enough manure strewn near (and within) the average courthouse to fertilize the neighboring twenty counties. This isn't just for equestrian kicks. The rewards of immediate gratification provide a constant check on honor. Still, for you, the question's the same: Regardless how wounded the patient, where do *you* wish to operate?

Though it might seem too quaint a vision, your reputation is pretty much all you'll have in law. If you lie to (...or mislead) other counsel (...or, God forbid, a judge), you can guarantee with a certainty that'd make an actuary quake that your standing in the legal community—and it *is* a community—will be pegged just half a notch above solidly convicted child rapists. Not a pleasant way to go about practice.

Think about it.

THE LAITY

Lying to clients is even less forgivable, but, unfortunately, it's also less uncommon...and less punished. I once perused an issue of the *California Bar Journal:* I was astounded at the sheer *volume* of reported disciplinary actions (...which, presumably, are only the tip of a malpractice iceberg). Worse, most of the problems were, from a law practice standpoint...*stupid*. Sitting on cases. Stealing clients' trust-account money. (*Gee*...now what do "client" and "trust" mean, again?) Self-dealing. *No* dealing.

Just what the hell are we doing? We cheat our clients. We take their money, without earning it. We lose their cases, without trying. We ignore them, without thought. We treat them like crap, and then wonder why the world suddenly rises against us.

We enter a noble guild—it should not be cause for embarrassment to think so—and then deceive ourselves into believing our own hype. Worse, we become so cynical we hardly believe the rules should apply to *us*...especially after we learn that they don't seem to apply, with any moral uniformity, to our clients. Our adversarial system is partly to blame—*All's fair in love, war, and, perhaps, winning?*—as well as our failure to steadfastly maintain perspective.

If *you're* a cheat, there's not much this book can do to change you. It'd be poetic to proclaim that you'll probably fail, but in life too many are rewarded for their dishonesty. As a Junior, though, the level of cheating skill required to snow *everyone* higher up is so high as to almost make it cynically justified.

You're on your own in this one. And you're among us.

YOU

Some of you *are* cheats. Not a pleasant thought, but true. Beginning with a taste in school for the benefits of unpunished fraud, the same avaricious lust for instant gratification that fills us all screams as well for a life of idle freedom from the chores of work. Lawyers in particular seem to think that they *deserve* the sinecure life. Aside from the moral issues, you should realize that, unless you've a guaranteed slot in your family's firm, it's highly improbable that you'll avoid the unpleasant realities of law practice. Even then....

Cynicism is not better than hypocrisy.

One problem with cheating—particularly if it's successful—is the powerful incentive it provides to cheat elsewhere...and often.

And the game never ends. It just gets more seductive. But, *hey,* I won't blow smoke at you. Remember the maxim we were all taught: "Crime doesn't pay." They *lied.* Crime pays. Darned well, too. Smart thieves—those who steal for serious money, rather than for drugs or rent—do quite a bit better than our teachers.

Lawyers are in positions of power ripe for abuse. Not only the obvious stuff, like self-dealing, but also the more mundane (and distressingly common) habits of overbilling, double-billing, and charging clients—full fare—for work done for, and paid by, another client.[149]

A force for most cheats is a contempt of those who are cheated, and who are usually ignorant (and thus defenseless) against professional chicanery. The sad truth is that it's all too easy to get away with it.

You might be tempted to dishonesty because you think it's good lawyering, or because you feel cheated by life. Either way, get a grip.

It is not good lawyering. It is not good lawyering. It is not good lawyering.

And even if you *were* cheated by life, which is a *generous* allowance of a *remote* possibility...take a look around. There's always someone else who's got it worse. A little perspective, please. As an attorney, you won't starve. Sure, you might have student loans that would've drowned your ancestors...who probably couldn't've afforded to go to school at all. Sure, you might have to work harder than the homeless folk you step over on your way to lunch.

Get a grip.

---

149 This last offense, in most firms, is taken for granted. It is seen as a nonissue— *Gee...Why should a client get the benefit of another client's previous expense?*—or it's not seen at all. It's *wrong.* Firms have tried—and, thus far, have succeeded—in capturing *all* of the economies possible in institutionalized law practice. That's gluttony, unwise, and, unless you've just saved the planet from annihilation, unjust.

THE EXPENSIVE LAWYER

One of the irritants clients face is the fear that they're being ripped off. Too often, this fear is soundly justified. Ever hear about the power plant mechanic, who presented the utility with a bill for $100,000.03?

Upon learning that all he did was tap on a pipe to avoid the meltdown, they exclaimed: "But that's ridiculous!"

To which the mechanic replied: "The tapping cost you three cents. The rest was knowing *where* to tap."

Lawyers know where, but should beware the temptation of charging too much for the tap.

No. That's much too mild.

Lawyers have been charging too much for taps... and acting as if every tiny rattle is a meltdown-in-progress, worthy of Olympian compensation. We've become so infatuated with rules—and loopholes—at the expense of reason that we easily lose sight of our purpose, which should be defined by the needs of our clients, and not of our egos (... or mortgage payments).

Worse, many lawyers aren't worth their *normal* rate.

Ever hear about the client who phones a high-powered attorney, only to learn of the counselor's thousand-dollar-per-hour rate?

"Fine," the prospective client replies, "as long as you can solve my problem in ten minutes."

Few are worth the price of six pounds of meat every six minutes of the working day. (Filet for Seniors; lesser cuts for the rest.) Those who *are* worth it... aren't worth it *every* six minutes of the working day. Yet that's what lawyers expect.

Some of you will counsel corporations and wealthy clients, who are used to the notion of lawyers-as-a-(high)-cost-of-doing-business. Even so, you can be sure that they won't be ecstatic over your bills. And, for less-than-wealthy clients, the strains stir closer to the surface.

Therein lies the tension: Lawyers want a life of luxury, and their clients want to retire on more than Social Security. No, that's too glib. When clients need lawyers, they usually need them under duress (or, at least, under unpleasant or stressful circumstances): Writing a will. *Reading* a will. A property dispute. A divorce. Buying a house. Selling a house. *Losing* a house. Suing someone. *Being* sued.

Not a pleasant situation among them. Adoption might be the only warm practice (and even that's subject to some distressing turns).

The answer?

Get as close to that ten-minute marker as you can. If you are truly good, and truly fast, and truly considerate, you will have little worry over disgruntled clients. A worthy goal for selfish reasons (staffing a complaints station isn't one of life's more enjoyable jobs), if not for altruistic ones.

Don't make it any worse than it already is.

THE GOOD LAWYER

The insults slung at lawyers are so incessant and biting, it's clichéd to expect the cinematic bad guy to be the pin-striped lawyer. *Why?* The reasons are manifold, but they all boil down into an undeniable truth: In life, lawyers are parents. And, as any normal, rambunctious non-parent knows, parents are a drag.

Worse, we parent not for love but for money.

The first thing we do, let's kill all the lawyers.

That unforgettable line is repeated again and again (usually with no light undertone of approval) at dinner parties the nation—no, the world—over. It's ironic, then, that few remember (and fewer convey) that those words were spoken by one Dick the Butcher, a follower of another, Jack Cade, a revolutionary who would be King.

Why kill all the lawyers? Had Dick had a run-in with a nasty divorce attorney? No, that'd be too poetic. Revolutionaries have enough to worry about, but they do need two things: a convenient scapegoat, and a free sword.

It is *we* who stand as the first line in defense of the kingdom's soul. True, the kingdom might be corrupt, and the King incompetent or malevolent. Yet it is the rare revolutionary who is better, and the rarer revolution that can *do* better.

Shakespeare was, perhaps unintendedly, paying our profession a supreme, if back-handed, compliment.

The difference between the Balkans (which only happens to be one of the hot spots *du jour*) and the rest of our world is not nearly as great as we delude ourselves into believing.

Law is a noble, pathetic calling. Noble because without it, civilization cannot exist. Pathetic because we're only partially civilized. The message of the Holocaust (which some now find expedient to deny) is not a memorial to those who died (which happens to include half of my ancestry), but a pledge by all who live that it won't happen again.

Yet it does, over and over.

It does where political demands—and the boundless seduction of rule by force—overpower the rule of law. When law is co-opted, which occurs all too easily, the innocent suffer. And the greater sin—with history as an icy guide—is that the guilty do not.

The list, shamefully, goes on.

In 1915, Armenians suffered nearly as grievously under Ottoman Turks as did the Jews under Nazi Germans. In 1937, the Japanese butchered some 100,000–300,000 Chinese (no one knows how many) in a few days after they took Nanking. The streets *flowed* with blood. (The purpose? A planned, preemptive punishment against the Chinese provisional capital.) Of course, the Chinese peasantry have fared little better under their *own* warlords. The Japanese continued their exploits against 140,000 or so Caucasian prisoners of war, with a near-genocidal vehemence expediently ignored by history, and they planned mass executions had the Allies invaded the Japanese mainland. (By the numbers, though, Stalin easily outranks Hitler.) If you'd like to fast-forward a bit, more than one million Cambodians—about a *seventh* of the population—perished under the Khmers Rouges between 1975 and 1979. More recently, the Rwandan Hutus decided the Tutsis had been around long enough. (The *logistics* of killing so many thousands of people, in such a short time—with *machetes*—is testament to our ability to overcome technical obstacles when the need, however evil, arises.) It's almost hopeless to try to track the goings-on in Bosnia—though apparently things were pretty dirty there, ethnically. (This is a lesson, too, in the by-product of a centuries-long clash of Levantine and European "civilizations".[150])

I'm leaving some folks out, no doubt...and that was just for *this* century. And, so you don't think I've forgotten our own, we've got: the native folk who beat us by a few thousand years (...and thus suffered the misfortune of being in the way), Americans of western, central, and southern-African descent, Americans of Irish descent, Americans of Japanese descent,[151] Americans of Chinese descent...*Hell,* Americans of Any-Subsequent-Descent.

The list, shamefully, goes on.

We the Species have a rather rude habit of pissing on each other. Most are too timid or weak to piss back. So long as there's at least one wolf about, law is the protector—however imperfect—of the sheep. And before you deign to look down on those many sheep, look around instead at all who are gentle. It is they you protect, however indirectly. *Hi, mom.*

The notion that human conduct is to be guided by a *commonly applied* set of rules—the Rule of Law—is almost mystical in its implications, and not at all predestined. Entropy is a powerful cosmic force, overcome only with the addition of energy.

In society, you're part of that energy. You toil to add predictability to life's goings-on. It might, at times, seem a frivolous waste, but the nihilistic alternative is far, far worse. Some lighter versions of this are evident in the rubble of the former Soviet empire, where the Rule of Law must now be built from scratch. In Albania, for example, lawyers were, essentially, outlawed. Not a pretty society...before or after.

---

150 ...and in the dangers of cleaving to group identity. Isn't it interesting the many *intra*-group disputes: North v. South Vietnam, East v. West Germany, North v. South Korea, Northern Ireland, East Timor. Odd how the adjective takes on a greater importance than the noun.

151 If you'd like to ponder the consequences of lawyers co-opted, take a look again at *Korematsu* (in which the Supreme Court approved the internment, without due process under even the standards of the time, of...*Americans*).

The energy needed to overcome our barbaric side is the subdued goodness of an impartial *system*—hardly the stuff of a more romantic yet inevitably hollow sheriff (played by John Wayne)—to protect the gentle, even cowardly, townsfolk. Though gentleness is the desired result, its *attainment* is a guarantee of relapse.

On the other side of Asia, in China, a long history of antagonism to the mere *suggestion* of the rule of law—seen, wrongly, as a sovereign or even cultural affront—belies a shadow system of justice that is becoming increasingly troublesome as the demands of commercial and diplomatic interaction overwhelm Chinese social institutions designed for a different purpose.

Totalitarian justice, for most, is no justice at all.

And, to reemphasize *your* role in all this, remember that Adolf relied on the active participation of Germany's best and brightest. It's a fine, perilous line we walk. Stride carefully.

THE COSTLY LAWYER

And for those condemning of the supposed economic disaster that is our profession (including many within the law who buy, uncritically, the criticism), ask them what, *exactly,* would they propose instead?

Don't let them off the hook with some whiny (or, worse, glib) solution. Give 'em a taste of the Socratic method. This ability to play the Devil's advocate is perhaps the single most annoying feature we lawyers exhibit. But, if judiciously displayed, it can educate.

Even if you *agree* with them, explain the possible complications from the *other side's* perspective. As bureaucrats know in their bones (and as everyone else happily rejects), the Devil is in the details.[152] Even a simple policy choice will complicate—sometimes severely—the administrative structure necessary to carry out whatever the policy majestically commands.

(I once drafted a new court procedure for citations, to replace an unwieldy one. I made the mistake of offering to the Chief Justice the option of automatically increasing the fine levied. He heartily agreed, and I was left to figure out the minutiae. That simple idea *tripled* the complexity of the rule. Although I too liked the goal, and I thoroughly enjoyed the drafting, I would have argued strongly against it.)

Law is social infrastructure. Expensive, intricate... and crucial.

It is less difficult to castigate than it is to construct. And it is even easier to blame the ills of humanity on the necessarily imperfect institutions that We the People did ordain and establish.

---

152 With all respect to Gustave, *God* may also be there, but it is not He who will make the mischief.

Of course law is inefficient. *Conflict* is inefficient. Law practice only serves to make it worse because it attempts to purify past conflict in an artificial truth machine, which, as often as not, backfires. As long as we have humans to deal with, a defensive instinct emerges to thwart any attempt to get to the "truth". This is a lesson, magnified manyfold, that frustrates jurists all.

True, our system overdoes much of the process, but chew on this: All economic development (...from, say, the Dark Ages on) is possible only with law as a midwife. All that we take for granted—fast cars, fancy houses, juicy cheesesteaks—*all* would be impossible (...for all but the most powerful) without the protective umbrella that law, and law alone, provides.

Who came up with the idea of a contract? What would life now be like without the simple notion of the ability to bargain... and to seek redress for another's breach?

Who cares?

We all should, for the idea of a contract—absurdly simple in principle—is perhaps the single most important factor in the pleasant reality that you will eat tonight, and not be murdered.

Huh?

Let's go through it, carefully. Contracts involve the transfer of things from one person to another. The Things may be real, or intangible. The Person may be real, or corporate. The Other may be friend or enemy. In the realm of commerce, it matters not.

But why should we so want to trade? If memories of grade-school trading-card victories don't ring true, how about the idea of spending your time lawyering for yourself. Farmer does not farm for you, or for the joy of it. He farms to feed his family. Banker does not lend him money for you, or for the joy of it. He lends to feed *his* family.

Do you lawyer for the joy of it?

We trade because we cannot each do everything, and shouldn't want to try. Still, we want whatever toys others have. Yet the process of transferring something of value to another, almost by definition, is ripe for conflict. If we can't get it peacefully—and easily—we get it less graciously: we *take* it. The choice is simple: trade or violence.

Ninety-plus percent of trades will be agreed, made, and forgotten, without second thought. Such is life. It is the other, smaller percentage of transactions where something goes awry to upset one, or both, of the parties. That's where we establish rules: The Law.

But so what? Why not just write off those few bad cases, and eliminate the need for irritating—and expensive—lawyers?

Indeed. Why not?

Because we are human. We cannot agree so merrily to shrug our shoulders over future conflicts, which, when they erupt, incite our baser instincts. Exasperation. Anger. *Vengeance.*

We also cannot abide our *own* agreements…to proper *behavior;* *im*proper behavior is too profitable. Thus a centuries-long, convoluted evolution of commercial law from the earliest days of proto-navigation to the mind-bogglingly complex intricacies of today's commerce.

All in our food chain depend on similar relationships with un-known others for the "essentials" in life. Yet without the promise that a transfer can take place, with assurance that what one gives will not be lost in vain, nothing—*nothing*—would exist but war, pestilence, famine, and death…and shimmering enclaves of those who've gotten theirs, and intend to keep it.

Think the logic simplistic? Consider the unrelenting demands of feeding, clothing, and housing the residents of any mid-sized city. Tens of thousands of cartons of food, per day. Thousands of liters of drink, per day. A few hundred liters of potable and waste water, per person, per day. Millions of kilograms of garbage. Megawatts of elec-tricity. And on and on.

Yet this logistical reality is comparable to the entire population of most nations a few centuries ago. The only exceptions of organized activity without the rule of law that come to mind involve either ex-treme (and usually contrived) external threat…or autocracy (and the very real threat of violence to anyone who gets in the way).

Should we reduce the complexity of our laws? Don't get me started. I'd take several dozen pairs of scissors—and a few industrial sharpen-ing wheels—to our codes. They are absurdly complicated. They should be accessible to, and understood by, the average citizen. Seriously.

Still, we're faced with the same dilemma: we live in a complicated society, with complicated possibilities. Yet it boils down to the basics. What about mortgages?

Before? *Nothing.*

After? The possibility of escape from perpetual serfdom.

The notion of possessing a thing before paying for it—*in full*—was as radical as it was—no, *is*—crucial to our on-going economic revolu-tion. Had it not taken hold, however, how could any other transaction (beyond handing over a twig for seisin) have developed?

Much as we resist the notion, life really isn't as complicated as we make it to be. In worldly matters, sustained economic development is preconditioned on some rather mundane policies, starting with enforceability of contracts and recognition of property rights.

Yeah, it's no fun evicting someone who's missed half a year's pay-ments, but how else can it be?[153]

---

153 Before you respond with the notion that, *Gee,* why can't we just be *nicer,* take it to its logical conclusion: In any community (of humans) greater than one, communism (in its true sense, not the folly of the Soviets or East Asians) *cannot* work. (To paraphrase Coolidge's prophetic, rhetorical comment: "Why should someone else work to feed me, without some benefit to himself?")

Even computers insist on hierarchy.

Yeah, it's no fun arguing about who gets custody, but what should we do with infantile parents...split the kids down the middle? (Might be better to do that with the *parents*.) What about wills, corporations, stocks, bonds, deeds, checks, recognition of foreigners and their possessions (no small historical development in itself), bills of lading....

What did I leave out? What did I *not?*

Better to argue, inefficiently, about blueberry subsidies than to kill, efficiently, over anything else. Unfortunately, that's pretty much the choice. America is a litigious place—not quite as bad as naysayers suggest—but litigious nonetheless, in both fact and spirit.

Why? To quote a *National Law Journal* editorial, "we are inculcated from early childhood with the belief that life is fundamentally fair, and in the isolated instances when it turns out not to be, those injustices must be corrected."

Well, life is *not* fair. Or, perhaps more cautiously, a large part of our frustration results from our disbelief that life is, fundamentally, neither fair nor unfair.

We are each are created *un*equal: each with talents, shortcomings, and circumstances different from all others. And in the process of living, these differences, *well*...make a difference.

Lest you again reply mentally that perhaps I'm being ideological (a role I decline), I'll respond more forcefully. With several dozen decades of economic reflection, we're presented with two choices: unequal distribution of wealth, or *more* unequal distribution of poverty. Which do you prefer?

Difficult questions *well* beyond the scope of this book are raised, true, but demagogues in fashion constantly manipulate the issues away from deeper truths. (Paradoxically, Adam Smith, who is credited with the crystallization of a pure *laissez faire* ethos, recognized the need for, and promoted, certain government oversight.) Capitalism works because it co-opts human nature; communism fails because it rejects it.

And this is only the beginning: add such concepts as freedom, democracy, the rule of law (and its protections against the cancers of favoritism, nepotism, and other insidious forms of corruption), and such other concepts so hackneyed to our modern ear we forget their importance. Add also to this dry analysis the human element.

Thus, an unhappy answer to Rodney King's plaintive plea: *No.*

A compulsion for *niceness* is understandable, and adolescent. In adulthood, especially in an institutional context, it is *dangerous*. Why? Because life is not a snapshot. It is instead a movie. *Many* movies, each with unfilmed endings. An adult must ask: "What are the *consequences?*" The Law is an *ultra*-adult: we cannot be concerned solely with a single conclusion, but must also consider its effect on all other like cases. Much to the disbelief of the parties, each case is a mere pixel in a grander picture. Thus...The System. This "System" should not be a bad word. Its relative goodness or evil rests with us; its absence is a guarantee of the latter.

The gods laugh. How easily we mortals unlearn.

Treating unequal people equally *under the law* is bound to be a difficult undertaking. In building a society, we can favor one set of jurisprudential interests, or the other.

Do we make it easier to convict, knowing that some innocent will be wrongly punished, or do we make it more difficult, knowing that some guilty will not? Do we make it easier to recover damages, knowing that some defendants—and society—will be drained, perhaps unfairly, or do we make it more difficult, knowing that many who are harmed will go without? Unfortunately, when such basic questions are posed, there are no answers. Only choices.

Worse, the law cannot be concerned with the proverbial pound of flesh because—much as we thirst for blood—the guilty ones are, more often than not, turnips. Thus, an endless battle to determine who *else* should pay. Not a pleasant prospect... or process.

Yes, there's *lots* of room for improvement. But destroying the system—or its actors—is not the answer.

Be strong enough to say, civilly, "I disagree." Then explain why. *Yes,* it might turn 'em off. So be it. As long as you don't go overboard, they'll respect your insight—because so few will have thought of the consequences—and they'll probably respect you. If not, they're not worthy of *your* friendship, are they? (You'd be surprised, though, at how *polite* assertiveness will stop 'em in their tracks.)

Either way, you might plant the seeds of thoughtful doubt in other listeners' minds to not be so quick to spout—or hold—simplistic solutions to complex and inherently conflicted problems.

THE MISUNDERSTOOD LAWYER

Now, there you are at that fancy dinner party and who should walk up but a physician (who's enduring his second malpractice suit in as many years)... *breathing fire.* (Better watch out. Better not cry. *Legal* malpractice is the next growth industry in law.) There's little you can do to assuage such anger, other than to sympathize, sincerely... and explain why the rules work as they do (and what would happen if we went back to the bad ol' days).[154]

In less-confrontational situations, explain, carefully, how the law relates to daily concerns. (This is one benefit of the bar exam, which forces you to truly *learn* The Law.) Criminal trials, for example, frequently make the news, and are just as often poorly reported, leading

---

154 But don't talk specifics; it will get everyone—especially *you*—into trouble. This is not, by the way, because you're being asked for a legal opinion—the product that puts food on your table—without being paid. Rather, it's that confidentiality evaporates, the question is probably poorly framed, you will likely give an incomplete (or entirely wrong) answer, and any answer you *do* give will almost certainly be misinterpreted, and misused.

to misconceptions and anger at our judicial system. That's not good. For example, it's important first to understand, and second to explain, that victims are *not* parties to a criminal action...they're *witnesses*. Indeed, this crucial distinction in criminal law is rarely understood even among lawyers: the state's interest is not the victim's interest. The state prosecutes for the benefit of its citizenry; the victim is only indirectly benefited (...if at all).

Yet because this goes against gut instinct,[155] the natural reaction to courtroom antics is disbelief and disgust.

Pay attention to the big picture, and convey its broad strokes, with care and dispassion, to curious non-lawyers.

THE FUNNY LAWYER

As a Junior, be careful around whom you repeat lawyer jokes. Most of us appreciate them, but many do not. Previous ABA bigwigs weighed in with proposals to limit them. Before you rustle through your special volume on First Amendment law, take a moment to ponder both sides. I like lawyer jokes (...and I like lawyers who like lawyer jokes), but it's important to not lose perspective. If jokes are too persistent, or are aimed too close to the soul, or are traded in disrespect rather than levity, then they're no longer funny.

An ability to laugh at oneself is among the highest signs of maturity. But, to be healthy, it must be laughter, not acid.

THE RADICAL

Some of you are resentful: Of the system. Of the hypocrisy. Of life. Some of you believe, sincerely, that the world doesn't have to be the way it is. Perhaps so. But, better yet...pull your head out of your ass.

When all is considered, it's *amazing* things aren't worse.

Yes, we should look for, and work towards, steady improvement. Yet the answer is not categorical denial. You need only carry it a few steps farther to realize that utopian rejection of reality is more idiotic than admirable. (I feel at liberty to be contemptuous because I am sympathetic with many of the same ideals.)[156] For the rest of you,

---

155 ...and common sense. For the record, I think our system is wrong. Instead, civil damages, in favor of the victim, should follow—*summarily*—a criminal conviction (and, possibly, even an acquittal). As long as I'm ranting: I think punitive awards are *wonderful*...but, rather than go to plaintiffs, should instead go, *sua sponte,* to a fund for victims unwise enough to have been harmed by impecunious defendants.

156 I made a difficult decision (...with strenuous editorial pushing), to yank *another* bonus chapter on bringing up Junior, law firm (mis)management, and law-as-a-business. It simply wasn't appropriate for this book, and would have been a disservice for you.

if you want the power, prestige, and perks that big-firm law provides, check in with Faust, first. You might not lose your soul.

But, then again...

THE LAWYER SAVANT

Few lawyers know the law as well as a lawyer should.

Be one of the exceptions.

THE CHASM

The technical lawyer perches in satisfaction on the ledge.

On either side, lined up in formation, nest those who assume that the law is just a bunch of rules, and those who just want the nice car. These lawyers can be competent, but only just.

High above, circle the dreamers. From their higher vantage, they scan the horizon for what lies beyond. Generally well-meaning, philosophical, and incompetent. They *can* become competent, but only with forced landings on the technical flats.

Know thyself. Broaden your horizons, if among the former, or narrow them (at least for now), if among the latter. *Combine the two*—a deep knowledge of the law with a deeper understanding of what's *really* important—to circle at all levels, and alight at will. *Your* will.

The Attorney

While you're at that party, be the wise counselor, not the boisterous braggart. No one likes a boor...and the law just begs for boorishness.

Wait until you're *asked* for an opinion before charming 'em with your wit and erudition.

Sure, law's not quite as rosy as this chapter paints—it has serious structural problems, and even more serious *lawyer* problems—but it's not the evil made of it everyday. It's a vital part of our and every society, and it separates us from the anthropoids whence we came.

Don't let it go to your head, but do take a little pride in what you do...and in who you are. It's important to your sanity, to your clients, and to society.

THE FOREST

One idea I hope you picked up is the central role of *people* in this law business. You will succeed under the guidance (...and occasional kindness) of Senior people. You will spend your working life assisting client people. You will battle mightily against adversary people. You will labor resolutely to convince court people. You will rely heavily on staff people. You will, eventually, supervise subordinate people. You will be respected—and scorned—by lay people. This is a lesson too rarely repeated in high-powered legal circles. Remember it when a nervous Junior faces you, years from now, in *your* Senior office.

THE LEGAL GRAIL

Though you're too deep in your own learning curve to see the depth of power politics in your firm, not all Partners are created alike; a pecking order exists. Still, no matter what's happening above you, you're now (again) at the bottom. Remember also: those wandering about will still be there *after* you make partner. And, more importantly, they'll still be *ahead* of you in the pecking order. Will you be happy at the bottom of the top? Even more fundamentally, do *you* really want to be partners with *them?*

The partnership aura is tinted with the blessing that partners bestow upon senior associates, but it's important that you invert the lens. You don't have to love them, but you do need to respect them and feel that you'll be treated fairly. Unless you're planning to use partnership as a stepping stone to something else, the better part of a dozen years is a helluvan investment to find out that you're still a powerless peon to unliked peers. At least Juniors know they're junior.

Remember too that your rainmaking talents will dominate the power and money equation among you and your partners. Not surprisingly, they'll have a serious head start. It usually boils down to how willing—and when—they are to give up credit (read: money) for your (then) clients.

MAKING PARTNER—PART II

You're offered the glories of Partnership. Then what? First, smile graciously towards your future partners, offer a toast of appreciation, and avoid throwing up. Bask in the warm glow of congratulations from officemates. Only when you return to your office may you dance the Dance of Joy. (Close your door, first.)

Sometime after you've celebrated with your S.O.—and *before* you sign any papers—*ask to see the books*. For the fifty-ninth time, serious responsibilities attach to law practice. As Seniors are now becoming acutely aware, serious responsibilities also attach to partners.

You should know much of this *long* before you're offered partnership. Keep your eyes and ears open. Fair or not, you'll be instantly on the hook for just about everything the firm's on the hook for.

Yes, firms are searching for ways to limit liability, and many are reorganizing to do just that. This problem might be moot eventually, but until then, beware.

THE LEAN AND HUNGRY LOOK

If you're still not sure whether you even *want* the partnership schtick, *do not voice your doubts*. If you do, you'll find yourself on a sidetrack, regardless of your true, eventual desires.

Many successful people fall into their vocations. You might not appreciate what you do until later, after you've acquired a taste for it. Keep your doubts to yourself... until *you* have decided, affirmatively, what you want; don't let them make your decision for you.

Hang in there. Don't despair at each of your inevitable setbacks. Think instead back to life's scarier parts—like losing sight of mommy at the store—and realize that the answer is neither to give up in frustration, assuming the world's against you, nor to shriek in panicky terror. Look around. You'll find her.

Don't despair. What seemed like boulders blocking your path look like pebbles, once you're past. (Or, if you prefer, *sic gorgiamus allos subjectatos nunc.* [157])

And don't be so quick to dislike law.

Of all the jobs you could have, it's not vile. It is, at times, irritating as hell. It is, more often, exasperatingly mundane. It is ceaselessly exhausting. But there's not much out there that's notably better.

And there *is* much out there that's notably *worse*.

...WHEN *YOU'RE* KING [158]

Maybe it's a bit early for you to start thinking about this. Fine, don't. Just observe... and realize that what makes some people more equal than others in life are nearly undefinable skills and characteristics that set them apart from—no, *above*—the rest.

---

[157] Two points to readers who recognize this line from *The Addams Family:*
"We gladly feast on those who would subdue us."

[158] *I know, I know,* I said I was gonna' yank this chapter. *Well,* I just couldn't help myself. Here are a few tidbits. (No extra charge. = :)

You can tell who they are. From a management perspective, it's kinda' like Justice Stewart's take on obscenity: He wasn't sure how to define it...but he knew it when he saw it.

Charismatic leaders are both born *and* raised. A good portion of "charisma" is probably just the right childhood reinforcement at just the right time for just the right, extroverted youngster. (Even that's probably too broad a generalization.) Still, what's important for you is to figure out where *you'd* like to be in the human food chain, and plan accordingly. For now, recognize that managing is not leading. Neither one is *lawyering*.

If you wish to rise to the top, you must perfect skills in *all*.

Law firms, businesses, empires, and marriages each suffer from the dull strains of day-to-day travails. Worse, these constant, tiny sufferings have a disproportionate effect, especially over time, on that mushy monster: morale. Dealing with these mundane complications is a Herculean task, for which many firms are woefully, and constitutionally, unprepared.

Sympathize with your Seniors.

Most, though skilled-to-superb lawyers, are ill suited to their unsolicited positions as mentors and personnel managers, thrust upon them by necessity. A different, albeit related, set of skills is required to teach than to do. Some possess both. But it's rare.

They've been trained in law, not management. Most compensate with common sense, which is the preferred response of any sentient being; one should not hide behind the cop-out (or snobbery) that a framed diploma is required for competence in any discipline.

Don't confuse intelligence with wisdom: Some of the wisest people you'll meet in life will be janitors...and some of the *dimmest,* JDs.

Many Seniors "manage" by neglect. They pay attention when attention must be paid, or when they feel unacceptably guilty for their inattention. Some don't act even then.[159]

In some firms you will be neglected to (...and sometimes beyond) the point of malpractice. Yes, this isn't a smart way to run a railroad. If *you* are in this type of environment, your chances of success will depend largely on your attitude and personality.

If you're an organization-type, who's oriented toward routine completion of routine tasks, you will probably survive with few scrapes. If you're a real go-getter, with a decisive goal and a decided interest, you'll take 'em by storm.

---

159 Here's another, less positive, tidbit: A proposed change to the disciplinary rules adds the responsibility of the firm to provide "reasonable" supervision of its members. Given the growing spectre of vicarious malpractice liability, this is not a bad plan. (Notably, this new rule still places less of a professional obligation on law firms than the law already places on *other* employers, via strict or near-strict liability, for employment-related goings-on.)

If, however, you're of the personality type least compatible with practice—a dreamer—then it's *imperative* to make a concerted effort to imitate the organization soul to survive, if for no other reason than that you will ask too many questions—of yourself as well as of others.

(If, however, you're a prima donna, disregard everything I've written and head for a firm with a "star system" culture. Then avoid being scorched by *another's* star.)

The important point for everyone is to spot the issues arising from your inexperience...and *solve* them.

THREE REASONS TO CARE

1. Proactivity is invigorating.
2. You *like* being a Junior?
3. Why bother consuming so much oxygen, anyway?

...and now, with Feeling !

One problem few Juniors consider goes beyond attitude:

To succeed in law, you must *want* to. If you're just on for the ride, chances are fair-to-good that it will be a bumpy one, and even better that you won't make it to the Junior finishline: partnership. This is not to say that all ambitionless souls wind up on the legal scrapheap, but that's the way to bet. More to the point, why waste everyone's time? (Including, especially, your *own*.) Don't spend your *life* doing something that makes you miserable. It really *is* too short.

If you do want to make partner...then give it all you've got, and keep your eyes and ears open.

If you don't know what you want when you start...that's okay. Indeed, it's normal.

If, however, you're still wandering after a few years, you really *should* search your soul. We are trained as lawyers to disregard—or at least pigeonhole—the subjective, but here is one time where it is needed in full force. A life is a terrible thing to waste.

The Law Zone is for loading and unloading only. Please don't leave your career unattended; it will be towed.

Talk with your friendly SO. This is an area in which they *can* help; they usually know a lot more about you than you do. When things have settled down a bit, take a long weekend and an even longer look at the firm in which you park your carcass for those zillion hours a week. On that subjective level, how good is the fit?

If you're happy, then you'll know it. Clap your hands.

THE MEANING OF LIFE[160]

If you're *not* happy, ask yourself why.

There's much discontent in the legal world, and even more reasons behind such hearty dissatisfaction. If *for you* it goes beyond a distaste with the work or colleagues, then think about future options outside practice, or outside of the law, entirely. Options abound; there is one with your name on it.

It is crucial to take this seriously, and soon: Our lives are littered with critical paths, each of which change all that follow, and erase all that pass. Of these many detours, frolics, and yellow-bricked roads, choose wisely.

If you *are* unhappy, and you know, deep down, that it won't get better with a change of place, plan ahead to leave. This is crucial. It is best to have your escape charted before a career crash. Like the adage about loans—*It's better to ask for money when you don't need it*—it is vastly easier to look for something else while you're still employed. This reality you must accept. If you do not, you almost certainly will suffer a fate of needless and life-wrenching torment.

If you *remain* unhappy, it is exceedingly unlikely that you will Make Partner.

The answer? Don't be unhappy. *Get* happy, or at least comfortable, in appreciation of the better parts of practice. If you cannot appreciate *any* part of practice, then cut your losses and Get Out.

Law can be a rewarding path to follow, for those who admire her many well-carpeted trails. But beware. Don't discount your opportunity cost: the trails you *didn't* take. When all has been seen and lived, the Worldy Grail of Partnership, or General Counsel, or whatever... ain't worth it if you never wanted to be there.

As someone once said, "All paths in life lead to the same place, so you may as well take one you'll enjoy." Don't glance back, after you've applied for Social Security, at a bitter life spent wandering the *wrong* path. And don't glare about, blaming others for your unhappiness.

Responsibility for your life, loves, and career is *yours*.

FIN

Whether your travels take you from Junior to managing Senior on the fast track, or in a roundabout way, or on a happy tangent to in-house counsel, teacher, Colonel, tycoon, or askew to who-knows-what south-southeast of Kathmandu, good luck.

---

160 Good thing we're not getting too big for our existential britches.

No animals were harmed in the writing of this book.[†]

[†] One insect, a small spider, *was* dispossessed of his home during editing of the manuscript, however.

LAW TREK
THE NEXT GENERATION

I hope this book has given you a helpful glimpse into the strange new world you're about to explore.

If you have travel logs or horror stories about your own adventures that you'd like to relay to The Next Generation, then live immortally through a subspace transmission, in care of The Entity:

THANE J. MESSINGER
C/O THE FINE PRINT PRESS, LTD.
350 WARD AVENUE, SUITE 106
HONOLULU, HAWAII 96814-4091

Your contribution will be appreciated (and cited, if you so desire). Sorry, but compensation is limited to one Piña Colada, Mai Tai, or comparable umbrella drink,* collectible at the author's island of residence.

Mahalo, fellow Traveller.

---

* ...or *three,* depending upon the quality—*very* subjectively judged—of the contribution (...and drinks).

INDEX

(Very) Advance Praise

FOR

The Young Lawyer's Jungle Book

"Taught me a thing or two."

—Clarence S. Darrow.

"I just *had* to dig myself out and buy a copy."

—John ("Johnny") Marshall.

"*Geez*...where was this book when *I* started?"

—William O. Douglas.

"It costs *how much?*"

—Johnny Marshall (...a few minutes later).

"No wonder I had so much trouble on the Court."

—Earl Warren.

"So good I cried."

—Perry Mason.

"...and he wasn't just acting."

—Perry's mother.

"*Mmm, mmm. Good!*"

—Mrs. Campbell.

"So buy this book. *What*...would it kill you?"

—Rabbi Maimonides.

"*Riveting! Spectacular!! Seat-of-the-pants adventure!!!*"

—Someone who thought this was Grisham's latest.

"The best book yet written."

—The author.

About the Author

Thane Messinger practices law in Honolulu, and is adjunct professor of business law at the University of Hawaii.

Mr. Messinger served as Court Counsel to the Kosrae Supreme Court in the Eastern Caroline Islands in the newly Federated States of Micronesia, somewhere west-southwest of Hawaii.

When not serving, he taught Entrepreneurship, Finance (and, if he behaved, Economics) at the College of Micronesia. He conducted a seminar for Micronesian judges on alternative dispute resolution, in Yap. (Yes, the island of Stone Money.)

Mr. Messinger received his law degree from the University of Texas Law School, where he served as an editor of the *Texas Law Review*. He studied at Oxford University and at Tunghai University, in Taiwan.

He is the author of an article in the *Denver University Law Review,* which has been read by at least four people (including the author, the proofreader, and both editors who'll admit to it).

Along the way, he picked up an M.B.A., a Spousal Unit (otherwise lovingly referred to as the "Commander, Domestic Forces"), and, from the side of a road, a soggy little kitten named "Lucky".

PROFESSIONAL REVIEWS

"A very helpful book for those planning legal careers."

"Each year 45,000 young lawyers graduate from one of the most grueling of all graduate programs only to enter one of the most hostile employment environments. If you did well in law school, and go with a top firm, its expectations will blow your mind. If you were only average, then you have a real job search on you hand. In either event, this book is filled with sound advice with a helpful optimistic tone."

"Every career field would benefit from a great book like this one on law."

Career Opportunity News 12 (Jan./Feb. 1997).

"As a young associate, I was anxious to read *The Young Lawyer's Jungle Book: A Survival Guide*. Like most associates starting out, I have quickly realized that three years of law school education did not adequately prepare me for legal practice. While volumes have been written about law school survival and how to get ahead in law school, books on associate survival are relatively few in number. Thus, it was refreshing to discover that Messinger's book is primarily addressed to that forgotten class of legal society."

"He offers his own tidbits and advice on everything from 'your place in the firm' to dealing with other attorneys, clients, secretaries, and staff to avoid the traps and pitfalls that await every young 'junior' in a firm."

"The book is loaded with common-sense advice for new associates, presented in a humorous, readable manner."

Joseph Lee, Esq., 51 *Washington State Bar News* 38-39 (Mar. 1997).

"New lawyers receive relatively little in the way of practical guidelines to the real world of practice: enter this title, which examines law practice operations and the young new lawyer's entry-level experience. From getting research and work done to handing projects, problems, and mistakes, this book covers all the basics."

12 *Midwest Book Review* 1 (Dec. 1996).

"Suggested reading for pre-law and law students, as well as attorneys beginning their first years of practice. Also of interest to legal recruiters, law firm administrators, personnel support, and law librarians."

"Messinger is encouraging and supportive throughout. *The Young Lawyer's Jungle Book* is highly recommended."

Michelle Schmidt, 13 *Research Advisor* 5-6 (Jan./Feb. 1998) (Ms. Schmidt is a librarian for Luce, Forward, Hamilton & Scripps, a law firm based in San Diego, California).